REHUMANIZING LAW:
A THEORY OF LAW AND DEMOCRACY

RANDY D. GORDON

# Rehumanizing Law

## A Theory of Law and Democracy

UNIVERSITY OF TORONTO PRESS
Toronto Buffalo London

© University of Toronto Press Incorporated 2011
Toronto Buffalo London
www.utppublishing.com
Printed in Canada

ISBN 978-1-4426-4229-4

∞

Printed on acid-free, 100% post-consumer recycled paper with
vegetable-based inks.

**Library and Archives Canada Cataloguing in Publication**

Gordon, Randy D., 1955–
Rehumanizing law : a theory of law and democracy / Randy D. Gordon.

Includes bibliographical references and index.
ISBN 978-1-4426-4229-4

1. Law and literature.   2. Law in literature.   3. Legal stories – History
and criticism.   4. Law – Political aspects.   I. Title.

PN56.L33G67 2011      809′.933554      C2010-906761-4

University of Toronto Press acknowledges the financial assistance to its
publishing program of the Canada Council for the Arts and the Ontario
Arts Council.

 Canada Council    Conseil des Arts
for the Arts    du Canada

 ONTARIO ARTS COUNCIL
CONSEIL DES ARTS DE L'ONTARIO

University of Toronto Press acknowledges the financial support of the
Government of Canada through the Canada Book Fund for its publishing
activities.

In Memoriam
Professor Sir Neil MacCormick
(1941–2009)


*For My Family: Lori, Breck, Connor, and the Dogs*

# Contents

# Acknowledgments

I've been thinking about aspects of this work for over twenty years, so properly acknowledging everyone who has helped me bring it to fruition is at once a daunting and futile task. But I must try, so let me begin with an apology to anyone whose influence and assistance I have overlooked. Since this book is about narrative, I think it only fitting to order my thanks according to my own personal narrative, but with a twist: told (mostly) backwards chronologically and anchored by place.

*In Edinburgh.* I researched and wrote the bulk of what follows during a delightful year in Edinburgh. Professors Zenon Bankowski and Neil MacCormick gave me indispensable advice at every step of the drafting process, from concept to completion. I am greatly in their debt and would never have finished this project without their generous guidance. Sadly, Neil passed away just after I finished the manuscript. He was a great man and good friend – we are all diminished at his passing. Professors Neil Walker and Bert van Roermund also gave me helpful comments on the penultimate draft. Having somewhere to read, write, and just contemplate was also important to my work, and for that I am grateful to the Institute for Advanced Studies in the Humanities, where I was housed as a Faculty Fellow during my time in Edinburgh. In especial, I thank the Institute's director, Professor Susan Manning, and her very helpful staff, including Ms Anthea Taylor, to whom I owe a special debt for finding me a flat! I also received considerable moral support while in Edinburgh, and for that I thank the Society of Writers to Her Majesty's Signet and its CEO, Mr Robert Pirrie, and the law firm of Dundas & Wilson, particularly Mr David Hardie and Mr Jim Moser.

*In Dallas and other points south.* I could not have undertaken this work – or spent the time in Edinburgh – without the generous institutional support of my colleagues at Gardere Wynne. I've also benefited from my long associations with Southern Methodist University (and its law school dean, Professor John Attanasio) and the Dallas Institute of Humanities and Culture (and its director, Dr Larry Allums). I have learned much from my students at SMU and from my fellow Fellows at the Dallas Institute – I thank both groups for listening to and improving my ideas. I must also thank my friend and occasional collaborator Professor Nancy Rapoport (formerly of the University of Houston, now of the University of Nevada, Las Vegas) for sounding out my ideas on interdisciplinary legal studies.

*In Kansas.* My interest in humanistic theory stretches back to my graduate student days at the University of Kansas, where I had the good fortune to come under the guidance of Professor G. Douglas Atkins, a steadfast mentor and now friend. Sine qua non. I also owe a debt to Professor Amy Devitt, with whom I have collaborated over the years and from whom I have learned much, particularly with respect to genre theory. Environmental historian Professor Donald Worster pointed me to a number of important resources concerning Rachel Carson and her legacy. I also thank Professors Victor Bailey and Michael Hoeflich for giving me helpful advice on studying in the UK. Though it is too long ago for me to remember with certainty, I think that some of the cases and concepts that are threaded through this work first came to my attention via a first-year course in legal method that I took from Professor L. Ali Khan at Washburn Law School – thanks for the memories. Before leaving this Kansas section, I must thank my parents – James and Rosemary Gordon – for indulging my myriad youthful interests in all things literary.

*In New York and other points north.* My first serious foray into legal theory came in a seminar that I took from Professor Kent Greenawalt at Columbia Law School. In addition to providing me with a solid introduction to legal philosophy, he – and other members of the class – helpfully sharpened my thinking about the relationship between legal and literary interpretation. As we say in Kansas and Texas, this book is my first trip to the rodeo, so I am thankful for the guidance I have received from the University of Toronto Press, especially in the form of helpful comments from two anonymous readers and the step-by-step advice of editor Daniel Quinlan.

*Around the house.* Above all others listed above, I thank my wife, Lori, for allowing me to run off to Scotland while we still had two teenagers in the house. Once she got past the 'Have you lost your mind?' phase, she gave me all the support I needed. Thanks, too, to Breck and Connor: to both for being good sports in my absence, and to Breck for graduating early from high school, enrolling at the University of Edinburgh, and eating my cooking without complaint on many a dark Scottish night!

REHUMANIZING LAW:
A THEORY OF LAW AND DEMOCRACY

# Introduction

'Law is institutional normative order.'[1] Nothing about this statement seems controversial. Indeed, it is hard to imagine any three-word definition of 'law' that would be more accurate. But each of those three words carries a second-order connotation that reveals as much about law's nature as its first-order denotation. To wit: Institutions have walls – sometimes literal, sometimes figurative – that keep things out. Norms are abstractions, distillations, and purifications that leave things out. Orders are systems, and systems seal things out. What are these 'things' that wind up outside the law (or, perhaps more to the point, must fight to get in)? There are many possible answers, but the one that I am concerned to examine in this work arises from *narrative*, which is one of the most fundamental modes of human expression. By keeping narratives at a distance or delay, law loses some of its essential humanity. My project is, then, an attempt to explain the relationship between law and narrative, and – in the end – to suggest ways to (re)humanize law by (re)connecting it to its narrative roots and certain cognates in the humanities.

The process of packaging law as bundles of rules is an exercise in relentless reduction. By the time a common law rule is stated or a statute is codified, it's impossible to tell from the face of that rule or statute what went into the mix that created it. What that mix includes, I submit, is a healthy dose of narrative. Thus, any account of law that ignores or skims over this fact is neither wholly valid nor completely accurate. The contention I will advance is designed to fill this lacuna, not to upend or supplant other descriptions of the law and its operation. In essence, I intend to do nothing more than peel back law's normative veneer just far enough to reveal its narrative foundation. To do this, I offer four related (and ultimately converging) propositions. First, though law is often posited to be 'autonomous,' that autonomy is not necessarily absolute, though it is quite potent. It is, therefore, a force requiring active resistance. Second, narratives often stand in the formative background of laws. This is true for statutory and common law alike. Third, the ability of a legal system to absorb and digest extrasystemic narratives serves democratic ends. Fourth, educating both lawyers and the general public to think of law 'narrativistically' (i.e., as something more than a system of rules to be extracted from texts) can help ameliorate the dehumanizing effect of the Rule of Law's inherent drive to universalize all that comes before it. This is the case I hope to make throughout the remainder of this book, which is broken into four parts, each of which engages one of the four central themes. The first three parts are essentially descriptive and are designed to show different aspects of the relations among laws, legal actors, and ordinary citizens and to demonstrate the significance of those relations for both law and democracy. The fourth is (at least partially) prescriptive and suggests ways to think, teach, and write about law in democratic ways that can, thereby, improve the entire justice system.

Part One begins with a look across the spectrum between full-blown theories of legal autonomy (like autopoiesis) and humanities-based accounts (like Percy Shelley's belief that legislation has a literary basis). Though it is impossible fully to reconcile the two extremes, narrative is a possible bridge between them because both law and the humanities often take a storytelling form. To illustrate this point, I offer a reading of Camus's *The Stranger*. Taking Shelley as a cue, I next consider whether literature can in fact prompt legislation. I conclude that it can, but the process is neither as simple nor as direct as Shelley would have it. By tracing Upton Sinclair's *The Jungle* and Rachel Carson's *Silent Spring* through legislative history, I am able to show that literary works can figure in the adoption of important legislation. I then take the first step toward explaining the process of literature-becoming-law by looking at an elaboration of Margaret Somers's seminal work on the interaction of personal narratives with higher-order, public narrative forms. This feeds into a discussion of narrative interaction based, once again, on *The Jungle* and *Silent Spring* and the historical record surrounding the principal actors (e.g., Teddy Roosevelt) involved in the legislative offshoots of those two works. Along the way I stop to consider whether the 'factual' versus 'fictional' nature of a narrative is solely determinative of its potential to impact law-making. (It is not.)

Part Two first considers Bernard Jackson's narrativistic account of rule formation and observes that account at work in specific case law. I follow that discussion with a reading of *Antigone* that cautions against dominant public narratives that – though consistent with a narrow definition of the Rule of Law – do not offer paths along which new narrative material can be absorbed into the system. I then move to a concrete application of my theoretical observations and show how personal narratives can become institutionalized as new rules (or modifications of old ones). The cases I examine to demonstrate this process ultimately suggest a link to Ronald Dworkin's chain novel metaphor and Stanley Fish's attack on it. I conclude that – though Dworkin's metaphor is not a complete description of rule building in all cases – it holds in at least some cases. But Fish is correct as well: law is a conservative institution – and one packed with generic constraints that cause it to lag behind other institutions in the face of change. We can see this at a linguistic level by looking at how slowly Scots law anglicized compared to other genres in the sixteenth and seventeenth centuries or, more recently, how scientific evidence gained currency in legal proceedings much later than when it was considered conclusive in other spheres. This elides into the question of what it means to 'find facts,' and I turn to Robert Browning's *The Ring and the Book* as a tool for answering that question and the related question of what it takes to 'justify' a decision.

Part Three is concerned with the relationship between law and democracy. It begins with an exploration of two concepts that are often linked in both popular and theoretical discussions: 'democracy' and the 'Rule of Law.' To show that the latter is not sufficient to the former, I offer a reading of Melville's *Billy Budd* that demonstrates the problematic nature of legal rules untempered by notions of proportionality, mitigation, and a larger sense of morality. This leads to an articulation of what a *democratic* Rule of Law must entail and how that can be achieved. For general insight, I invoke Jürgen Habermas's discourse theory of democracy and show how that 'discourse' can take a narrative form. Specifically, I show how the American jury system adds a democratic dimension to the legal system by ensuring that non-elites participate in matters of public import. Fish's theory of 'interpretive communities' provides the theoretical backdrop for this discussion, which focuses on the famed O.J. Simpson and Rodney King cases. This part concludes with observations on 'objectivity' in the interpretation of legal narratives and how a proper conception of objectivity can have pro-democratic consequences.

Part Four begins with a discussion of the relationship between legal and moral reasoning. I conclude – as have many others – that legal and moral reasoning are both branches of practical reasoning and that the occasional gaps that appear between their results can be explained by attending closely to how each process creates narratives. To anchor the discussion, I examine several cases in detail to show how legal narratives leave out material that moral narratives might include. I attend in particular to the formal features of appellate opinions (which by design squeeze narratives beyond recognition) and suggest that – because appellate opinions are the primary tool that lawyers use to learn and practise law – they come to define the common boundaries of the interpretive community to which lawyers belong. The lawyer-ly way of seeing the world is valuable, but it is also constraining. To loosen these constraints, I offer some modest suggestions for opening legal reasoning and analysis through education reforms (in the broad-est leadership sense) – reforms that might well strengthen democratic institutions.

This, in outline, is the account of law that I will offer in this work. I stake no claim to a Grand Unified Theory of either law or humani-ties, but I do believe that storytelling – when considered as a method of arguing – can expand our understanding of how some laws come to be, other laws come to be changed, and how many laws come into democratic institutions in ways that strengthen and perpetuate those institutions. But stories are not everything. Though they help us make the world intelligible by suggesting agency and causation, they suffer the inherent limits of all things metaphoric. Other accounts – physics, for example – often offer more complete and accurate pictures (almost inevitably, another metaphor) of 'how things really are.' Most of us do not, however, have the mathematical skills to understand phys-ics in anything other than an indirect, trope-laden way. So we must do with what works, all the while realizing that our descriptions are incomplete.

And what holds at the universal level holds at the narrative level as well: our law-stories can be incomplete in devastating ways. Let me illustrate and close – appropriately enough, I think – with a story about a story (infected with multiple levels of hearsay and attendant unreliability). A few years ago I represented a number of the defendants in an antitrust class action. The case settled, and – as the law requires – the judge to whom the case was assigned held a final fairness hearing to ensure that the settlement was fair, adequate, and reasonable to the members of the class. Some small detail that I can't even remember now caused the judge to want to modify the proposed judgment that the parties had negotiated; this occasioned a brief delay in the hearing. While the papers were being edited and copied, the judge decided to divert us with a yarn about his first murder trial, which had taken place many years before when he was a newly minted prosecutor. It was an open-and-shut case. The defendant had viciously knifed his victim multiple times, and there was overwhelming evidence of his guilt. The judge told us about his meticulous preparation, masterful handling of the actual trial, and – as a crowning achievement – his brilliant summation, in which he stood before the jury and, in a final flourish, pretended to plunge the knife into his own chest over and over again. He then sat down, at once exhausted and pleased. His opposing counsel slowly rose and – addressing the court – said, 'Move to dismiss the indictment, Your Honor; the State hasn't proved that anyone died.' Alas! Our fearless young prosecutor had forgotten an element of his case and thereby learned a lesson that should serve to caution us as well: a good story is not always a legally sufficient story. (Oh, by the way, the court allowed our young friend to reopen his case and prove that the victim had died, which shows, I guess, that even a good lawyer sometimes needs a good editor.)

# 1 Law and Narrative: Re-examining the Relationship

Is law an autonomous discipline? That question animates much that follows here, and my answer – an equivocal 'it depends on whose definition of "autonomy" we're using' – gets at much of the theoretical disagreement about what law is and what it can reasonably be expected to achieve in complex modern societies. I despair that law may have become more closed than I believe desirable; this despair flows from a deep-seated belief that law has suffered from overreaching experiments that have tried to refashion every area of human inquiry into a 'science.'[1] Now I do not mean to deny that law is not 'different' in meaningful ways from what we think of as the humanities or the social sciences, but I will argue – and I hope demonstrate – that law shares common, fundamental features with them, the most important being a narrative element. But first, let me stake some metes and bounds. Two decades ago, Charles Fried struck back at the ascendance of what is now broadly referred to as 'interdisciplinarity' in legal studies and practice by arguing that judges and law professors had lost sight of the signal, yet unassuming, role that lawyers had traditionally played in the social order:

> I would like to propose the picture of lawyers, not as the architects of society, but as its janitors. I would like to suggest that we are modest people, laboring in the basement of the building of society, doing really important work, while the great things that happen, happen up in the upper stories, and that they are done by entrepreneurs, by businessmen, by artists, by painters, by politicians, by poets, and by philosophers and economists, as well. One of the really bad things that has happened is that we have tried to get out of the basement. In an earlier day, a kind of bargain was struck

with lawyers. If they would stay in the basement, doing something rather boring and technical (the picture is of Bartleby, the Scrivener), then we would be partially left alone, honored after a fashion and paid quite well. Now I think we have welshed on the deal. We insist, these days, on being paid well and running the show too. I think law studies should once more be hard, rigorous, full of memorization and that we should see far fewer citations in law reviews to Derrida and Foucault.[2]

As the references to Derrida and Foucault suggest, Fried's target here was the Critical Legal Studies (CLS) movement that had found some traction in the 1970s and 1980s. But that is not, in my view, the (sole) ground upon which law's autonomy should be adjudicated. For even if we concede that some mischief has been done in the law reviews in the name of deconstruction or some other faddish theory, lawyers have continued to learn and apply rules, and judges have continued to justify their decisions with precedent and principles of logic. What I am proposing is that law and the humanistic disciplines share certain deep structures and that some of law's features can be explained by insights derived from the humanities, especially the literary humanities. My ultimate aim is to give a partial explanation of what law is, how it works, and how it changes, and – in the end – to suggest how a properly institutionalized and humanistically informed legal order contributes to democracy.

To be clear, I am not proposing that law *is* one of the humanities. To that extent, I agree with the position that Judge Richard Posner has taken from time to time in his influential critiques of the law and literature movement.[3] But I don't agree with his further belief that law is just 'a technique of government.'[4] I think, rather, that law is in some respects an 'applied' humanity, in much the same way that, for instance, electrical engineering is applied physics.[5] James Boyd White comes close to the mark when he states that judicial and literary texts can each be seen 'as a kind of argument with its culture, or, better, as an argumentative reconstitution of it.'[6] In other words, White proposes that the two types of text run on parallel tracks and, moreover, that the arrow of cultural influence is not mono-directional. The humanities and the law both inform and sustain culture, but they are themselves in the process reciprocally refreshed by that culture and (perhaps only indirectly) by each other.

But before we can begin to reach conclusions (or even see them off on the horizon), we must stop to consider what 'autonomy' may or may not mean when applied to the law. Let's return to Fried's jeremiad for a moment. He is not (really) saying that law is or should be hermetic – his complaint is that, with the Realists and after, philosophy and economics 'erupted' into the law in ways that led to false conceptions of it (e.g., that 'it is not possible to work with doctrines and precedents and texts'). I'm not sure that anyone ever seriously advanced a claim of doctrinal-precedential-textual irrelevancy as an absolute (or that very many people took it seriously even if it was made), but we need to keep in mind that Fried's underlying lament is that much of the 'interdisciplinary' work he had reviewed was in fact 'undisciplined': 'I think one of the worst effects ... of the huge amount of philosophy and economics and political science and sociology leaking into law is the poor quality of the philosophy and the economics and the sociology which we see there.'[7] And this should stand, I think, as an indictment of poor scholarship, teaching, and opinion writing, not as proof that law is better off when it is in some sense sealed off from other disciplines.

Perhaps the simplest way into a discussion of law's autonomy is to look at the impetus for Fried's argument, which was an influential article by Judge Richard Posner that had recently appeared in the *Harvard Law Review*.[8] In that article, Posner traded on the notion that law historically had been (more accurately, I should probably say, 'law historically had been treated *as if it were*') an autonomous discipline, both in practice and as a matter of training:

> The idea that law is an autonomous discipline, by which I mean a subject properly entrusted to persons trained in law and in nothing else, was originally a political idea. The judges of England used it to fend off royal interference with their decisions, and lawyers from time immemorial have used it to protect their monopoly of representing people in legal matters. Langdell in the 1870s made it an academic idea. He said that the principles of law could be inferred from judicial opinions, so that the relevant training for students of the law was in reading and comparing opinions and the relevant knowledge of what those opinions contained. He thought that this procedure was scientific, but it was not in the modern sense at any rate.[9]

Posner suggests that the Langdellian project was really just a form of Platonism (e.g., a contract decision embodies the concept of a contract) and notes that even in its heyday that project was properly assailed by Holmes, 'who pointed out that law is a tool for achieving social ends, so that to understand law requires an understanding of social conditions.' But Posner also notes that Holmes's assault fell short: it took another sixty years or so for serious breaches to appear in the law's citadel. Posner traces the relatively recent decline of law's autonomy to a variety of sources, ranging from the shattering of political consensus in the Vietnam era, to the proclivity of the United States Supreme Court to stray into areas that had traditionally been marked off as 'political,' and to – most important for our discussion – 'a boom in disciplines that are complementary to the law, particularly economics and philosophy.'

As Posner's analysis indicates, the question of law's autonomy resolves into two overlapping inquiries, one having to do with how law functions (i.e., how lawyers and judges go about doing the business of law), the other with what legal teachers–scholars–theorists do. The first inquiry looks at law from a process perspective and asks questions like these: How are legal arguments constructed? How are legal decisions made and justified? And, even more telling, are legal arguments and decisions different from other types of arguments and decisions? The second inquiry looks at law as an object of study and pedagogy and asks questions like these: Should legal scholarship and teaching focus on anything other than doctrine? Can legal thought be enriched by insights and approaches developed in other disciplines? Should a law student be taught 'to think like a lawyer' (and little else), and what does that mean anyway?

## Describing Law in Terms of Autonomy

Brian Bix proposes that law's autonomy (or lack thereof) be viewed through three lenses: one descriptive, one analytic, one prescriptive.[10] This multiperspective approach ensures that an investigation of a particular legal system will describe the level of autonomy assumed or encouraged by that system, analyse whether claims of autonomy can withstand heavy scrutiny, and prescribe greater or lesser interdisciplinarity in legal reasoning, decision making, or education. This makes sense to me, and I have loosely adopted it as a method of testing my own predilection in favour of interdisciplinary enterprises. I do this while recognizing that the case in favour of interdisciplinarity can never be more than partial. For at bottom I agree with Neil MacCormick that 'law is an argumentative discipline' and that 'legal arguments are always in some way arguments about the law, or arguments about matters of fact, of evidence, or opinion, as these have a bearing upon the law, or as the law has a bearing on them.'[11] But MacCormick's description is, I think, just a statement of limitation – he doesn't mean it as a statement of law's wholesale autonomy.

At this point it may be useful to consider theories that – at least on their face – tend toward either the 'autonomous' or 'non-autonomous' pole of our discussion. In 'A Declaration of Rights,' the Romantic poet Percy Shelley proposed that 'law cannot make what is in its nature virtuous or innocent, to be criminal, any more than it can make what is criminal to be innocent. Government cannot make a law, it can only pronounce that which was law before its organization, viz. the moral result of the imperishable relations of things.'[12] In other words, law is anterior to government. Is anything anterior to law? Shelley would say 'yes' and draw our attention to the literary humanities, poetry in particular. In Shelley's most famous hyperbole, Shelley asserted (Paul Fry tells us) that 'the progress that culture owes to poetry and that poetry partakes in consists in the forging of ever new and better legislation. Shelley's favorite example of how this progress works is the literature of "chivalry" in the Middle Ages, mainly that of Dante, which advanced the conditions both of slaves and of women towards equality.'[13]

Behind this assertion was Shelley's bedrock belief that 'institutionalized laws, whether scientific, moral, or political, cannot change ... because they are inert. They can be altered only from without, by revolution or by some kind of revolutionary poetry.'[14] Shelley's positions are of course indefensible in their breadth, but they are of a sort not unique to him. White, for example, has much more recently argued that 'law can be best understood as a set of literary practices that at once create new possibilities for meaning and action in life and constitute human communities in distinctive ways.'[15] Defensible in whole or not, positions like those of Shelley and White raise at least a couple of related questions worth investigating – namely, can law be changed in important ways from without, and do the humanities in some sense forge larger cultural institutions via the mediating force of law-as-instrument?[16]

Before seeking answers to these questions, we should glance toward the other end of the spectrum and one of the cases that has been advanced in favour of law as an insular system. 'Autopoiesis' is the notion that many systems (biological, ecological, even social) contain self-reflexive mechanisms that allow those systems to self-govern.[17]

Put broadly, 'an autopoietic system produces and reproduces its own elements by the interaction of its elements.'[18] When applied to law, as Zenon Bankowski maintains, this means that

> the law is a system of meaning which creates its own objects and criteria of truth. It is those that determine its cognition. All input coming from other systems such as the economy, politics and even individual actors (psychic systems for the theory) is filtered through these criteria. It cannot properly be called knowledge of the other system at all since the legal system has transformed it into *legal* knowledge. It does not even perceive the input as knowledge. Rather it senses an irritation, a noise, to which it adapts.[19]

I think that the law's adaptability in the face of 'noise' suggests a middle ground between the law-as-humanity and law-as-closed-system camps. Hugh Baxter signals this possibility when he discusses the idea of 'relative autonomy':

> While [Niklas] Luhmann [one of the seminal autopoietic theorists] expressly refuses the term 'relative autonomy,' his work can nonetheless be understood as an attempt to capture theoretically the intuition behind that enigmatic phrase. Despite his emphasis on 'operative closure,' Luhmann readily acknowledges that social subsystems, among them the legal system, are at the same time 'cognitively open' and able to 'observe' one another. He insists, further, that the legal system is connected – 'structurally coupled' – to other social subsystems, particularly the economic and political systems. Luhmann's account of the law's simultaneous openness and closure, and its simultaneous distinction from and 'coupling' to other systems, corresponds to the opposing impulses that the phrase 'relative autonomy' expresses.[20]

If law remains open to other systemic influences, can one of those influences be the humanities? And if so, exactly how does this process work?[21] And – even more interesting, I think – does such an influence have a collateral influence on the institutions necessary to ensure the possibility of democracy?

## Narrative as the Basis of Law and the Humanities

My answers to these just-posed questions are in the affirmative and turn on the fact that both the law and the humanities often transmit information in narrative form. In the end, I conclude that law may be conservative and resistant to outside influence, but it is not autonomous in the sense of 'hermetically sealed.' This is not to say that narrative 'noise' from another system can automatically be transcribed as legal norms – or, more generally, legally useful information – but narratives can and do 'get through' to the system. They do so through a process of translation and assimilation, not direct absorption.[22] Accordingly, a legal system cannot comprehend a 'story' in its raw, natural form, be that in the form of a play, a novel, or personal confession.[23] It must first be massaged into a legal shape through things like questions-and-answers at trial, cross-examination, and compliance with the rules of evidence – in short, it must undergo an alchemic process[24] through which it is transformed into a *legal* narrative.[25] This suggests that legal narratives are subject to generic restrictions only slightly less stringent than those associated with literature. They are not as structured as, say, sonnets, but they are nonetheless conventional.

As a further complicating factor, we must remember that a narrative has not only an author (or many) but an auditor or reader (or many) as well. Thus the 'meaning' and consequent legal significance of a narrative is a function of the interpreter, the context, and author's selection of facts and construction of those facts into a story. (This is of course just an application of Aristotle's rhetorical triangle of ethos–pathos–logos.) To make this a little more concrete, let's look at an example. Albert Camus's *The Stranger* neatly illustrates both the power of narrative forms and the dangers inherent in them.[26] These dangers arise because, simply put, we are gullible. We too quickly equate a coherent narrative with a complete (or truthful) narrative. But that is not always the case, as Camus shows us through the process of what might be called comparative renarration. Here's how it works as a matter of structure. The novel is broken into two parts, each of which – among other things – casts the same series of facts into a different narrative form and within a different interpretive context.

Part One of the novel is told from the first-person point of view of the protagonist, Meursault. It begins with one of the most famous opening paragraphs in Western literature, a paragraph that immediately alienates readers from Meursault:

Maman died today. Or yesterday maybe, I don't know. I got a telegram from the home: 'Mother deceased. Funeral tomorrow. Faithfully yours.' That doesn't mean anything. Maybe it was yesterday.[27]

By carefully accreting details of his behaviour at the vigil, funeral, and period of mourning for his mother, Meursault confirms our first impression of him: he is an outsider. In his conversations with others and in his description of the events leading up to Maman's funeral, he reveals that he didn't know her age, that he put her in a retirement home against her will, that he didn't want to see her body before the burial, and that he slept and breached other social conventions during the vigil:

> The caretaker turned the switch and I was blinded by the sudden flash of light. He suggested I go to the dining hall for dinner. But I wasn't hungry. Then he offered to bring me a cup of coffee with milk. I like milk in my coffee, so I said yes, and he came back a few minutes later with a tray. I drank the coffee. Then I felt like having a smoke. But I hesitated, because I didn't know if I could do it with Maman right there. I thought about it; it didn't matter. I offered the caretaker a cigarette and we smoked.[28]

Even at this early point in the novel, we understand that Meursault will be judged on his indifference. We learn as much when his mother's friends come into the vigil and are seated as if they were a jury: 'It was then that I realized they were all sitting across from me, nodding their heads, grouped around the caretaker. For a second I had the ridiculous feeling that they were there to judge me.'[29] And so they were, just as all of us are in our daily social interactions.

After Meursault returns home from the funeral, he continues to violate social norms. He goes swimming at a public beach, where he meets up with his soon-to-be lover, Marie, and then takes in a movie – a comedy. Soon thereafter, he helps a neighbour of dubious character (he's a reputed pimp), Raymond, execute a plan to exact revenge on Raymond's former mistress, an Arab. Raymond winds up beating the woman and getting himself tangled up with the police. To get out of this fix, Raymond needs Meursault to testify 'that the girl had cheated on him,' a fact of which Meursault has no personal knowledge. But Meursault readily agrees to testify anyway, and Raymond gets off with a warning because the police 'didn't check out [Meursault's] statement.' Despite Meursault's willingness to flout convention at the urging of his physical appetites and to comply blindly with improper requests on behalf of others, we learn that he is not a scofflaw. In fact, he's actually something of a rule follower: he worries about breaking even petty dictates like the general prohibition in his office against taking personal phone calls, and he declines to accompany Raymond to a whorehouse 'because,' as he explains, 'I don't like that.'[30] From all this we conclude that Meursault is perhaps selfish and egoistic – maybe even something of a lout – but we don't see him as a sociopath or menace to society. Unfortunately for Meursault, though, his real troubles have not yet begun.

Soon after the incident with the Arab woman, Raymond invites Meursault and Marie to spend a Sunday at the beach house of Raymond's friend, Masson. It will not be a relaxing day, though, because they have been followed by the Arab woman's brother and a friend. They meet three times on the beach. In the first encounter, Raymond and Masson provoke a fight that results in the Arabs being thrashed until one of them pulls a knife, with which he slashes Raymond. Once Raymond is bandaged, he sets off again for the beach, this time with a gun. Meursault follows him, and they again encounter the Arabs at the far end of the beach, lying next to a spring. Raymond reaches for his gun, but Meursault wisely counsels Raymond to reconsider:

> Raymond asked me, 'Should I let him have it?' I thought that if I said no he'd get himself all worked up and shoot for sure. All I said was, 'He hasn't said anything yet. It'd be pretty lousy to shoot him like that ...' Then Raymond said, 'So I'll call him something and when he answers back, I'll let him have it.' I answered, 'Right. But if he doesn't draw his knife, you can't shoot.' Raymond started getting worked up ... 'No,' I said to Raymond, 'take him on man to man and give me your gun. If the other one moves in, or if he draws his knife, I'll let him have it.'[31]

Here, Meursault evinces at least some sense of morality (it would be 'lousy' to shoot an unarmed man), as well as a tacit feel for the law of self-defence. His stance is nonetheless equivocal, because once the gun is in his hand, he 'realized that you could either shoot or not shoot.' None of this is yet put to the test, though, because the Arabs slip away, and Meursault and Raymond head back towards Masson's bungalow.

But Meursault makes it no farther than the steps leading from the beach up to the bungalow. Echoing his statement about shooting/not shooting, he finds himself 'unable to face the effort it would take to climb the wooden staircase and face the women again ... To stay or go, it amounted to the same thing.' Throughout the entire time on the beach, the sun's intensity has risen like a drumbeat that impels him back down the beach to his doom. Accompanied by a final burst of synesthesia (the sun not only dazzles his eyes but presses on his back, burns his skin, and crashes like cymbals), a disoriented Meursault again confronts the Arab:

> The sun was the same as it had been the day I'd buried Maman, and like then, my forehead especially was hurting me, all the veins in it throbbing under the skin. It was this burning, which I couldn't stand anymore, that made me move forward. I knew that it was stupid, that I wouldn't get the sun off me by stepping forward. But I took a step, one step, forward. And this time, without getting up, the Arab drew his knife and held it up to me in the sun. The light shot off the steel and it was like a long flashing blade cutting at my forehead ... All I could feel were the cymbals of sunlight crashing on my forehead and, indistinctly, the dazzling spear flying up from the knife in front of me. The scorching blade slashed at my eyelashes and stabbed my stinging eyes. That's when everything began to reel ... My whole being tensed and I squeezed my hand around the revolver. The trigger gave; I felt the smooth underside of the butt; and there, in that noise, sharp and deafening at the same time, is where it all started ... I knew that I had shattered the harmony of the day, the exceptional silence of the beach where I'd been happy. Then I fired four more times at the motionless body where the bullets lodged without leaving a trace. And it was like knocking four quick times on the door of unhappiness.[32]

Part One of the novel thus ends with Meursault having narrated two key events: his mother's funeral (and its immediate aftermath) and the killing of the Arab. Part Two examines the relationship of the former to the latter within a larger narrative context.

As I think the discussion thus far has shown, Part One involves two types of acts by Meursault: those observed by others and reported by Meursault-as-narrator (e.g., the vigil and the funeral), and those that are unobserved by others yet narrated by Meursault (e.g., the shooting on the beach). Part Two complicates this structure by placing another interpretive and narrative lens between the 'facts' and our interpretation of them. And lenses always both refocus and distort what passes through them. In *The Stranger*, this happens in two ways. First, in the investigation phase of Meursault's case, he learns from his lawyer that 'there had been some investigations into [his] private life' and that 'the investigators had learned that [he] had "shown insensitivity" the day of Maman's funeral.'[33] Meursault is unable to rebut the charge of insensitivity, and he makes matters rather worse for himself in the trying:

> He asked if I felt any sadness that day ... I answered that I had pretty much lost the habit of analyzing myself and that it was hard for me to tell him what he wanted to know. I probably did love Maman, but that didn't mean anything. At one time or another all normal people have wished their loved ones were dead. Here the lawyer interrupted me and he seemed very upset. He made me promise I wouldn't say that at my hearing or in front of the examining magistrate.[34]

Meursault is of course correct in noting that 'none of this had anything to do with my case,' but he grossly miscalculates the power of a narrative that is coherent (though irrelevant) and the ability of others to read this narrative as anything other than evidence of a black heart.

Meursault fares no better with the examining magistrate, who is willing to help him but demands an explanation for the group of four shots that Meursault fired after the Arab was already down (and probably dead). That is an explanation that Meursault cannot give, especially since the magistrate demands that it be in the form of a Christian confession, lest Meursault's narrative infect his own:

> I vaguely understood that to his mind there was just one thing that wasn't clear in my confession, the fact that I had hesitated before I fired my second shot ... I was about to tell him that he was wrong to dwell on it, because it didn't really matter. But he cut me off and urged me one last time, drawing himself up to his full height and asking me if I believed in God. I said no ... He said it was impossible; all men believed in God, even those who turn their backs on him. That was his belief, and if he were ever to doubt it, his life would become meaningless. 'Do you want my life to be meaningless?' he shouted. As far as I could see, it didn't have anything to do with me, and I told him so.[35]

After this meeting, 'the magistrate seemed to have lost interest in me and to have come to some sort of decision about my case.' That decision is, of course, that Meursault should be tried for premeditated murder.

Meursault's trial in some sense tracks – in reverse order – the narratives first constructed in Part One of the novel. Thus the trial begins with the presiding judge simply reading from a dossier the narrative of what Meursault had done and verifying its accuracy with Meursault every few sentences. Those facts are undisputed, so the remainder of the trial is focused on the issue of intent and collateral questions

such as why Meursault had returned to the spring and why he was
armed when he did. The prosecutor's approach is to elicit testimony
– and thereby sponsor evidence – that he can recraft into a narrative
of evil. He therefore calls to testify people who were present with
Meursault at his mother's vigil and funeral and in the days thereafter.[36] For example, the prosecutor elicits testimony from an unwitting
Marie that he is able to summarize in a single damning sentence at
the end of her examination: 'Gentlemen of the jury, the day after his
mother's death, this man was out swimming, starting up a dubious
liaison, and going to a movie, a comedy, for laughs.'[37] Armed with this
and other similar building blocks, the prosecutor, in his summation,
constructs a narrative edifice that even Meursault concedes is coherent
and plausible:

> He reminded the court of my insensitivity; of my ignorance when asked
> Maman's age; of my swim the next day – with a woman; of the Fernan-
> del movie; and finally of my taking Marie home with me. It took a few
> minutes to understand the last part because he kept saying 'his mistress'
> and to me she was Marie. Then he came to the business with Raymond. I
> thought his way of viewing the events had a certain consistency. What he
> was saying was plausible. I had agreed with Raymond to write the letter
> in order to lure his mistress and submit her to mistreatment by a man 'of
> doubtful morality.' I had provoked Raymond's adversaries at the beach.
> Raymond had been wounded. I asked him to give me his gun. I had gone
> back alone intending to use it. I had shot the Arab as I planned. I had
> waited. And to make sure I had done the job right, I fired four more shots,
> calmly, point-blank – thoughtfully, as it were.[38]

All the basic facts underlying this narrative are true, but it is not *the*
truth. How do we know this? It's because we've already read the story
and reached our own conclusions. Those conclusions may vary from
reader to reader, but more often than not readers convict Meursault
of rather venal sins, not ones that lead the presiding judge to declare,
after receiving the jury's verdict of guilty, 'that [Meursault] was to
have [his] head cut off in a public square in the name of the French
people.'[39] What, then, is the difference between the readerly and judicial judgments? Context, I think.[40] That is, readers have more context
within which to view Meursault's behaviour and to assess it as odd,
yet relatively benign, and certainly not as conclusive (or even relevant)
proof that Meursault acted with murderous intent on the beach. Read-

ers believe Meursault because he gains our narrative trust through his brutal honesty, which is aimed – more often than not – at himself. The jurors do not have the advantage of this critical perspective.

The point here is that good stories – and even legally cognizable stories – are not always true stories. So if we are to improve the odds of doing justice, we must always – because the warp and woof of law is so often of narrative origin – be on the lookout for additional facts, contexts, and perspectives that can help us better to weave and interpret stories in ways that are truthful (or, if that is an ideal that must remain merely aspirational, then at least accurate). Where better to start this excursion than with a consideration of the discipline-artform that is mainly concerned with stories: literature?

### Shelley's Case, Part 1: Law of *The Jungle*

One of the principal criticisms of the law and literature movement has been that it doesn't really prove anything meaningful about the relationship between the two.[41] Yes, *To Kill a Mockingbird* has a trial in it, and understanding law can add a subtle dimension to a reading of that novel. Yes, Justice Cardozo and Lord Denning wrote with what might be called a literary flourish, and recognizing their effective use of tropes and other rhetorical devices leads to a better understanding of why some case law is more persuasive than others. And yes, critical theory offers valuable insights into modes of interpretation that are as applicable to legal texts as to literary texts. But none of this demonstrates a typical claim of the movement: that literature plays a noteworthy role in the development of the law. In the following pages I hope to contribute something concrete to the discussion. My claim at this point is a narrow one: sometimes literary works at least partially *cause* the enactment of legislation.

Shelley was not the first literary figure to suggest that literature influences the development of the law. Ben Jonson had made the same claim nearly two centuries before:

I could never think the study of Wisdom confined only to the Philosopher; or of Piety to the Divine: or of State to the Politic: but that he which can feign a Commonwealth (which is the Poet), can govern it with counsels, *strengthen it with laws*, correct it with judgments, inform it with religion, and morals, is all these. We do not require in him mere Elocution, or an excellent faculty in verse, but the exact knowledge of all virtues, and their contraries; with ability to render the one loved, the other hated, by his proper embattaling them.[42]

This accords with what most serious writers think about their work (i.e., that it rises above mere entertainment), but how do we move from the level of assertion to that of accomplishment? An answer – but perhaps not the *only* answer – can be found in legislative history, which has been kept with increasingly meticulous care in the United States since the late nineteenth century.

In 1906, Upton Sinclair published *The Jungle*, a socialist screed aimed specifically at the Chicago meatpacking industry and more generally at the plight of American workers.[43] Though the novel often descends into melodrama, episodes in the first few chapters are crafted with a stark realism that effectively portrays the ghastly conditions in which much of the United States' meat supply was then produced. These few pages stir the reader's conscience – and raise her ire – on a number of fronts: the horrors of animal slaughter, the back-breaking misery of work on an ever-quickening production line, the lack of competition in the packing industry, the open and wanton environmental pollution practised by the packers, and the disgusting genesis of processed food. To make this all a bit more tangible, it is perhaps wise to pause and look carefully at a few groups of excerpts from the novel, each directed to a particular ill associated with Chicago's Union Stockyards.

A guided tour of one of the plants in the Stockyards offers the occasion for readers to witness the carnage visited upon an array of unwitting hooved creatures – a carnage that, through personification, portends still greater ills to be suffered by the novel's protagonist (Jurgis Rudkus), his family, and his fellows:

> Once started upon [the mechanized death] journey, the hog never came back; at the top of the wheel he was shunted off upon a trolley, and went sailing down the room. And meantime another was swung up, and then another, until there was a double line of them, each dangling by a foot and kicking in frenzy – and squealing … One by one, they hooked up the hogs, and one by one with a swift stroke they slit their throats. There was a long line of hogs, with squeals and lifeblood ebbing away together; until at last each started again, and vanished with a splash into a huge vat of boiling water.[44]

It is the mechanized nature of the slaughter (in an eerie anticipation of the First World War) that Sinclair finds most disturbing. He sees it as a breach of a grand social contract, one extending beyond humans and including animals:

> It was all so very businesslike that one watched it fascinated. It was pork-making by machinery, porkmaking by applied mathematics. And yet somehow the most matter of fact person could not help thinking of the hogs; they were so innocent, they came so very trustingly; and they were so very human in their protests – and so perfectly within their rights! They had done nothing to deserve it; and it was adding insult to injury, as the thing was done here, swinging them up in this cold-blooded, impersonal way, without a pretense at apology, without the homage of a tear. Now and then a visitor wept, to be sure; but this slaughtering-machine ran on, visitors or no visitors. It was like some horrible crime committed in a dungeon, all unseen and unheeded, buried out of sight and out of memory.[45]

Sinclair goes on to describe ever more horrifying atrocities, including the 'knocking pens' in which cattle are stunned with sledgehammers, then rolled onto 'killing beds' to be disembowelled while still alive. Through textual juxtaposition and elaboration, this callous indifference to life foreshadows the protagonist's own doom. And because Jurgis is a sort of Everyman, the animals-to-the-slaughter imagery extends and applies with equal force to an entire class of American worker.

Sinclair pointedly develops this aspect of his critique by widening his scope beyond Jurgis. The humiliations of workers in the packing yards are manifold and – even in some literal sense – equal to those of the animals. First, there are the physical injuries:

> There was another interesting set of statistics that a person might have gathered in Packingtown – those of the various afflictions of the workers ... The workers in each [part of the plant] had their own particular diseases. [A] wandering visitor ... could not be skeptical about these, for the worker bore the evidence of them about on his own person – generally he had only to hold out his hand ... Worst of any, however, were the fertilizer men, and those who served in the cooking rooms. These people could not be shown to the ordinary visitor, – for the odor of a fertilizer man would scare any ordinary visitor at a hundred yards, and as for the other men, who worked in tank rooms full of steam, and in some of which there were open vats near the level of the floor, their particular trouble was that they fell into the vats; and when they were fished out, there was never enough

of them left to be worth exhibiting, – sometimes they would be overlooked for days, till all but the bones of them had gone out to the world as Durhams' Pure Leaf Lard![46]

These physical ailments are, of course, merely symbolic of a more general maleficence:

The peculiar bitterness of all this was that Jurgis saw so plainly the meaning of it. In the beginning he had been fresh and strong, and he had gotten a job, the very first day; but now he was second-hand, a damaged article, so to speak, and they did not want him. They had got the best of him – they had worn him out, with their speeding-up and their carelessness, and now they had thrown him away! And Jurgis would make the acquaintance of others of these unemployed men and find that they had all had the same experience … They had been overworked and underfed so long, and finally some disease had laid them on their backs; or they had cut themselves, and had blood poisoning, or met with some other accident. When a man came back after that, he would get his place back only by courtesy of the boss. To this there was no exception, save when the accident was one for which the firm was liable; in that case they would send a slippery lawyer to see him, first to try to get him to sign away his claims, but if he was too smart for that, to promise him that he and his should always be provided with work. This promise they would keep, strictly and to the letter – for two years. Two years was the 'statute of limitations,' and after that the victim could not sue.[47]

In the beginning, however, Jurgis is thrilled to be part of the Durham meatpacking firm and is swelled with corporate pride. The business represents for him the apotheosis of freewheeling American capitalism, a portal to the American Dream: 'Now he had been admitted – he was part of it all! He had the feeling that this whole huge establishment had taken him under its protection, and had become responsible for his welfare.'[48] We, of course, know better, and Jurgis himself later learns the truth: namely, that the entire meatpacking industry is – in antitrust terms – nothing short of a massive horizontal conspiracy targeting its workers, its suppliers, and its customers:

So guileless was he, and ignorant of the nature of business, that he did not even realize that he had become an employee of Brown's, and that Brown and Durham were supposed by all the world to be deadly rivals – were even required to be deadly rivals by the law of the land, and ordered to try to ruin each other under penalty of fine and imprisonment.[49]

Once or twice there had been rumours that one of the big houses was going to cut its unskilled men to fifteen cents an hour, and Jurgis knew that if this was done, his turn would come soon. He had learned by this time that Packingtown was really not a number of firms at all, but one great firm, the Beef Trust. And every week the managers of it got together and compared notes, and there was one scale for all the workers in the yards and one standard of efficiency. Jurgis was told that they also fixed the price they would pay for beef on the hoof and the price of all dressed meat in the country ...[50]

The narrator also reports of collateral consequences flowing from the meatpackers' socially casual way of conducting business. We learn, for instance, of air thick with soot and other pollutants and a landscape that recalls the bareness of winter even at high summer. But the Stygian vision of the Chicago River that he summons is the most stunning:

'Bubbly Creek' is an arm of the Chicago River, and forms the southern boundary of the yards; all the drainage of the square mile of packing houses empties into it, so that it is really a great open sewer a hundred or two feet wide. One long arm of it is blind, and the filth stays there forever and a day. The grease and chemicals that are poured into it undergo all sorts of strange transformations, which are the cause of its name; it is constantly in motion, as if huge fish were feeding in it, or great leviathans disporting themselves in its depths. Bubbles of carbonic acid will rise to the surface and burst, and make rings two or three feet wide. Here and there, the grease and filth have caked solid, and the creek looks like a bed of lava; chickens walk about on it, feeding, and many times an unwary stranger has started to stroll across, and vanished temporarily. The packers used to leave the creek that way, till every now and then the surface would catch on fire and burn furiously, and the fire department would have to come and put it out.[51]

Ultimately, Sinclair is most effective in his food polemic. He makes what is essentially a two-pronged attack on food quality – one directed to regulatory misfeasance, another to corporate malfeasance. First, he criticizes lax inspection and ineffective legislation:

It was late, almost dark, and the government inspectors had all gone ...

That day they had killed about four thousand cattle, and these cattle had come in freight trains from far states, and some of them had got hurt. There were some with broken legs, and some with gored sides; there were some that had died, from what cause no one would say; and they were all to be disposed of, here in darkness and silence. 'Downers,' the men called them; and the packing house had a special elevator upon which they were raised to the killing beds, where the gang proceeded to handle them, with an air of businesslike nonchalance which said plainer than any words that it was a matter of everyday routine. It took a couple of hours to get them out of the way, and in the end Jurgis saw them go into the chilling rooms with the rest of the meat, being carefully scattered here and there so that they could not be identified.[52]

Though condemned meat slips through the net because of the packers' chicanery, Sinclair makes it clear that inspection laws of the day were deeply, conceptually flawed and easily circumvented anyway:

The people of Chicago saw the government inspectors in Packingtown and they all took that to mean that they were protected from diseased meat; they did not understand that these hundred and sixty-three inspectors had been appointed at the request of the packers, and that they were paid by the United States government to certify that all the diseased meat was kept in the state. They had no authority beyond that; for the inspection of meat to be sold in the city and state the whole force in Packingtown consisted of three henchmen of the local political machine.[53]

But even if the laws had not been drafted so as to be meaningless in application, the haphazard system of inspection would have eviscerated them:

Before the carcass was admitted [to the dressing line], it had to pass a government inspector, who sat in the doorway and felt the glands of the neck for tuberculosis. This government inspector did not have the manner of a man who was worked to death; he was apparently not haunted by a fear that the hog might get by him before he had finished his testing. If you were a social person, he was quite willing to enter into conversation with you, and to explain to you the deadly nature of the ptomaines which are found in tubercular pork; and while he was talking with you you could hardly be so ungrateful as to notice that a dozen carcasses were passing him untouched. This inspector wore a blue uniform, with brass buttons, and he gave an atmosphere of authority to the scene, and, as it were, put the stamp of approval upon the things which were done at Durham's.[54]

The second prong of Sinclair's attack on food quality was the one that resonated most deeply with the public. And it is the depictions of adulterated and unsanitary foodstuffs that are to this day most often invoked in the popular press when the novel is recalled at all. In due course, we will explore why this might be so. For now, it is enough to note how skilfully Sinclair weaves metaphor, irony, and naturalistic detail into a rhetorically powerful appeal to shared values and experience:

They were regular alchemists at Durham's; they advertised a mushroom-catsup, and the men who made it did not know what a mushroom looked like ... And then there was the 'potted game' and 'potted grouse,' 'potted ham,' and 'deviled ham' – de-vyled, as the men called it. 'De-vyled' ham was made out of the waste ends of smoked beef that were too small to be sliced by the machines; and also tripe, dyed with chemicals so that it would not show white; and trimmings of hams and corned beef; and potatoes, skins and all; and finally, the hard cartilaginous gullets of beef, after the tongues had been cut out. All this ingenious mixture was ground up and flavored with spices to make it taste like something.[55]

There was never the least attention paid to what was cut up for sausage; there would come all the way back from Europe old sausage that had been rejected, and that was moldy and white – it would be dosed with borax and glycerine, and dumped into the hoppers, and made over again for home consumption. There would be meat that had tumbled out on the floor, in the dirt and sawdust, where the workers had tramped and spit uncounted billions of consumption germs. There would be meat stored in great piles in rooms; and the water from leaky roofs would drip over it, and thousands of rats would race about on it. It was too dark in these storage places to see well, but a man could run his hand over these piles of meat and sweep off handfuls of the dried dung of rats. These rats were nuisances, and the packers would put out poisoned bread for them; they would die, and then rats, bread, and meat would go into the hoppers together. This is no fairy story and no joke; the meat would be shoveled into carts, and the man who did the shoveling would not trouble to lift out a rat even when he saw one – there were things that went into the sausage in comparison with which a poisoned rat was a tidbit.[56]

As these excerpts plainly show, *The Jungle* was (and is) a comprehensive indictment of American business practices. In theory, then, the work could have inspired cries for reform in each of the regulatory areas that correspond to the passages we just reviewed: animal rights, workers' rights, antitrust, environmental standards, and pure food requirements. Sinclair himself sought to effect radical change across the board and, in especial, to improve the lot of the working class. To that end, the bulk of the work is devoted to following the devolution of a representative, hapless immigrant, one quickly eaten up and spit out by the meatpackers. But as Sinclair later bemoaned, he missed the mark with respect to the largest target: 'I aimed at the public's heart and by accident hit it in the stomach.'[57] For as we will presently see, there is a direct and demonstrable connection between publication of *The Jungle* and adoption of the Meat Inspection Act and the Pure Food and Drugs Act, both of 1906, but no others.

From a literary and rhetorical perspective, Sinclair's various commentaries on the wide range of bad acts that constitute the packing industry are narrated with equal skill (even if you conclude, as have many critics, that Sinclair was not particularly skilful). Why, then, did *The Jungle* take hold in only one relatively narrow area? In other words, why didn't Sinclair's novel – which plainly had a considerable impact on the public imagination and concomitant political ramifications – lead to immediate, widespread legislation? What we find, instead, is that landmark legislation that would have reformed an array of practices in the packing industry (or, in some cases, in business generally) did not follow close on the heels of *The Jungle*. For example, the Packers & Stockyards Act (antitrust) was not adopted until 1921, the Occupational Safety and Health Act (worker's health and safety) until 1970, the Clean Water Act (putting teeth into older environmental legislation like the Water Pollution Control Act of 1948) until 1972, and the Humane Slaughter Act (abolishing certain gruesome butchering practices like 'knocking') until 1972. I will ultimately suggest that – as I hinted at before – it is all a matter of context. Literature – even persuasively powerful literature – does not operate in a void: conditions must be ripe if it is to draw energy from the social milieu and thereby attain a kinetic force capable of influencing the law. This, as I will argue, requires an alignment of narratives: the literary narrative with the larger cultural narrative within which it subsists. But before turning to that subject later in this chapter, we must take a closer look at how a literary work can actually 'cause' legislation and, even more important, demonstrate that this in fact happens.

The late eighteenth century and all of the nineteenth century witnessed massive changes to social structures in the West. As societies industrialized and urbanized, attendant changes appeared in widely disparate areas, from the rise of the novel as a literary form to the rise of the modern regulatory state as a method of governance.[58] Single causes are always difficult to isolate in the context of social change, but there is general agreement that scientific and technological advances were the principal impetus behind the movement from rural, agrarian structures to urban, industrial structures. With these 'advances' came a host of consequences, many unanticipated and, it follows, unintended: 'Discoveries in chemistry, for example, led to new synthetic medicines and altered radically both the growing and the processing of food. Transportation developments brought processed food to an increasingly national market, making the growth of giant cities possible. The residents of those cities lost the ability villagers had possessed of being first-hand judges of the food they ate.'[59]

It was within this temporal gap between raw food (meat on the hoof/vegetables in the ground) and the table that much mischief could be worked. Some of chemistry's impact on food production was benign – even salutary in many cases – but it also permitted unscrupulous latter-day alchemists to transform vile, inedible dross into slightly less vile, semi-edible (and marketable) dross. Think, for instance, of Sinclair's descriptions of 'ham' with no ham in it, spoiled sausage treated with borax then recycled, or rancid butter 'oxidized' to remove its smell before being returned to grocery shelves. None of this was completely lost on lawmakers or the public – even prior to Sinclair's emergence on the scene. For example, a Senate report from 1890 cautioned that 'it has only been since the great opportunity for fraud provided by modern science ... that the sophistication of articles of commerce has reached its present height.'[60] But it is equally clear that, prior to publication of *The Jungle*, 'pure food crusaders' had had little success in pushing effective legislation through Congress, despite numerous journalistic exposés (including Sinclair's own 1905 serial publication of what was to become *The Jungle* in a socialist newspaper) recounting the horrors of Chicago's Union Stockyards.[61]

All this changed in 1906 with the publication of *The Jungle* in book form, which 'spurred a mighty reaction in the body politic that, in four months, led to the enactment of two laws.'[62] The confluence of several factors contributed to the novel's rapid public acceptance. As historian James Harvey Young capably demonstrates, both Sinclair and his publisher, Doubleday, extensively and effectively promoted the novel.[63] But even more important, Sinclair, Doubleday, and two key political figures, James R. Garfield and Senator Alfred J. Beveridge, put the novel into the hands of President Theodore Roosevelt.[64] The trust-busting Roosevelt – still stinging from failed attempts to dismantle the beef trust under the Sherman Act – was predisposed to read the (perhaps any) novel that offered another opportunity to bring the packers to heel. And after Roosevelt's own investigators independently verified the major contours of Sinclair's allegations (and in some instances supplemented them),[65] the road to legislation was cleared.[66]

At this point, one may ask: In what sense did *The Jungle* 'cause' passage of the Meat Inspection Act and Pure Food and Drugs Act? The novel was not, of course, what in legal parlance would be termed the 'sole proximate cause,' but the record makes it reasonably clear that it was a significant contributing cause. For evidence of this type of causation, we can look first to the legislative history of the acts. Though Sinclair is never mentioned by name in the floor debates attendant to the Meat Inspection Act, at least one senator alluded to him and his novel.[67] There is, moreover, a wealth of indirect evidence of provocation in the legislative history. In the House hearings, much energy was devoted to attacking or buttressing the conclusions of the Neill-Reynolds Report, which was generated at Roosevelt's request either to confirm or to refute the factual assertions upon which Sinclair based his book. Roosevelt ordered the independent investigation at Sinclair's behest, as his directive to Secretary Wilson reveals: 'I would like a first-class man to be appointed to meet Sinclair, as he suggests; get the names of witnesses, as he suggests; and then go to work in the industry, as he suggests.'[68] Sinclair himself hoped that the final report would give 'a sort of governmental sanction to *The Jungle*.'[69] Thus, the official report became something of a stalking horse for the novel: criticism or praise levelled at it was in essence criticism or praise of its original impetus, the novel. Of this, there is ample evidence in the legislative history, including the report itself and the testimony of its two authors.[70]

There is also considerable contemporaneous evidence outside the official record that the novel had a powerful impact. Roosevelt's correspondence cited above is, of course, germane, as are the recollections of many of the key players in the political scene of the time.[71] These included, for example, Harvey W. Wiley, the Chief of the Bureau of Chemistry, and Sinclair himself.[72] Most historians, after combing the relevant archives, have ascribed a 'causal' relationship between *The*

*Jungle* and the Meat Inspection Act and, perhaps as a collateral consequence, the Pure Food and Drugs Act.[73] Case law is to similar effect.[74] And two economists recently concluded – after performing an econometric analysis of Senate voting patterns – that 'the muckraking press [including Sinclair] eventually galvanized widespread consumer interest in food and drugs regulation and broke the [then existing] impasse, allowing the [food and drugs] law to be finally enacted.'[75]

What this proves, then, is that literature can have a demonstrable – not merely posited – impact on the law. I could pile up dozens of other examples from the humanities and social sciences (Harriet Beecher Stowe, Karl Marx, Ralph Nader, Jonathan Swift, and on and on), but there would be little point now that the basic point is made. I do think, however, that one more fairly detailed example will prove useful, if only because it will figure prominently in the next stage in my argument – that is, the question of *why* certain humanistic works serve as legislative flashpoints. That work, Rachel Carson's *Silent Spring*, differs from *The Jungle* both in genre (literary broadside as opposed to novel) and in purpose (reforming a single area as opposed to fomenting a wide-ranging socialist revolution).

Before turning there, though, I want to again emphasize that I'm using the concept of 'causation' loosely. The literary narratives we are considering do, I think, have demonstrable causal force. But they are themselves the products of other discourses. So the best we can say is that they are part of a causal complex. Perhaps a bit of forewarning from Tolstoy (excessive, perhaps, in its strict historical determinism) will help us keep this in perspective:

Had Napoleon not taken offense at the demand that he should withdraw beyond the Vistula, and not ordered his troops to advance, there would have been no war; but had all his sergeants objected to serving a second term then also there could have been no war. Nor could there have been a war had there been no English intrigues and no Duke of Oldenburg, and had Alexander not felt insulted, and had there not been an autocratic government in Russia, or a Revolution in France and a subsequent dictatorship and Empire, or all the things that produced the French Revolution, and so on. Without each of these causes nothing could have happened. So all these causes – myriads of causes – coincided to bring it about. And so there was no one cause for that occurrence, but it had to occur because it had to. Millions of men, renouncing their human feelings and reason, had to go from west to east to slay their fellows, just as some centuries previously hordes of men had come from the east to the west, slaying their fellows.

Nothing is the cause. All this is only the coincidence of conditions in which all vital organic and elemental events occur ... Equally right or wrong is he who says that Napoleon went to Moscow because he wanted to, and perished because Alexander desired his destruction, and he who says that an undermined hill weighing a million tons fell because the last navvy struck it for the last time with his mattock. In historic events, the so-called great men are labels giving names to events, and like labels they have but the smallest connection with the great event itself. Every act of theirs, which appears to them an act of their own will, is in an historical sense involuntary and is related to the whole course of history and pre-destined from eternity.[76]

## Shelley's Case, Part 2: *Silent Spring*

In 1962, Rachel Carson published *Silent Spring*, a call to arms aimed specifically at the by then widespread use of pesticides, more generally at the civil responsibilities of scientists, and even more generally at the post-Enlightenment belief in technological progress. Though her work has a more than sufficient scientific basis, it gains its greatest force from its 'literary' qualities. It begins with an epigraph from Keats ('The sedge is wither'd from the lake / and no birds sing') before opening the text proper with what Carson herself dubbed a 'fable,' a cautionary vision of Middle America stricken not by the then feared nuclear holocaust, but by the insidious – and purposeful – use of pesticides:

There was once a town in the heart of America where all life seemed to live in harmony with its surroundings. The town lay in the midst of a checkerboard of prosperous farms, with fields of grain and hillsides of orchards where, in spring, white clouds of bloom drifted above the green fields ... The countryside was, in fact, famous for the abundance and variety of its bird life, and when the flood of migrants was pouring through in spring and fall people traveled from great distances to observe them. Then a strange blight crept over the area and everything began to change. Some evil spell had settled on the community: mysterious maladies swept the flocks of chickens; the cattle and the sheep sickened and died. Everywhere was a shadow of death ... There was a strange stillness. The birds, for example – where had they gone? ... It was a spring without voices. On mornings that had once throbbed with the dawn chorus of robins, catbirds, doves, jays, wrens, and scores of other bird voices there was now no sound; only silence lay over the fields and woods and marsh. On the farms the hens brooded, but no chicks hatched ... The apple trees were coming into bloom but no bees droned among the blossoms, so there was no pollination and there would be no fruit. The roadsides, once so attractive, were now lined with browned and withered vegetation as though swept by fire. These, too, were silent, deserted by all living things. Even the streams were now lifeless. No witchcraft, no enemy action had silenced the rebirth of new life in this stricken world. The people had done it themselves.[77]

What Carson brought to the debate was a keen sense of literary style, coupled with a jargon-stripped exposition of scientific principles. Even a general reader of the time could understand the salient features of her argument: namely, that synthetic chemicals indiscriminately kill life forms, often with unimagined consequences, and that, moreover, these chemicals circulate – and move up through the food chain – far beyond their intended targets:

Sprays, dusts, and aerosols are now applied almost universally to farms, gardens, forests and homes – nonselective chemicals that have the power to kill every insect, the 'good' and the 'bad,' to still the song of birds and the leaping of fish in the streams, to coat the leaves with a deadly film, and to linger on in soil – all this though the intended target may be only a few weeds or insects. Can anyone believe that it is possible to lay down such a barrage of poisons on the surface of the earth without making it unfit for all life? They should not be called 'insecticides' but 'biocides.'[78]

In the less than two decades of their use, the synthetic pesticides have been so thoroughly distributed throughout the animate and inanimate world that they occur virtually everywhere ... They have entered the bodies of fish, birds, reptiles, and domestic and wild animals so universally that scientists find it almost impossible to locate subjects free from such contamination. They have been found in fish in remote mountain lakes, in earthworms burrowing in soil, in the eggs of birds – and in man himself. For these chemicals are now stored in the bodies in the vast majority of human beings, regardless of age. They occur in the mother's milk, and probably in the tissues of the unborn child.[79]

No dry scientific treatise this. It reads, from a rhetorical standpoint, much like Sinclair's meatpacking exposé, full of tropes, literary allusions, and appeals to shared values. Her technique is transparently literary: she weaves into her fabric a host of mini-narratives ranging from the pathetic (a boy and his dog stricken by the insecticide endrin; two small boys – cousins, even – killed at play by another insecticide, parathion) to the archetypal (retelling the myth of the sorceress Medea and her robe of 'death by indirection' to illustrate the mechanics of 'systemic insecticides'). In an excerpt worth quoting at some length, she even slyly invokes the authority of law when she appropriates a story from the outdoor biography of a United States Supreme Court Justice:

> Justice William O. Douglas, in his recent book *My Wilderness: East to Katahdin*, has told of an appalling example of ecological destruction wrought by the United States Forest Service in the Bridger National Forest in Wyoming. Some 10,000 acres of sagelands were sprayed by the service, yielding to pressure of cattlemen for more grasslands. The sage was killed, as intended. But so was the green, lifegiving ribbon of willows that traced its way across these plains, following the meandering streams. Moose had lived in these willow thickets, for willow is to the moose what sage is to the antelope. Beaver had lived there, too, feeding on the willows, felling them and making a strong dam across the tiny stream. Through the labor of the beavers, a lake backed up. Trout in the mountain streams seldom were more than six inches long; in the lake they thrived so prodigiously that many grew to five pounds ...
>
> But with the 'improvement' instituted by the Forest Service, the willows went the way of the sagebrush, killed by the same impartial spray. When Justice Douglas visited the area in 1959, the year of the spraying, he was shocked to see the shriveled and dying willows – the 'vast, incredible damage.' What would become of the moose? Of the beavers and the little world they had constructed? A year later he returned to read the answer in the devastated landscape. The moose were gone and so were the beaver. Their principal dam had gone out for want of attention by its skilled architects, and the lake had drained away. None of the large trout were left. None could live in the tiny creek that remained, threading its way through a bare, hot land where no shade remained. The living world was shattered.[80]

Powerful as the contrast between the pastoral lyric prose and its antithesis might be, Carson does not rest her argument solely on her ability to persuade through rhetorical devices and logic. Indeed, she raises the ante a few pages later by locating the overarching issue *in law* – specifically, as a clash of competing private commercial and public environmental rights. Once again, she cloaks herself in Justice Douglas, but this time using *his* words to make the operative point, not her own:

> Justice Douglas tells of attending a meeting of federal field men who were discussing protests by citizens against plans for the spraying of sage-brush ... These men considered it hilariously funny that an old lady had opposed the plan because the wildflowers would be destroyed. 'Yet, was not her right to search out a banded cup or a tiger lily as inalienable as the right of the stockmen to search out grass or a lumberman to claim a tree?' asks this humane and perceptive jurist. 'The esthetic values of the wilderness are as much our inheritance as the veins of copper and gold in our hills and the forests in our mountains.'[81]

Though Carson herself had little hope that *Silent Spring* would make a deep impact (she wrote to a friend that 'it would be unrealistic to believe that 1 book could bring a complete change'), reality proved otherwise.[82] Just as Sinclair struck the mark with respect to unsanitary and adulterated food, Carson found it with respect to pesticides and – even more generally – the whole range of environmental issues. Like Sinclair, she was vilified by the industry whose products she impugned, but – also like Sinclair – she found a powerful reader in the then sitting President, John F. Kennedy. At a press conference in the summer of 1962 – in response to the question whether he would ask a government agency to investigate the long-term effects of DDT – Kennedy stated: 'Yes, and I know that they already are. I think particularly, of course, since Miss Carson's book, but they are examining the matter.'[83] In fact, Kennedy asked his Scientific Advisory Committee to investigate Carson's claims. That committee's report, issued in May 1963, largely vindicated Carson's work, particularly in condemning indiscriminate pesticide use and calling for additional research into potential health hazards.[84] The committee chair, Dr Jerome Wiesner, minced no words, calling the uncontrolled use of poisonous chemicals a 'potentially ... much greater hazard' than radioactive fallout.[85]

Where did all this lead? By the end of 1962, dozens of state legislatures had taken up bills regulating pesticides; and by the end of the decade, at least three states had banned DDT.[86] Of greater ultimate importance, however, were the wheels set in motion at the federal level. First, the committee's report exposed loopholes in the federal regulatory scheme through which, for example, pesticides that had been denied approval by the U.S. Department of Agriculture could still slip though and reach the market and, thereby, the environment. The more gaping loopholes of this type were almost immediately closed.[87] Second, government-sponsored research on pesticides markedly increased after the publication of *Silent Spring*; these studies led to agency regulations sharply curtailing DDT use.[88] Third, Senator Abraham Ribicoff introduced a bill (S. 2792) proposing omnibus federal control over pesticide use and manufacturing. Carson testified before the Senate subcommittee holding hearings on the bill,[89] and – though that bill did not become law – her suggestions, including for a ban on DDT and the establishment of the Environmental Protection Agency, were ultimately adopted in subsequent legislation.[90] Finally, and in some ways most interesting, *Silent Spring*'s influence did not stop at the U.S. border: Carson's work was cited several times in 1963 before the House of Lords, resulting in significant controls on a number of chlorinated hydrocarbons (e.g., aldrin and dieldrin). The book is generally credited with provoking environmental legislation in dozens of countries.[91]

How is it that literary works like *The Jungle* and *Silent Spring* can have a deep and direct impact on a process as formalized as the legislative? Just as interesting, why did those works succeed so well in some areas but not in others? After all, Sinclair had the Chicago River in flames in 1906, but it took a relatively minor oil fire on the Cuyahoga River in 1969 to spur Congress to take serious action to clean up America's waterways. The answer, I submit, lies in *narrative* – or, more specifically, in an alignment or misalignment of narratives, as the case may be. To that subject, and a new subsection, we now turn.

### Law, Literature, and Narrative

Roland Barthes once remarked that narrative 'is simply like life itself … international, transhistorical, transcultural.'[92] This cultural invariance invites us to consider what it is about culture – or indeed, human nature – that impels the narrative turn. For Hayden White, 'so natural is the impulse to narrate, so inevitable is the form of narrative for any report of the way things really happened, that narrativity could appear problematical only in a culture in which it was absent – absent or, as in some domains of Western intellectual and artistic culture, programmatically refused.'[93] One domain that has resisted – even if it has not quite refused – narrative accounts of its operation is the law.

Some have suggested that the conceptual coupling of law and narrative is of recent vintage – that is, just another outcrop from the law and literature vein.[94] That is probably true, if one is thinking purely in terms of volume of legal scholarship. But it is equally true that, at least as far back as the Romans, lawyers have recognized the central importance of facts to legal decisions: *da mihi facta, dabo tibi ius* (give me the facts, then I will give you the law).[95] Not surprisingly, then, most scholars have focused on 'storytelling' in the litigation context, particularly as a strategy for 'outsiders' to achieve legal ends that would not be available solely with reference to rules and logic.[96] But this, it seems to me, cuts the potential for a narrative-based jurisprudence far short and sets an easy target for those critics – like Judge Posner – who hold the law and literature movement to be something of an oversell.[97]

Before conceding all this ground to the Posnerians, though, we should take time to survey it and then – without attempting to defend the entire field – fence off a corner here and a parcel there that can withstand their attacks. Many scholars working the borderland between law and literature distinguish between studies involving law *in* literature and those involving law *as* literature.[98] Roughly put, the former suggests that there are literary texts (often plotted around legal incidents or themes) that warrant the attention of legal scholars; the latter maintains that legal texts and practices should be probed with the tools of literary criticism. There is no sharp divide between these two approaches – indeed, one often implicates the other – and collectively, the two comprehend a range of practices. Kieran Dolin proposes a more fine-grained list of 'structures and associations' that have caught the attention of law and literature scholars:

1. literary representations of legal trials, practitioners and language, and of those caught up in the law;
2. the role played by narrative, metaphor and other rhetorical devices in legal speech and writing, including judgments;
3. how the supposed freedom of literary expression is contained and regulated by laws;
4. the circulation of legal ideas in literary culture, and vice versa in various periods and societies;
5. the effects of social ideologies such as race and gender in legal language;
6. theory of interpretation;
7. the use of theatricality and spectacle in the creation of legal authority;

8. the culture and political consequences of new technologies of communication, such as writing, the printing press and the Internet;
9. legal storytelling or narrative jurisprudence.[99]

As this list suggests (and as reflected in the subtitle of Ian Ward's book), the 'possibilities and perspectives' of the law and literature enterprise are practically unbounded.[100] And though Judge Posner is correct that some of the claims of particular participants in the movement are not sustainable, the best work in the area holds up quite well under critical pressure.

My own view is that aspects of narrative theory (point 9 on Dolin's list) are especially useful. Before getting to specifics, though, it would be helpful to run a quick course through a couple of other, related areas (the first is really just an aspect of the second) on Dolin's list that have been particularly successful and that sceptics like Judge Posner would concede as worthwhile. First, works of literature are cultural artefacts, and some of them gain secondary status as part of our general storehouse of shared knowledge. Lawyers and judges reach into this storehouse from time to time and pull out novels, poems, and plays, to which they then allude as part of their rhetorical strategies in particular cases.[101] In this context, literary works operate as a sort of shorthand: *Bleak House* stands for judicial inefficiency or litigation's procedural mazes, *The Merchant of Venice* for the limits of contract formation or enforcement, *1984* for doublespeak or governmental intrusions on privacy, and so on. Given this common use of literary allusion in legal discourse, I think it is fair to say – as a baseline – that most lawyers (including those who are generally unconvinced) would acknowledge some minimal interaction between the two disciplines. For even Judge Posner (as *Judge* Posner) does it![102]

Second, if we extrapolate a bit from these citation-to-literature examples, we find that they are part of a wider law and literature intersection – namely, the one between law and rhetoric. This strain of law and literature studies is perhaps the least controversial (because the connections are so apparent on their face), but it is also an area rich in possibilities.[103] Dolin illustrates this richness with a reading of a literature-infused case from the United States Supreme Court, *Plaut v. Spendthrift Farm*.[104] The case began as a securities fraud suit that was dismissed on statute of limitations grounds. After the dismissal, Congress amended the securities laws to provide that a case like the Plauts' (which had been dismissed based on a then recent Supreme Court holding) could be reinstated. The Plauts quickly moved to do so, but to no avail because the District Court held the act of Congress unconstitutional – a holding that the Court of Appeals and the Supreme Court affirmed.

This sketch of the facts is sufficient to reveal a quintessential American tug of war: Congress versus the judiciary. In the Supreme Court's majority opinion, Justice Scalia offers a paean to the separation of powers doctrine, which functions as 'a prophylactic device, establishing high walls and clear distinctions because low walls and vague distinctions will not be judicially defensible in the heat of interbranch conflict.'[105] His metaphor of the 'wall' summons up images of citadels past, from Troy to Rome and beyond. The implicit warning is, of course, that if the walls come down even slightly (by trickery or through lack of diligence), the barbarians standing ready will indeed flood over. But he goes on to locate insulated branches of government as something beyond the grasp of the historical wall metaphor: 'separation of powers, a distinctively American political doctrine profits from the advice authored by a distinctively American poet: good fences make good neighbors.'[106] As Dolin astutely notes, Justice Scalia 'grounds the authority of the law of separation not just in legal precedent, but in the national cultural heritage, which he assumes to be shared and to include Robert Frost's "Mending Wall."'[107] The poem thus takes on an almost normative significance.

But that's not the end of it. Justice Breyer – though concurring in the result – believes that the majority has overstated the wall-like characteristics of the separation doctrine. He, too, invokes Frost's poem and offers a variant reading of it: 'One might consider as well that poet's caution, for he not only notes that "Something there is that doesn't love a wall," but also writes, "Before I built a wall I'd ask to know / What I was walling in or walling out."'[108] The poem becomes something of a contrapuntal score, with each of the two Justices sounding the opposing notes. Interesting as that is, it's still not all. For as Dolin goes on to show, the Justices have actually assumed the two roles around which Frost casts his dramatic dialogue, in which two neighbour-farmers (one of whom is also the narrator) go about the business of repairing a rock fence along their common boundary:

> Something there is that doesn't love a wall,
> That sends the frozen-ground-swell under it,
> And spills the upper boulders in the sun;

And makes gaps even two can pass abreast.
The work of hunters is another thing:
I have come after them and made repair
Where they have left not one stone on a stone,
But they would have the rabbit out of hiding,
To please the yelping dogs. The gaps I mean,
No one has seen them made or heard them made,
But at spring mending-time we find them there.
I let my neighbor know beyond the hill;
And on a day we meet to walk the line
And set the wall between us once again.
We keep the wall between us as we go.
To each the boulders that have fallen to each.
And some are loaves and some so nearly balls
We have to use a spell to make them balance:
"Stay where you are until our backs are turned!"
We wear our fingers rough with handling them.
Oh, just another kind of out-door game,
One on a side. It comes to little more:
There where it is we do not need the wall:
He is all pine and I am apple orchard.
My apple trees will never get across
And eat the cones under his pines, I tell him.
He only says, "Good fences make good neighbors."
Spring is the mischief in me, and I wonder
If I could put a notion in his head:
"Why do they make good neighbors? Isn't it
Where there are cows? But here there are no cows.
Before I built a wall I'd ask to know
What I was walling in or walling out,
And to whom I was like to give offence.
Something there is that doesn't love a wall,
That wants it down. I could say "Elves" to him,
But it's not elves exactly, and I'd rather
He said it for himself. I see him there
Bringing a stone grasped firmly by the top
In each hand, like an old-stone savage armed.
He moves in darkness as it seems to me,
Not of woods only and the shade of trees.
He will not go behind his father's saying,

And he likes having thought of it so well
He says again, "Good fences make good neighbors."[109]

In playing their respective roles, Justices Scalia and Breyer show us something about themselves as readers, something about political structures, and something about the relationship between law and literature. Justice Scalia simply mines the poem for a catchy aphorism, with no regard for the context in which the aphorism is stated (and thereby undermined). Justice Breyer appreciates the aphorism's local context, which cautions against the unquestioned rebuilding of the wall. He's thus crowded into the uncomfortable position of agreeing with Justice Scalia on the applicability of the separation of powers doctrine to the case at hand and disagreeing with him on the proper interpretation of the poem. In Dolin's reading of the Justices' readings, 'Breyer's opinion exposes a rift between the poem and the law: to agree on the law but disagree on the poem either cancels out the significance of the poem or it undermines the metaphoric separation of powers doctrine.'[110]

At this point, I'll leave Dolin's masterful analysis of *Plaut*/'Mending Wall,' recommend that my own readers take it up in due course, and turn back to the question of why this type of discussion is important. Of the many potential points of contact between law and literature, which are worth the time to explore? There are at least three such points (in addition to law rhetoric, which we've already considered) that are readily apparent from Dolin's analysis. First, there's the issue of interpretation, often considered under the catch-all 'hermeneutic criticism of law.' Though it's not a particular focus of my study, interpretation cuts across nearly all theoretical discussions of the law, so it is omnipresent in what follows. Second, there's the issue of context, both the local context of a text bite (e.g., 'Good fences make good neighbors' within the poem as a whole) and the historico-cultural context in which any utterance is made or transcribed. As an instance of the latter, we can glance back at 'Mending Wall.' The narrator tells us of the neighbour that 'Good fences make good neighbors' is 'his father's saying.' It's received wisdom (as are legal rules) that neither the neighbour nor Justice Scalia stops to consider. Part of what I'm asking us to do is to rethink borders/boundaries before we reconstruct them (as we do each time we apply a legal rule). Third – and this is the most common currency of my theory – there's the issue of narrative. As Dolin observes, Justice Scalia's 'rhetorical flourish' in *Plaut* confirms Robert Cover's insight that 'no set of legal institutions or prescriptions exists apart from the narratives that locate it and give it meaning.'[111] Each of these three points interpenetrates the others, so each steps out of the background from time to time. But for now I would ask us to focus on the concept of narrative and to consider its bearing on the law – without ignoring some of the well-placed criticisms that have been lodged against certain 'narrative' strains of law and literature commentary.

## What Is Narrative?

'Narrative' is a slippery concept, one capable of generalization to the point of functional meaninglessness. It is therefore necessary to look carefully at some of the competing definitions offered in (mostly) recent scholarship and then arrive at a definition that will serve as the starting point for further discussion:

- 'a story of events arranged in time sequence and offering some sort of meaning'[112]
- 'the organization of material in a chronologically sequential order and the focusing of the content into a single coherent story … its arrangement is descriptive rather than analytical and … its central focus is on man not circumstances'[113]
- 'first a "selective appropriation of past events and characters"; second, a temporal ordering that presents these events with a beginning, a middle and an end; and third, an overarching structure that contextualizes these events as part of an opposition or struggle'[114]
- 'a recognizable discourse or operation … that … can be abstracted from [its] medium [of expression] as in the plot summary'[115]
- a story[116]
- 'a metacode, a human universal on the basis of which transcultural messages about the nature of a shared reality can be transmitted'[117]

The common thread here is the basic idea of a 'story,' a relational and temporal ordering of selected *human* events that culminates in 'closure.' Though we may refine this a bit as we go on, this is a serviceable definition for most of our purposes.

The connection between law and narrative is obvious (perhaps too much so) and has spawned a school in the law and literature stream known as, among other things, 'legal narratology,' or 'narrative jurisprudence.' The claims of this school are many and vary among its adherents, but a number of statements recur. Here's a paraphrase of the list that Binder and Weisberg propose:

1. Humans perceive, store, and retrieve information in narrative form.
2. The same events can give rise to competing events.
3. Legal arguments and judgments are based on selected facts delivered in narrative form.
4. Legal procedures repress competing stories.
5. The stories most often repressed reflect the values and perspectives of subordinated groups.
6. Legal discourse denies that it privileges some stories over others.
7. In their drive to appear objective and impartial, legal actors and institutions employ rules that abstract away particulars of human experience that narrative foregrounds.
8. By suppressing particulars, rules make law 'morally obtuse.'
9. The authority of rules flows from implicit narratives that link those rules to authoritative decision makers and that explain how those decision makers came to have authority.
10. The inclusion of narratives – whether factual or fictional – in legal scholarship will improve the law morally, subvert its claims to objectivity and impartiality, and advance the interests of the disenfranchised.[118]

As the tone of this list suggests, Binder and Weisberg are out to undercut 'some of the extravagant and sentimentalist claims made on … behalf' of narrative legal scholarship.[119] Richard Weisberg, to the contrary, genuinely believes that literary narratives can help us understand (1) how a lawyer communicates, (2) how a lawyer treats people and groups outside the power structure, (3) how a lawyer reasons, and (4) how a lawyer feels.[120] Is there any common ground here? I think so. Binder and Weisberg agree that narrative can inform our understanding of law: 'Narrative is the aspiration that guides us, the tradition that commits us, the hollow-seeming hope that accommodates us to the limits we live within. It is the order we submit to, the law by which we govern ourselves.'[121] Indeed, their deepest criticism is that some law and literature scholars have posited a false dichotomy between law and literature – one that they then busy themselves to tape back together. So where do we find this common ground? I submit that we must look not just at what particular narratives say but also at how they work. We'll come to specific examples in the next chapter, but by way of preview, I'll note that the confluence of narrative and feminist theory has been especially generative in areas of the law dealing with abusive domestic relationships (e.g., the law of provocation as applied to battered spouses).[122] What we'll find is that, engaging as some of these individual stories may be, they work changes in the law for reasons larger than themselves (or how they are told). To me, this suggests that the 'outsider' storytelling model, though important, is incomplete.

But the biggest drawback, in my view, to cabining narrative legal theory within an advocacy-based 'storytelling' framework is that it misses a larger conceptual and practical point: law is a system existing within and alongside other systems. It exerts its own force over those systems, but it is also subject to the gravitational forces of the others. The graviton here is narrative. And like all natural forces, narrative is morally neutral. There are good narratives and bad narratives. Narrative is not just a method for the oppressed to receive justice. Hitler slipped his genocidal programs quite easily into the myth of Lohengrin and the related narrative of a glorious and heroic Teutonic past (as well as the post-1918 'stab in the back' theory of Germany's defeat in the First World War). The aim, then, should be to develop an understanding of how narratives work on and within the law generally – not just within the courtroom.

By further way of groundwork, we must make additional distinctions among categories of narrative falling under the general definitional umbrella. There are, for instance, larger cultural narratives and smaller individual narratives. This is not to suggest that there is a bright line between narratives big and small – to the contrary, I hope to show that one influences the other in ways essential to the making of law. Jonathan Hearn, following Margaret Somers, has developed a useful framework within which to examine narrative forms and how particular narratives interact.[123] For both Hearn and Somers, narrative is an antidote to 'identity politics,' a way of explaining human experience and interaction without wholesale resort to arbitrary or ambiguous labels such as race, ethnicity, class, and gender. The focus thus shifts away from labels, toward a picture of the narratives that both individuals and groups participate in, and toward the web of social relationships into which this picture is woven. Under the Hearn–Somers rubric, narrativity has two aspects: 'emplotment' and 'evaluative criteria.' Emplotment – unlike, for instance, an 'annal,' which is nothing more than a list of dates and events – locates events on a contextual matrix: 'To make something understandable in the context of narrative is to give it historicity and relationality. This works for us because when events are located in a temporal (however fleeting) and sequential plot we can then explain their relationship to other events. Plot can thus be seen as the logic or syntax of narrative.'[124] Embedded in emplotments are 'evaluative criteria,' which extract the important from the trivial and bring about narrative coherence: 'In the face of a potentially limitless array of social experiences deriving from social contact with events, institutions, and people, the evaluative capacity of emplotment demands and enables *selective appropriation* in constructing narratives. A plot must be thematic.'[125]

Thus conceived, narrative is a tool that mediates between raw experience and efforts to articulate that experience by, as Barthes explains it, 'ceaselessly substitut[ing] meaning for the straightforward copy of the events recounted.'[126] In other words, narrative is a way to make sense of it all. But making sense is not a one-size-fits-all proposition. To help sort all this out, both Hearn and Somers identify four main dimensions to narrativity: ontological, public, metanarrative, and conceptual. *Ontological* narratives are narratives that individuals use for making sense of their lives, sometimes by fabricating new narratives, sometimes by investing in existing ones. Hearn explains that this process often involves 'appropriating and customizing "public narratives": those narratives attached to cultural and institutional formations larger than the single individual, to intersubjective networks or institutions, however local or grand.'[127] By way of example, a *public* narrative might trace the ups and downs of families like the Medici, the Churchills, or the Kennedys; or the rise and fall of empires; or periods of great prosperity or famine. *Metanarratives* 'are meant in much the sense made popular by Lyotard (1989), as master narratives that encompass much or all of human history – either as master frameworks for explanation, for example, the Individual versus Society, or progressive stories of the rise (and sometimes fall) of Nationalism, Liberalism, Socialism, Globalization, and the like.'[128] The final dimension, the *conceptual*, concerns the modes of analysis that social scientists conceive in their efforts to understand society, both past and present. As Hearn aptly notes, conceptual 'narratives often interpenetrate with metanarratives.'[129] Indeed, Somers's entire enterprise seems designed to extend the notion of metanarrative to a purely conceptual plane, one 'that is more sensitive to human variability, one that recursively appreciates the role of narrativity both in social theory and throughout social life.'[130]

But Somers does not intend to leave things at the level of concept; her ultimate goal is to offer a description of agency that traces social interaction down through the ever more specific narrative dimensions until ultimately arriving at the ontological level: 'So basic to agency is ontological narrativity that if we want to explain – that is, to know, to make sense of, to account for, perhaps even to predict, anything about the practices of social and historical actors, their collective actions, their modes and meanings of institution-building and group-formations, and their apparent incoherencies – we must first recognize the place of ontological narratives in social life.'[131]

It is at this point that Hearn begins to diverge from Somers, if only to supplement her scheme in two key respects. First, Hearn tasks himself with putting forth a more concrete description of how the various dimensions of narrativity interact. He accordingly offers a redefinition of agency, one that strives for a fuller apprehension of how agency works in practice: 'For persons, agency is not simply either raw potential for action, or the actual expression of action, but something that is deeply felt as an existential need to act, that is either being frustrated or realized in general. We need another, mediating concept that directs our attention to this middle ground between the potential for and performance of agency, to our dispositions towards agency.'[132] Second, Hearn notes that narratives also typically have protagonists. And it is the protagonist that gives a narrative shape and texture, which are the features that permit individuals to invest and participate in higher-order narratives. For Hearn, a troping process is at work: 'A metaphorical link is forged between individual and collective identities. It is because public and meta-narratives have key protagonists – the nation, the class, the race, the gender, the members of the profession, the leaders and employees of the corporation, the great people of "this city" – that individuals identify with them. It is through an isomorphism between the individual and the collective as protagonist that people become attached to narratives.'[133] We can often observe shifting narrative sands by watching protagonists move on and off the stage of great public legal debates as they are embodied in case law. Let's take as an example the continuing battle over abortion at the United States Supreme Court.

In *Roe v. Wade*, the Court sought to free itself of 'emotion' and 'predilection' by inquiring into and placing emphasis on 'medical and medical-legal history.'[134] The Court considered a range of non-legal materials, including the Hippocratic Oath, the then current position of the American Medical Association, and advances in medical technology that had reduced the risk of physical harm associated with abortion procedures. Almost inevitably, then, 'The Physician' emerges as the protagonist in the drama, a looming presence with whom a woman must consult in weighing all the factors that go into an abortion decision. And indeed, the Court aims its holding as much at a physician's right to practise as at a woman's right to privacy: 'The decision vindicates the right of the physician to administer medical treatment according to his professional judgment.'[135] Within two decades, opponents of abortion mounted an assault on *Roe*. In the Supreme Court's opinion in that case, *Planned Parenthood of Southeastern Pa. v. Casey*, the physician all but disappears into the background, replaced by 'The Woman,' whose 'personal decisions,' 'right,' and 'liberty' are at stake.[136] In some cases, she is a tragic victim, one who might suffer bodily injury from an abusive spouse were she to have only a fettered right to abortion (the statute at issue had, *inter alia*, a spousal notification provision). In the Court's most recent foray into the thicket, *Gonzales v. Carhart*, the woman, who must be protected from a choice she may come to regret, gives way to the 'Unborn Child' (aka 'The Infant Life' and 'The Baby'), who is on a quest to enter the world and must be protected along the way (by Congress-as-St George) from a barbaric procedure known as a partial birth abortion.[137] Interestingly, the physician takes another turn across the boards, but this time in the role of villain, not protagonist. No longer is he the reasonable and compassionate 'consultant'; now he is a comrade of Hitler's infamous Angel of Death, Dr Josef Mengele:

> Dr. Haskell went in with forceps and grabbed the baby's legs and pulled them down into the birth canal. Then he delivered the baby's body and the arms – everything but the head. The doctor kept the head right inside the uterus ... The baby's little fingers were clasping and unclasping, and his little feet were kicking. Then the doctor stuck the scissors in the back of his head, and the baby's arms jerked out, like a startle reaction, like a flinch, like a baby does when he thinks he is going to fall. The doctor opened up the scissors, stuck a high-powered suction tube into the opening, and sucked the baby's brains out. Now the baby went completely limp ... He cut the umbilical cord and delivered the placenta. He threw the baby in a pan, along with the placenta and the instruments he had just used.[138]

These cases illustrate quite well, I think, Hearn's point that a narrative's rhetorical power flows just as much from *who* it is about as *what* it is about.

Hearn goes on to suggest that ontological narratives can bind with higher-order narratives because the higher-order narratives 'appeal to us according to how they explain, justify, and resonate with our actual experiences of agency, of empowerment and disempowerment.'[139] This means, I think, that there is much to learn from examining narratives with a 'nexus' approach – that is, from measuring narratives at any given time against one another to see whether they are congruent, complementary, or contradictory. For law, this means that lower-order narratives can become actualized only when they align with a higher-order, dominant narrative. This is not to say, however, that the accretive force of lower-order narratives cannot incrementally shift dominant higher-order narratives into an ultimate position of alignment:

> Ontological narratives are, above all, social and interpersonal. Although psychologists are typically biased toward the individual sources of narrative, even they recognize the degree to which ontological narratives can only exist interpersonally in the course of social and structural interactions over time. To be sure, agents adjust stories to fit their own identities, and, conversely, they will tailor 'reality' to fit their stories. The intersubjective webs of relationality sustain and transform narratives over time. Charles Taylor calls these 'webs of interlocution,' others call them 'traditions,' I call them 'public narratives.'[140]

To illustrate how this plays out in practice, let's turn to some specific examples, including our two literary works.

### How Narratives Interact to Influence Legislation

As I already demonstrated, *The Jungle* is composed of a number of mini-narratives, each of which could in theory have led to legislative reforms. Each is as compelling as its fellows, at least in terms of rhetoric and style. And taken collectively, the overall narrative could have inspired a socialist revolution, a complete revamping of the legal and social systems in the United States. But this didn't happen. The question is 'Why?' The answer is complicated, but it turns on narrative.

First, let's revert to the adulterated food issue and the legislation that *The Jungle* inspired. Federal food and drug regulation was a long time coming in the United States. From the early years of the republic, health and safety regulation was presumed to reside in the states; consequently, most federal officials thought (to the extent that they thought about it at all) that the federal government lacked legislative jurisdiction over the subject matter.[141] But two overlapping narratives were destined to converge in Congress and to clash with the dominant narrative of nineteenth-century America: *laissez-faire* capitalism.[142] The unlikely narrative partnership arose from, on the one hand, a series of fragmented yet slowly coalescing consumer-oriented stories; and from, on the other hand, entrepreneurial businesses trying to elbow their way to a seat at the table of commerce. Young puts it this way:

> The attempt to secure a broad national law to protect citizens of the United States from the expanding threat of adulterated food, drink, and drugs began in 1879 and continued through a quarter century, by turns waxing and waning in intensity, before reaching fruition in 1906. During this extended campaign, two kinds of voices urged the necessity for action. The reform voice, sometimes shrill, concerns itself with the welfare of consumers, and, while bemoaning the way in which adulteration cheats the public, puts major stress on hazards to health. The business voice speaks in less frenetic tones, downplays danger, exempts from regulation harmless adulterants sanctioned by long trade practice, and defines more serious secret adulteration as a morally indefensible economic practice that pinches the consumer's purse and pushes the honorable entrepreneur, unable to compete, to the brink of bankruptcy. The reform and business voices criticize each other, as well as castigating their mutual enemies.[143]

This dance of narratives continued throughout the closing years of the nineteenth century, with the partners drawn closer by a confluence of key persons and events. First, it is hard to overestimate the work of Dr Wiley, who was the chief chemist in the Department of Agriculture from 1883 until 1912. His obituary in *Science* described him as both a tenacious crusader and an astute observer of the human condition: 'a very mountain among men, a lion among fighters, [a] keen student of human nature, [and a] prince of good fellows.'[144] Wiley was by all accounts not only a solid scientist but as well – and probably more important – a capable bureaucrat and an effective public speaker and writer. He skilfully used the press, and his 'Poison Squad' – whose human volunteers experimented on themselves with food preservatives – enlivened the public imagination. But according to his biographer, Oscar Anderson, Wiley's greatest contribution was his ability to stay the course: 'He was the one individual who gave continuity to the struggle for pure food and drugs, the one leader who consistently saw the big picture. Wiley was in large part responsible for the fact that food and drug legislation came when it did and in the form that it did.'[145]

Soon after the turn of the century, Wiley's concerns about chemical food adulteration and about the quackery associated with patent medicines converged with the interests of the muckraking press. Chief among Wiley's muckraking collaborators was Samuel Hopkins Adams, who penned a widely followed polemic aimed at the patent medicine industry. The first instalment of Adams's series appeared in *Collier's* magazine in October 1905 and ran through February 1906. While collecting information for his articles, Adams consulted with Wiley, and later – when Congress took up the pure food and drug bill – he travelled to Washington to support Wiley's efforts to secure passage of the legislation.[146] But as Robert Crunden has shown, Adams left Roosevelt, who felt that journalistic hyperbole had poisoned the pure food issue, unpersuaded.[147] This, coupled with Roosevelt's suspicion of science in general and of Wiley's science in particular, might have kept the president on the legislative sidelines had the food and drug bill arrived in a vacuum. It did not, however: 'Furor over *The Jungle*, and public identification of meat and food bills as a "single effort" ... led Roosevelt to push hard for them both.'[148] An unanswered question hovers above here: Why did the meat legislation resonate with Roosevelt in a way that the food and drug legislation did not? An answer may be found – to return to Somers's vocabulary – in Roosevelt's ontological narrative.

In April 1898 the United States declared war on Spain. An expeditionary force decamped for Cuba in June and won two major battles on 1 July. Soon after, the Americans devastated the Spanish fleet in Santiago harbour, thereby bringing a quick end to the Spanish-American War. The American forces stayed on for a few weeks and in the process suffered nine times as many casualties from disease as from the period of combat. The reason? In almost every respect, the army was ill prepared to wage a tropical war. Provisions in general and bad beef in particular formed an area of special complaint. One mother of a soldier wrote in a letter to President McKinley: 'We are living under a generous Government, with a good, kind man at its head willing to give the Army the best possible, and yet thieving corporations will give the boys the worst.'[149]

McKinley, who had already been reading newspaper accounts of the food scandal, quickly appointed a special commission (the Dodge Commission, named for its head, General Grenville M. Dodge) to investigate the Cuban food debacle. Based on testimony before that commission, McKinley subsequently established a court of inquiry (the Wade Court, named for its head, Major General James Wade) to probe the mounting evidence of malfeasance in the provisioning of beef. In testimony before the Dodge Commission, Major General Nelson A. Miles coined the catchphrase by which army beef would thereafter be referred:

> There was sent to Porto Rico 337 tons of what was known as, or called, refrigerated beef, which you might call embalmed beef, and there was also sent 198,508 pounds of what is known as canned fresh beef, which was condemned ... by nearly every officer whose commands used it.[150]

In his autobiography, *Always the Young Strangers*, the poet Carl Sandburg recalled with little relish his own experiences with 'embalmed beef':

> What we called 'Red Horse' soon had all our country scandalized with its new name of 'Embalmed Beef.' It *was* embalmed. We buried it at sea because it was so duly embalmed with all flavor of life and every suck of nourishment gone from it though having nevertheless a putridity of odor more pungent than ever reaches the nostrils from a properly embalmed cadaver.[151]

Sandburg was not the only soon to be public figure to have suffered the torments of embalmed beef. Indeed, the embalmed beef fiasco left a lifelong impression on someone crucial to our larger discussion of consumer legislation: Theodore Roosevelt.

Roosevelt was a lieutenant colonel at the time of the Spanish-American War, which brought him into the limelight as the daring leader of a group of volunteers known as the Rough Riders. Prior to that group's famed charge up San Juan Hill, Roosevelt was faced with grousing from his troops about the canned roast beef they were being fed. Roosevelt later (by then Governor of New York) recounted these incidents in testimony before the Wade Court. He particularly recalled challenging a red-haired Kentuckian whom he caught in the act of discarding his meat ration. 'I can't eat the meat,' the soldier explained. Roosevelt retorted: 'If you are a baby, you had better not have come to the war. Eat it and be a man.' The soldier attempted to comply, and vomited.[152] Roosevelt first suspected that the problem was confined to the delicate stomachs of the volunteers, but he soon found that the regular cavalry also despised canned beef. He even 'tried to eat some of it myself when I was hungry and found that I could not,' finding the substance 'slimey ... stringy and coarse ... like a bundle of fibers.'[153] Upon returning from the war, the only surprise Roosevelt felt in learning of the raging public debate over 'embalmed beef' was that there was any debate at all, given that he had never heard an affirmative argument put forward: 'I never, in the cavalry division, or in the few infantrymen with whom I came in contact, from the generals down to the privates, heard anybody speak of the canned roast beef when they did not take it as a matter of course that it was a bad ration.'[154]

At the end of the day, the findings of the Dodge Commission and the Wade Court were inconclusive and in many key respects exonerated the packers: yes, there had been problems with the food supplied during the Spanish-American War, but no, the packers had not poisoned the beef supplied to the expeditionary force with preservatives. But none of that really mattered. For as Young aptly remarks, 'few Americans, certainly not Theodore Roosevelt, forgot "embalmed beef."' Indeed, the embalmed beef story was absorbed into a growing anti-packer public narrative, as it was into Roosevelt's own ontological narrative. And there it lay dormant for several years, awaiting an impetus like Upton Sinclair's *The Jungle* to reinvigorate it. We can thus see that the 1906 legislation was possible only because of a felicitous alignment of three narratives: Roosevelt's ontological one, which contained an 'embalmed beef' strand; a public one that increasingly portrayed the beef-packing industry as corrupt; and a literary one that sparked these other narratives to life (in the form of legislation).

## Text in Context

To remark on these felicitous narrative alignments and the law they produced is to remind ourselves that both law and narrative are historically situated. As Brook Thomas states it, laws and literature both 'grow out of a particular place and time.'[155] This suggests that one way to examine the intersection of various narratives and laws is with the tools of historicism, be it traditional (e.g., the historical determinism of Hippolyte Taine) or 'New' (e.g., the cultural poetics of Stephen Greenblatt). For Taine, independent forces – not a summoning and exercise of personal will – compel human actors to act as they do.[156] With respect to writers, three factors are at work: race, milieu, and moment.

Race 'consists of those innate and hereditary dispositions which man brings with him into the world and which are generally accompanied with marked differences of temperament and of bodily structure. They vary in different nations.'[157] Milieu (environment) scoops up sub-factors as diverse as climate, political events, and social/religious conditions: 'man is not alone in the world; nature envelops him and other men surround him; accidental and secondary folds come and overspread the primitive and permanent fold, while physical or social circumstances derange or complete the natural groundwork surrendered to them.'[158] Moment (epoch) signifies 'the acquired momentum' at any given point in time. For 'when national character and surrounding circumstances operate it is not on a tabula rasa, but on one already bearing imprints. According as this tabula is taken at one or at another moment so is the imprint different, and this suffices to render the total effect different.'[159]

There is much to criticize in this formulation, but it gets us to an important point – namely, that any historical artefact bobs in a causal pool. It is both producing and produced. Through reverse engineering of artefacts, then, we can learn something about how they issued and what they may have in turn influenced. With respect to literature, Taine says that a 'work is not a mere play of the imagination, the isolated caprice of an excited brain, but a transcript of contemporary manners and customs and a sign of a particular state of intellect.'[160] But this isn't just a way of thinking about literature. It applies as well to 'the large stiff pages of a folio volume, or the yellow leaves of a manuscript, in short, a poem, a code of laws, [or] a confession of faith.'[161] Each 'is simply a mold like a fossil shell, an imprint similar to one of those forms embedded in a stone by an animal which once lived and perished.' So just as we can study a fossil to develop some idea of the animal that formed it, so may we study a document to comprehend its author. Taine privileges literature, but only because its depth and subtlety allow us to draw a 'moral history' from it in a way not possible with other documents: 'there is nothing approaching [remarkable sensitiveness] in constitutions or religions; the articles of a code or of a catechism do no more than depict mind in gross and without finesse; if there are documents which show life in spirit or politics and in creeds, they are the eloquent discourses of the pulpit and the tribune, memoirs and personal confessions, all belonging to literature, so that, outside of itself, literature embodies whatever is good elsewhere.'[162] Under this way of thinking, any document can be described as a momentary fix and snapshot of then extant cultural cross-currents. Thus, contra strict textual constructionists, 'it is a mistake to study [a] document as if it existed alone by itself. That is treating things merely as a pedant, and you subject yourself to the illusions of a book-worm.'[163]

Historicism à la Taine as a mode of literary criticism died out in the middle of the last century in favour of text-based formalism (which I'll return to later in a discussion of New Criticism). Around 1980, though, historical criticism began a resurgence, particularly in Renaissance Studies, more particularly in the work of Stephen Greenblatt and Louis Montrose.[164] The practitioners of this New Historicism are many, and 'to group and define these wildly individual efforts would demand a craz[y] yearning.'[165] In fact, there are a number of schools of influence at work, ranging from Foucault, to Marx, to Benjamin, to Bakhtin and beyond.[166] Nonetheless, there are some common approaches that I'll try to quickly round up before turning to the implications that New Historicism may have for law.

New Historicist critics often assume that a literary work is not stable in the sense of self-containment. The text points outward to the world, but the world points back as well. And these referential cross-currents are not just between works of literature. Greenblatt and Catherine Gallagher put it this way: 'We are intensely interested in tracking the social energies that circulate very broadly through a culture, flowing back and forth between margins and center, passing from zones designated as art to zones apparently indifferent or hostile to art, pressing up from below to transform exalted spheres and down from on high to colonize the low.'[167] Greenblatt's technique, as Brook Thomas describes it, is to accrete historical details ('thick descriptions' in New Historicist lingo) before directly engaging a literary work. 'Starting with the analysis of a particular historical event, he then cuts to the analysis of a particular literary text. The point is not to show that the literary text reflects the historical event but to create a field of energy between the two so that we come to see the event as a social text and the literary text as a social event.'[168] In the hands of a New Historicist, then, a Shakespearean play can be seen as a political event, and royal pageantry can be read as a dramatic act.[169]

The application of a New Historicist method to law 'means both that the law's supposedly prosaic, instrumental process of weighing interests and defining entitlements is a contested social process of self-definition, and that the law's literary legibility in no way implies its refinement or transcendence of venality.'[170] Gregg Crane offers a useful way of approaching the task: 'Instead of theorizing an essential barrier between [legal and literary] discourses, one might situate these discourses in the historical moment (for example, the proximity of each to state power, the various roles that each has played in reproducing or challenging dominant notions of the social order, the types of institutional and material support each has received, and the effects on each of commercial or professional development).'[171] The point would be to 'trace the patterns of influence between law and literature' by 'analyzing their points of thematic and figural intersection.' To fix these abstractions somewhat and to show how the interplay of incongruent social discourses can influence legal outcomes and rules, I want to pick a hoary evidence case, *Mutual Life Ins. Co. of New York v. Hillmon*,[172] that fits neatly with my own ontological narrative as well as a couple of others. The case begins, as do I, on the Great Plains of Kansas, only a few years before my grandfather (who lived until the late 1980s) arrived in Kansas in a covered wagon with his parents and siblings. (I thus come by vast amounts of frontier/pioneer lore both genetically and by indoctrination!) To keep the length of this story manageable, I'll have to compress and condense considerably, but Marianne Wesson has written at great length about the case as part of an investigation that is ongoing, and her efforts are readily available to round out the story for the curious.[173]

Toward the end of 1878, John W. Hillmon purchased $25,000 of life insurance (a considerable sum in those days) before setting out from Lawrence, Kansas, for points west. The ostensible purpose of his trip was to meet up with a friend, John H. Brown, who would accompany him on an expedition to find and purchase land for a ranching operation. Brown and Hillmon connected in Wichita sometime in February 1879 and around 5 March headed southwest toward Medicine Lodge, where they stayed for a few days before decamping for a relatively unpopulated area called Crooked Creek. There, tragedy befell Hillmon: Brown's rifle discharged as he was unloading it from a wagon and a bullet struck Hillmon in the head. The coroner at Medicine Lodge – after personally visiting the campsite – convened an inquest (two, actually). Witnesses at the inquest testified that they knew Brown and Hillmon from an earlier trip and that they recognized the body as that of Hillmon. The verdict was 'accidental death.' That probably would have been that had not Hillmon's wife of less than six months, Sallie, made a claim on the insurance policies, setting in motion a litigation of *Bleak Housian* proportions, one that spawned six trials (and two trips to the Supreme Court) and that spanned the turn of a new century.[174] Only one of those trials, the third, will be our object of study.

On its face, Sallie Hillmon's claim bore indications of fraud: Hillmon was of relatively modest means (compared to the amount of insurance), a relative had paid part of the insurance premiums, the couple had been married only a short time, and Hillmon's 'death' came right on the heels of the multipolicy purchase. Unsurprisingly, given these circumstances and a general proliferation of insurance fraud in the late nineteenth century (apparently, insurance fraud was something akin to current-day employment scams on craigslist or Nigerian Prince e-mail blasts), the insurance companies refused to pay voluntarily, and litigation ensued. In 1888, after two trials had resulted in hung juries, the third trial came on as a consolidation of three separate actions (one against each insurance company).

At trial, Sallie's case rested on evidence supporting the gun-fell-out-of-the-wagon story that I just described. Defendants, however, 'introduced evidence tending to show that the body found in the camp at Crooked creek on the night of March 18th was not the body of Hillmon, but the body of one Frederick Adolph Walters.'[175] There was 'much conflicting evidence' on the point, but in the defendants' telling, 'Walters left his home at Ft. Madison, in the state of Iowa, in March, 1878, and was afterwards in Kansas in 1878, and in January and February, 1879; that during that time his family frequently received letters from him, the last of which was written from Wichita; and that he had not been heard from since March, 1879.' To tie Walters to the corpse at Crooked Creek, the defendants tried to introduce two letters from Walters, one written to his sister, one to his fiancée. The sister's letter had been lost, but the fiancée's letter was available. The trial court refused to allow the sister to testify as to the contents of her letter or to allow the contents of the fiancée's letter to be read to the jury. For the Supreme Court's purposes, the two letters contained evidence of the same operative fact, so I'll focus on the letter that was physically available.

The fiancée, Alvina D. Kasten, testified that she was twenty-one years of age, a resident of Fort Madison, and engaged to Walters, whom she last saw in March 1878. After Walters left, she corresponded regularly with him, receiving a letter about every two weeks until 3 March 1879, the date on which she received his final letter. That letter was dated at

Wichita, 1 March 1879, and signed by Walters; the envelope was post-marked 'Wichita, Kansas, March 2, 1879.' Here's what it said:

> Dearest Alvina: Your kind and ever welcome letter was received yesterday afternoon about an hour before I left Emporia. I will stay here until the fore part of next week, and then will leave here to see a part of the country that I never expected to see when I left home, as I am going with a man by the name of Hillmon, who intends to start a sheep ranch, and, as he promised me more wages than I could make at anything else, I concluded to take it, for a while at least, until I strike something better. There is so many folks in this country that have got the Leadville fever, and if I could not of got the situation that I have now I would have went there myself; but as it is at present I get to see the best part of Kansas, Indian Territory, Colorado, and Mexico. The route that we intend to take would cost a man to travel from $150 to $200, but it would not cost me a cent; besides, I get good wages. I will drop you a letter occasionally until I get settled down. Then I want you to answer it.[176]

The trial court ruled that this letter (and the one to Walters's sister) was inadmissible hearsay. So when Sallie prevailed at trial, the defendants included this evidentiary ruling as a point of error on appeal. They didn't really need it, though, because the Supreme Court held that the trial court had committed a fatal procedural error when – after consolidating the three separate cases – it made the defendants share three peremptory challenges to the prospective jurors rather than allowing them three each.

But despite the Supreme Court's usual reluctance to answer questions not necessary to the disposition of a matter, it went on to take up the evidentiary ruling. I don't want to spend much time with the matter here, but Wesson makes a convincing argument that it was not so much the author of the opinion, Justice Gray, who was interested in the evidentiary point as his clerk, Ezra Ripley Thayer (later Dean of Harvard Law School), and Thayer's father, James Bradley Thayer, a noted evidence scholar at Harvard.[177] Intriguing as that side story is, I want us to drill into the evidentiary ruling itself and consider why it was fashioned the way it was. For leaving aside that Thayer and his father might have been interested in this particular instance of hearsay as representative of a class, one can imagine that it would not have been difficult to convince the Court that it should take a position on the letters, given that an evidentiary battle over the letters was 'so likely to arise upon another trial.'[178] So I'm not sure that Thayer would have had to do much smuggling, since common sense and even mild pragmatism would have suggested that a pen stroke now could cut off an appellate point later, especially because the issue had to recur in one form or another on retrial.

In the Court's view, '[t]he matter chiefly contested at the trial was the death of John W. Hillmon' – that is, 'whether the body found at Crooked creek on the night of March 18, 1879, was his body or the body of one Walters.' The defendants introduced evidence tending to show that Walters was at Wichita in early March, that he had not been heard from since, that his body had been found at Crooked Creek, and that he went to Crooked Creek between early March and 18 March. Thus,

> [e]vidence that just before March 5th he had the intention of leaving Wichita with Hillmon would tend to corroborate the evidence already admitted, and to show that he went from Wichita to Crooked Creek with Hillmon. Letters from him to his family and to his betrothed were the natural, if not the only attainable, evidence of his intention. [And] whenever the intention is of itself a distinct and material fact in a chain of circumstances, it may be proved by contemporaneous oral or written declarations of the party.[179]

Thus is born the modern 'statement of intention' exception to the hearsay rule. This exception has been much criticized, and it does seem overbroad. (Could a statement that 'I'm going to do my homework' be used later as collateral proof that the dog did eat it?) So why did the Court (largely) invent this exception? Wesson makes a good structuralist (without using that term) argument that 'narrative exigencies' rather than 'policy views' drove the Court's decision.[180] Specifically, she argues that the Court was compelled to read the story before it as a 'romance,' into which the 'Dearest Alvina' letter (in its very artlessness) fits perfectly as a signifier of truth. Without disagreeing with this assessment, I would offer something different, tied back to the idea of a public narrative.

In *The Significance of the Frontier in American History*, a book that influenced more than a generation of American historians and literary critics (and gave rise to American Studies as a discipline separate from either), Frederick Jackson Turner equated the frontier with lawlessness: 'I have refrained from dwelling on the lawless characteristics of the frontier, because they are sufficiently well known. The gambler and desperado, the regulators of the Carolinas and the vigilantes of California are types of that line of scum that the waves of advancing civilization bore before them, and of the growth of spontaneous organs of authority where legal authority was absent.'[181] When Jackson says that the lawlessness of the frontier was 'sufficiently well known,' I think he's simply identifying the public narrative that had grown up to both describe and define life on the frontier (especially to those not living there).[182] If that's right, then the Supreme Court was in some sense constrained to read the facts of the *Hillmon* case in light of that narrative. As a consequence, the Court created a rule of evidence that would allow the construction of a better, more truthful story – one in which John Hillmon was a murdering, thieving desperado who preyed on a hapless young adventurer out to 'strike something better' on the frontier. But as Wesson shows, that's probably not the case: the 'Dearest Alvina' letter was either an outright fake or at best full of lies.[183] In either case, it was probably an invention of the insurance companies.

In a later chapter I'll explain how the process of constrained interpretation works; for now, it's enough for us to examine the result. The *Hillmon* opinion, like a work of art, is a historical product, which is to say that it is a product of a multiplicity of discourses – of narratives. Thus its authors (I'll assume more than one hand in the opinion) could not stand outside that narrative stream as 'objective' observers of the evidence. Rather, they read the evidence in light of (among other things) a stock public narrative of the lawless frontier and the artless young seekers who were lured there by the promise of 'something better.' ('Go West, young man, and grow up with the country!')[184] In that light, the 'Dearest Alvina' letter made it easier to find 'facts' that fit into a story that coordinated with that public narrative. In other words, the letter *had to be* admissible. And so it was.

### What's Truth Have to Do with It?

If narrative alignments can cause shifts in the law, what is it about a literary narrative that 'gets it in the game?' Some have suggested that literature is most effective when it is 'truthful.' That seems a dubious proposition, given literature's (mostly) fictional nature, but it is not something we need resolve for purposes of our present discussion. I would submit, rather, that a literary work can effect great change when it is *plausible* under a public narrative that is on the cusp of becoming dominant. In other words, a story doesn't need to be *true* to be an agent of change; mere plausibility is sufficient.[185] This much may reasonably be derived from our discussion of the pure food narratives, but it may be more instructive to discuss an example in which a legislation-inducing narrative is demonstrably false.

In the middle of a summer's day in 1969, a stretch of the Cuyahoga River passing through Cleveland, Ohio, burst into flames. Former Environmental Protection Agency administrator Carol Browner spoke for many of us of a certain age when she said: 'I will never forget a photograph of flames, fire, shooting right out of the water in downtown Cleveland. It was the summer of 1969 and the Cuyahoga River was burning.'[186] The photograph in question then stood and still stands as graphic proof that the then current system of environmental regulation (mostly state/local legislation and common law) was woefully deficient, which militated in favour of sweeping new legislation at the federal level.

And that legislation quickly followed in the form of, *inter alia*, the Federal Water Pollution Control Act of 1972.[187] Even today, the image of the fire is regularly invoked both as a cautionary tale and as a yardstick against which to measure how far we have come in our efforts to reclaim the environment. For example, as a testament to the continuing iconic status of the Cuyahoga fire, CNN broadcast this report on the thirtieth anniversary of the conflagration:

Three decades ago, an event occurred that would galvanize the U.S. environmental movement: the Cuyahoga River became a river of fire. A nauseating brew of flammable pollutants from steel mills, paint factories, chemical plants and sewage burst into flame. Today, mother ducks swim in the Cuyahoga with their offspring, blue herons have returned to the river banks, and rowing teams practice – all testament to an astonishing ecological [re]covery.[188]

This contrasts nicely with media reports of the pre-duck era, including this one from the 1 August 1969 issue of *Time*:

Some River! Chocolate-brown, oily, bubbling with subsurface gases, it oozes rather than flows. 'Anyone who falls into the Cuyahoga does not drown,' Cleveland's citizens joke grimly. 'He decays.'... The Federal Water Pollution Control Administration dryly notes: 'The lower Cuyahoga has no visible signs of life, not even low forms such as leeches and sludge worms that usually thrive on wastes.' It is also – literally – a fire hazard.[189]

A tidy narrative, this. Except that it never happened – at least not like we think it happened. The Cuyahoga was indeed polluted in 1969, as were all American rivers in the Rust Belt. They had been since the nineteenth century. And the Cuyahoga did briefly catch fire on 22 June 1969, as it had from time to time for over a hundred years.[190] But the fire, which arose when sparks from a passing train ignited a small oil slick and debris, was relatively minor, was quickly extinguished, and caused only about $50,000 in damage to two train trestles.[191] How can that be, one might ask, especially in light of the famous photograph of a wall of flames, a towering plume of smoke, and valiant firefighters pouring tens of thousands of gallons of water onto the inferno? The answer is simple: that's a photograph of the 1952 fire, a serious fire that caused over $1.5 million in damage.[192]

Why is it, then, that the 1969 fire provoked such outrage when its much more significant predecessors like the 1952 fire (or Sinclair's fictional fires on the Chicago River in the early 1900s) hardly registered? Jonathan Adler suggests – correctly, I think – that it was all a matter of timing:

> The 1969 fire was a catalyst for change because it was the wrong event at the right time. It was neither an impressive fire, nor one with a significant ecological impact. It may have brought greater attention to the serious environmental problems of the time, but it did not represent a continuing decline in water quality, let alone worsening environmental degradation nationwide. Contrasted with the relevant [sic] indifference to burning rivers in decades past, the public outcry over the 1969 fire signified that increasingly wealthy Americans now wanted to devote greater resources to environmental protection – and they likely would have even in the absence of federal regulations.[193]

Put differently, a public environmental narrative sufficient to flower into legislation in the presence of a catalyst like the 1969 fire did not exist prior to the 1960s. And even then, the putative narrative catalyst was not itself sufficient without some dressing up – some supplemental narrativizing – as we have seen.[194]

**Whose Story to Believe?**

If the Cuyahoga example shows that a narrative must be fleshed out (from time to time with fiction) to have legal consequences, sometimes the issue is one of contradictory narratives competing for legal recognition. *Silent Spring* presents one such case. As we already noted, the book challenged one of the prevailing myths of the Industrial Revolution and its successors: the notion of technological progress. It came as no surprise, then, that the chemical industry and its allies deployed that prevailing narrative as a block against *Silent Spring*'s potential to influence legislation. Monsanto Chemical Company, which was a major producer of DDT, published a 'fable' that parodied the introduction to *Silent Spring* and that presented an apocalyptic vision of a world overrun with insects.[195] An industry spokesman, Robert White-Stevens, invoked a typical image of devolution: 'If man were to faithfully follow the teachings of Miss Carson, we would return to the dark ages, and the insects and diseases and vermin would again inherit the earth.'[196] Even government officials warned of crops that could not be grown, staples that could not be maintained in abundant supply, and public health standards that could not be maintained in the absence of pesticide use.[197] Again, all this seems expected.

But it is not all. The most virulent criticism of *Silent Spring* came packaged in two of the era's most dominant public narratives: gender differences and communism.[198] Former Secretary of Agriculture Ezra Taft Benton is 'credited' with launching these lines of attack in a letter to Dwight Eisenhower, in which he wondered 'why a spinster with no children was so concerned with genetics?' The answer: she was 'probably a Communist.'[199] As Linda Lear explains, Benton's opening volley had serious consequences in the court of public opinion: 'The question reflected increasing attention on Carson's gender by those who commented on *Silent Spring* and its reserved author. The press was inordinately interested in Carson's marital status. She was, after all, physically attractive, quiet, and feminine.'[200] In the end, Carson's sex came to colour every argument against her scientific conclusions:

> Finally, mixed in with all the other arguments was Carson's gender. She kept cats and loved birds. She was a nature writer, a mystic, a devotee of the balance of nature. Her arguments were exaggerations born of hysteria at worst and an overly sensitive nature at best. Reason had been sacri-

ficed to sentiment. Behind these charges was understandable resentment of Carson's aggressive attack on the scientific establishment and on male dominated technology. Among her other errors, Miss Carson had over-stepped her place.[201]

Carson's narrative ultimately swamped those of her critics, but her struggle is in many respects representative. In the next chapter, we will look more closely at narrative combat and how the winners come to be institutionalized, sometimes for good, sometimes for ill, and sometimes at great cost. For now, it is enough that we remain both open to and on guard against narrative's raw power, especially where that power is actuated through forms in which the human dimension has either atro-phied or become wholly stereotyped. And we must be mindful, too, that narratives exist in a web-like complex; advancing one can sum-mon up others far different from those predicted or intended, as Rachel Carson and her acolytes learned. On that note, I close this section with an appropriate admonishment from Robert Penn Warren's *All the King's Men:*

> The world is all of one piece ... The world is like an enormous spider web and if you touch it, however lightly, at any point, the vibration ripples to the remotest perimeter and the drowsy spider feels the tingle and is drowsy no more but springs out to fling the gossamer coils about you who have touched the web and then inject the black, numbing poison under your hide. It does not matter whether or not you meant to brush the web of things. Your happy foot or your gay wing may have brushed it ever so lightly, but what happens always happens and there is the spider, bearded black and with his great faceted eyes glittering like mirrors in the sun, or like God's eye, and the fangs dripping.[202]

# 2 Institutionalizing Narratives*

In the last chapter, we observed how narratives interact with one another and with legal institutions to influence legislation. Next, we move out onto a broader plane to consider the similar – but not fully congruent – question of how narratives figure in common law decisions. This will allow us to examine the process by which narratives can actually *become* (not just influence) legal rules. This process of narrative institutionalization is complicated, but we can tease out at least some of the knots by looking both at specific case law examples and at useful theoretical accounts from inside and outside the law. As a launching point, it may prove helpful to consider one of the most common ways in which legal philosophers account for the application of law: the 'normative syllogism,' the major premise of which is a universal and normative rule of law – the minor allegations or findings of fact.[1]

## Narrative and the Normative Syllogism

In *Law, Fact, and Narrative Coherence*, Bernard Jackson offers a narrativisitic account of law that challenges the notion that legal decision making and justification can properly proceed via deductive reasoning.[2] The thrust of Jackson's argument is twofold. First, he asserts a 'strong' objection to the traditional view based on a structuralist linguistic argument that reference is merely a pragmatic truth claim. For example, a witness's testimony does not actually 'refer' to past events; rather, that testimony is a present, rhetorical construct designed to convince others that it corresponds to 'what really happened.' Testimonial evidence is therefore never more than an unverifiable claim to truth. Jackson recognizes that this represents 'a highly skeptical epistemology,' and he offers it more as a point of provocation than as a candidate for immediate practical implementation (e.g., he concedes that 'it would require a severe paradigm shift').[3]

Second, he asserts a 'weak' objection that does not entail wholesale acceptance of the radical conclusions (e.g., rejection of any correspondence theory of truth) that are inherent in the 'strong' objection. The weak objection turns not on the relationship between present testimony and past events but rather on the one between what a legislator has pronounced and facts that are subsequently adjudicated. His essential point is that there is an inevitable mismatch between the facts adjudicated and the law applied. This is so, he argues, because laws nowadays are expressed in universal and abstract terms that do not refer to particular cases; rather, they do no more than tie abstract legal conditions to specified legal consequences. Thus, according to Jackson, there is a fatal flaw in the traditional mode of legal reasoning because the major premise cannot be said to 'refer' to the facts in the minor premise, for the simple reason that the major premise exists first in time.

As Neil MacCormick has effectively demonstrated, this criticism is misplaced, for the following reason. Jackson takes as his working example the classical textbook case of Socrates and blasphemy:

All persons who blaspheme the gods are liable to be executed;
Socrates has blasphemed the gods;
Therefore Socrates is liable to be executed.[4]

The problem, as Jackson sees it, is that the major premise, as a universal, does not refer to any particular case, yet the minor one does. How, then, can the former authorize a conclusion as to the latter without risking violence to the Rule of Law, in particular its insistence on prospectivity?[5] MacCormick concedes that there is a problem here, but he identifies it as one of 'sense,' not 'reference.'[6] Thus, in the adjudicative context, the Rule of Law is upheld so long as the dictate of the major premise and the facts of the case at hand are used in the same sense. This presents, then, not an irresolvable problem of reference, but a mandate to *interpret* the standards set forth in the major premise and to *classify* the facts set forth in the minor premise in a manner that ensures that an adverse conclusion (i.e., liability) arises only if the general and the particular are used in the same sense.[7] To return to Jackson's example, Socrates is liable to be executed only if his particular conduct ('blasphemed the gods') qualifies as an instance of the general conduct proscribed ('blasphemed the gods'), with the operative phrase, 'blasphemed the gods,' used in the same sense in each premise.

Despite this problem in Jackson's criticism of the normative syllogism, his predicate assumptions involving the narrative roots of law – be they expressed in legislation or in common law rules – are well taken and signal a path along which we may discover how narratives become institutionalized as laws. In especial, we may learn a great deal from what Jackson tells us about the narrative form of rules:

> In almost any collection of ancient or medieval laws, the predominant form of expression we find is that commonly called by legal historians the 'casuistic' form – the conditional sentence in which the protasis expresses a hypothetical situation (the conditioning facts), while the apodosis states the conditioned consequences ... The following verse from the Bible is typical: 'If a thief is found breaking in, and is struck so that he dies, there should be no blood guilt for him ...' ... The assumption is often made that the origin of the pattern reflects actual adjudication: a case of this kind actually came up for decision, and as a result a rule was stated applying to everyone.[8]

Jackson expresses some doubt about this final proposition – at least as a universal – but for our purposes it doesn't matter whether a narrative embedded in a rule is adjudicative, literary, or of some other stripe. For the question we want to answer turns not on the origin of law-producing narratives, but rather on how narratives come to produce laws at all.

## The Narrative Nudge

We can look first to Justice Holmes, who understood that logic and narrative are not simply labels for competing paradigms: they are instead complementary facets of a single enterprise. In *The Common Law*, he noted a 'paradox' inherent in the development of the law that remains worthy of consideration:

> In form its growth is logical. The official theory is that each new decision follows syllogistically from existing precedents. But just as the clavicle in the cat only tells of the existence of some creature to which a collar-bone was useful, precedents survive in law long after the use they once served is at an end and the reason for them has been forgotten ... On the other hand, in substance the growth of the law is legislative. And this in a deep-

er sense than that what the courts declare to have always been the law is in fact new. It is legislative in its grounds ... Every important principle which is developed by litigation is in fact and at bottom the result of more or less definitely understood views of public policy; most generally, to be sure, under our practice and our traditions, the unconscious result of instinctive preferences and inarticulate convictions, but none the less traceable to views of public policy in the last analysis.[9]

By locating legal developments in 'public policy' and in 'adopting new principles from life,' Holmes in some sense anticipates Jackson's narrative theory of rule formation and emendation. For what are life principles if not compact expressions of life *stories?* A couple of specific examples, followed by a more general discussion suggested by Zenon Bankowski and Martha Nussbaum's readings of *Antigone*, should help us close this loop.

The appellate opinions in the famous case of *Hynes v. New York Central Railway Company* are instructive. At the intermediate appellate level, the court began its opinion with a brief description of the case as an 'action ... for alleged negligence, in causing the death of plaintiff's intestate, by being struck by electric wires which fell from a cross-arm of a pole maintained by defendant along its railroad,' followed by a rote statement of facts:

Decedent, a boy 16 years old, with two other boys, had swum across this ship canal from the Manhattan bank on July 8, 1916. He had climbed upon defendant's wooden-faced bulkhead, and finally walked out on a springboard projecting over the water. It was a plank 2' x 12' spiked down on the bulkhead, from which it ran back about 4 feet, so that the shore end was let into the soil. About 11 feet overhung the water. Its front end was about 3 feet above high tide. As Decedent was about to dive from the end, the wires came down. One struck him; others, falling on the plank, broke it off at the bulkhead; deceased was thrown into the water and died. The front of the plank protruded beyond defendant's boundary line from 3 to 6 feet. Who had manually placed this springboard did not appear. It had been there about three years. Employees of defendant and others had used it. On the land side defendant had maintained a fence along its right of way. Warnings that it was not a thoroughfare had also been posted along the railroad track, near this waterfront.[10]

From this pedestrian factual recitation, Putnam, J. quickly disposes of the case by agreeing with the trial court's holding that the plank was part of defendant's property, and was so annexed as to become part of the realty. Decedent's entry upon defendant's close from the waters of the ship canal was an unlawful intrusion. On this plank, he was still a trespasser – even when he stepped outward across defendant's technical boundary line and stood near the outer end, over the waters of the ship canal.[11]

As justification for this conclusion, Putnam, J. offers a series of rules designed to defeat the argument that the plank – or at least the part upon which Hynes was standing when struck by the wires – was not actually part of the railroad's property because it extended out over the property line. This series includes (1) the ancient rule that tree branches overhanging a property line belong to the owner of the tree, (2) the rule that the owner of a wharf or pier that runs out beyond the proper exterior line has a good right against trespassers, and (3) the rule that possession – even without title – is good against a trespasser.[12] As a consequence of these rules, Hynes was a trespasser and, therefore, the railroad owed him no duty of care upon which to predicate a negligence claim.

This holding is deeply dissatisfying, mainly because there is a misalignment of what Jackson calls 'narrative frameworks.'[13] In other words, one intuitively knows that the rule about tree branches arose from facts very different from those presented in *Hynes* (most often, to hazard a guess, having to do with neighbours fighting over the ownership of fruit on branches hanging over a property line). On subsequent appeal, Justice Cardozo recognized that blindness to the narratives in which abstract rules are grounded can work an injustice no less than a refusal to hear the full narrative offered at trial.[14] Accordingly, Cardozo begins his opinion with a very different narrative, one putting life to the abstractions of the lower-court opinion (notice, e.g., in the following excerpt that the 'plaintiff's intestate' becomes 'a lad of 16,' the 'plank' becomes a 'springboard,' the 'deceased ... struck and thrown into the water' becomes a 'diver ... flung ... from the shattered board and plunged ... to his death.'):

On July 8, 1916, Harvey Hynes, a lad of 16, swam with two companions from the Manhattan to the Bronx side of the Harlem River, or United States Ship Canal, a navigable stream. Along the Bronx side of the river was the right of way of the defendant, the New York Central Railroad, which operated its trains at that point by high-tension wires, strung on poles and cross-arms. Projecting from the defendant's bulkhead above the waters of the river was a plank or springboard, from which boys of the neighborhood used to dive. One end of the board had been placed under a rock on the defendant's land, and nails had been driven at its point of contact with the bulkhead. Measured from this point of contact the length behind was 5 feet; the length in front 11. The bulkhead itself was about 3 1/2 feet back of the pier line as located by the government. From this it follows that for 7 1/2 feet the springboard was beyond the line of the defendant's property and above the public waterway. Its height measured from the stream was 3 feet at the bulkhead, and 5 feet at its outermost extremity. For more than five years swimmers had used it as a diving board without protest or obstruction.

On this day Hynes and his companions climbed on top of the bulkhead, intending to leap into the water. One of them made the plunge in safety. Hynes followed to the front of the springboard, and stood poised for his dive. At that moment a cross-arm with electric wires fell from the defendant's pole. The wires struck the diver, flung him from the shattered board, and plunged him to his death below.[15]

Once Cardozo completes the factual picture, he turns to matters of logic, first by showing the absurdity of the lower court's decision to draw an outcome-determinative distinction between a boy standing on the end of the springboard and one standing directly beneath it in the water:

> The defendant was under a duty to use reasonable care that bathers swimming or standing in the water should not be electrocuted by wires falling from its right of way. But to bathers diving from the springboard, there was no duty, we are told, unless the injury was the product of mere willfulness or wantonness – no duty of active vigilance to safeguard the impending structure. Without wrong to them, cross-arms might be left to rot; wires highly charged with electricity might sweep them from their stand and bury them in the subjacent waters. In climbing on the board, they became trespassers and outlaws … Rights and duties in systems of living law are not built upon such quicksands.[16]

But Cardozo does not end with this *reductio ad absurdum*. He constructs yet another argument, this one buttressed with a pair of hypothetical mini-narratives, one revealing a logical gaff in the lower court's opinion, the other revealing the absence of a causal connection between the facts proven (viz., Hynes was killed by the railroad's improperly maintained wires) and the defence offered (viz., because Hynes was standing on the plank, he was a trespasser to whom the railroad owed no duty of care):

> Bathers in the Harlem River on the day of this disaster were in the enjoyment of a public highway, entitled to reasonable protection against destruction by the defendant's wires … A plane of private right had been interposed between the river and the air, but public ownership was unchanged in the space below it and above … Duties are thus supposed to arise and to be extinguished in alternate zones or strata. Two boys walking in the country or swimming in a river stop to rest for a moment along the side of the road or the margin of the stream. One of them throws himself beneath the overhanging branches of a tree. The other perches himself on a bough a foot or so above the ground. Both are killed by falling wires. The defendant would have us say that there is a remedy for the representatives of one and none for the representatives of the other. We may be permitted to distrust the logic that leads to such conclusions.
>
> There will hardly be denial that a cause of action would have arisen if the wires had fallen on an aeroplane proceeding above the river, though the location of the impact could be identified as the space above the springboard. The most that the defendant can fairly ask is exemption from liability where the use of the fixture is itself the efficient peril. That would be the situation, for example, if the weight of the boy upon the board had caused it to break and thereby throw him into the river. There is no such causal connection here between his position and his injuries.[17]

Cardozo concludes with a brief discussion of the limits of rules in hard cases.[18] Though he does not use the phrase 'hard cases,' I think he is concerned with both senses of the phrase as we currently use it (i.e., the older usage that refers to cases in which application of a legal standard would lead to particular hardship on a losing party, and the Dworkian usage that refers to cases posing particular difficulties of interpretation).[19] And this concern intersects with that of Jackson and Holmes, in that it exhorts judges to recall the animating force – the narratives – that gave birth to particular laws and to be keenly attuned to changes in public narratives. In *Hynes*, the narrative roots of rules are of critical importance in two respects: in the selection of the rule of decision (is the tree branch doctrine really pertinent?) and in the adaptation or extension of existing rules to fit a new situation (has the public narrative that valorizes property rights above all shifted?):

There are times when there is little trouble in marking off the field of exemption and immunity from that of liability and duty. Here structures and ways are so united and commingled, superimposed upon each other, that the fields are brought together. In such circumstances, there is little help in pursuing general maxims to ultimate conclusions. They have been framed alio intuitu. They must be reformulated and readapted to meet exceptional conditions. Rules appropriate to spheres which are conceived of as separate and distinct cannot both be enforced when the spheres become concentric. There must then be readjustment or collision.[20]

## When Narratives Clash

What Cardozo has identified here is the dilemma posed when narratives clash, a subject that both Zenon Bankowski and Martha Nussbaum have treated effectively in the context of *Antigone*.[21] To dress the stage, I offer a brief summary of the play's plot. The play begins in mediis rebus. Oedipus' sons, Eteocles and Polynices, had agreed to rule Thebes by turns. Eteocles breaches the agreement and remains in power. Polynices flees to Argos and there raises a force with which he attacks Thebes. In the ensuing battle, both brothers are killed. Creon, the brothers' uncle, reluctantly takes the throne. His first official act is to deny funeral rites to Polynices, on the ground that he is an enemy of the city. But Antigone, the brothers' sister, disregards this decree in favour of what she sees as a superior family obligation. Creon sentences her to death by entombment, even though she is betrothed to Creon's son, Haemon. The blind prophet Tiresias ultimately convinces Creon of his folly, but it is too late: Antigone has already hanged herself, Haemon has committed suicide upon finding her dead, and Euridice, Haemon's mother and Creon's wife, then kills herself as well.

In law and literature courses, *Antigone* is typically read as a dramatization of the systemic clash of two legal regimes: positive law and natural law. As Bankowski notes, Nussbaum's reading differs from the traditional readings in that she does not view Antigone as an unalloyed heroine or the conflict simply as one between different orders of laws. Thus in Nussbaum's telling – as with that of Hegel, to which she is in part reacting – Antigone is also flawed. In his earlier reading, Hegel had cast the drama as a dialectical struggle between the family and state, with Creon standing for the state, Antigone for the family. Under this view, each is bound to the other, right in his or her own terms but wrong in those of the other's system.[22]

Both Creon and Antigone clearly articulate what each sees as a cardinal virtue. Creon believes that concern for the civic well-being is paramount:

And whoever places a friend
above the good of his own country, he is nothing:
I have no use for him. Zeus my witness,
Zeus who sees all things, always –
I could never stand by silent, watching destruction
march against our city, putting safety to rout,
nor could I ever make that man a friend of mine
who menaces our country. Remember this:
our country *is* our safety.
Only while she voyages true on course
can we establish friendships, truer than blood itself.
Such are my standards. They make our city great.
Closely akin to them I have proclaimed,
just now, the following decree to our people
concerning the two sons of Oedipus.
Eteocles, who died fighting for Thebes,
excelling all in arms: he shall be buried,
crowned with a hero's honors, the cups we pour
to soak the earth and reach the famous dead.
But as for his blood brother, Polynices,
who returned from exile, home to his father-city
and the gods of his race, consumed with one desire –
to burn them roof to roots – who thirsted to drink
his kinsmen's blood and sell the rest to slavery:
that man – a proclamation has forbidden the city
to dignify him with burial, mourn him at all.
No, he must be left unburied, his corpse
carrion for the birds and dogs to tear,
an obscenity for the citizens to behold!
These are my principles. Never at my hands
will the traitor be honored above the patriot.
But whoever proves his loyalty to the state –
I'll prize that man in death as well as life.[23]

Creon is well aware of the evaluative terms with which fifth-century Athenians staked out the world of praxis: good/bad, pious/impious, just/unjust, friend/foe, and the like. According to Nussbaum, this terminology would have been familiar to and employed by the spectators of the play. Moreover, the spectators would have understood that these terms can conflict with one another (friendship may require one to be unjust) and that even a single virtue may place different demands in different contexts (justice of the city may conflict with justice of the dead).[24] One would expect, therefore, the play to open with Creon suspended in an irresolvable tension between his duties as ruler and those as relative. But Creon appears to have no conflict at all, no painful tension and deliberation. How is this, Bankowski asks? The answer lies in the passage I have just quoted: all virtues are subordinated to the welfare of the city. Thus what is good, pious, and just is that which serves the welfare of the city.

Though to our eyes Antigone makes morally superior choices, she is not wholly blameless. Her views are as one-sided and narrow as Creon's:

> It wasn't Zeus, not in the least,
> who made this proclamation – not to me.
> Nor did that Justice, dwelling with the gods
> beneath the earth, ordain such laws for men.
> Nor did I think your edict had such force
> that you, a mere mortal, could override the gods,
> the great unwritten, unshakable traditions.
> They are alive, not just today or yesterday:
> they live forever, from the first of time,
> and no one knows when they first saw the light.
> These laws – I was not about to break them,
> not out of fear of some man's wounded pride,
> and face the retribution of the gods.
> Die I must, I've known it all my life –
> your death-sentence ringing in my ears.
> And if I am to die before my time
> I consider that a gain. Who on earth,
> alive in the midst of so much grief as I,
> could fail to find his death a rich reward?
> So for me, at least, to meet this doom of yours
> is precious little pain. But if I had allowed
> my own mother's son to rot, an unburied corpse –
> that would have been an agony! This is nothing.

> And if my present actions strike you as foolish,
> let's just say I've been accused of folly
> by a fool.[25]

At bottom, Antigone is as guilty as Creon of what Nussbaum calls 'ruthless simplification.' She, too, selects only those facts that produce the outcomes she desires under the rules she valorizes. To hear her talk, as Bankowski observes, we would not know there had been a war, caused by one of her brothers. All we know is that her brother has been desecrated and that, *as a matter of family*, this cannot stand.

What does all this mean for the law generally and for our discussion in particular? First, I would suggest that we are presented with more than a simple clash of legal systems. It is, rather, a clash of narratives born of overweening, false piety (when Antigone refers to 'the great unwritten, unshakeable traditions' she is – as Somers has taught us – using a phrase synonymous with 'public narratives'). This über-piety leads to legal formalisms that have disastrous consequences. Second, and more important, Creon and Antigone offer up what prove to be impenetrable ontological narratives. The problem here is that – because he is the sole arbiter of the law – Creon's ontological narrative *is* the law (and in some sense the *only* public narrative, or at least the only one capable of receiving official sanction). But for positive law to be more than a matter of taste, bias, or whim, it must be permeable enough to allow the interpenetration of other narratives. We will return to this issue in greater detail when we more fully take up the question of how narratives become institutionalized in ways that are congenial to democracy. For now, though, it is enough to recognize the mischief that arises when a hermetic ontological narrative is coterminous with law. That is, in the public sphere, a dominant narrative consistent with the Rule of Law must bear receptors that allow the addition of new narrative material. It must, in Bankowski's terms, 'bring[] the outside in.'[26] For example, in the case of *Antigone*, if Antigone's narrative could have even slightly injected itself into Creon's, perhaps both could have been satisfied by allowing Polynices to be buried, but beyond the city walls.[27]

## Changes in Narrative, Changes in Law

Though legal narratives often directly clash (as in *Antigone*), there are many cases where the intersections are much more oblique and multifarious – messy even. In substantial part, this is because common laws are made via a process somewhat like that by which literature is made and very much like that by which history (in the sense of historical writing) is made. Depending on one's orientation, that perhaps is or is not a bold statement, but it is one that I think I can in the main defend. To push us down this avenue, let's pick up with one of the themes with which we ended the last chapter: the growing (some times grudging) institutional receptiveness to feminine narratives throughout the twentieth century. Two of the largest struggles of that period involved pro-business, *laissez-faire* capitalist narratives, on the one hand, and anti-feminist, paternalistic narratives on the other. The two crossed from time to time, often to weird effect. For instance, in *Lochner v. New York*, the United States Supreme Court struck down a state statute providing that no employee in a bakery could work more than sixty hours in one week or ten hours in one day.[28] The reason? The statute interfered with 'the freedom of master and employee to contract with each other.'[29] Three years later, the same court was asked to pass on the constitutionality of another state law limiting to ten the number of hours per day that a woman could work in a laundry.[30] Same result? Of course not. And why not? To protect women from the rapacious instincts of men *and* to ensure the continued well-being of the entire human race!

That woman's physical structure and the performance of maternal functions place her at a disadvantage in the struggle for subsistence is obvious. This is especially true when the burdens of motherhood are upon her. Even when they are not, by abundant testimony of the medical fraternity, continuance for a long time on her feet at work, repeating this from day to day, tends to injurious effects upon the body, and, as healthy mothers are essential to vigorous offspring, the physical wellbeing of woman becomes an object of public interest and care in order to preserve the strength and vigor of the race. Still again, history discloses the fact that woman has always been dependent upon man. He established his control at the outset by superior physical strength, and this control in various forms, with diminishing intensity, has continued to the present ... It is impossible to close one's eyes to the fact that she still looks to her brother, and depends upon him. Even though all restrictions on political, personal, and contractual rights were taken away, and she stood, so far as statutes are concerned, upon an absolutely equal plane with him, it would still be true that she is so constituted that she will rest upon and look to him for protection; that her physical structure and a proper discharge of her maternal functions – having in view not merely her own health, but the wellbeing of the race – justify legislation to protect her from the greed, as well as the passion, of man ... The two sexes differ in structure of body, in the functions to be performed by each, in the amount of physical strength, in the capacity for long-continued labor, particularly when done standing, the influence of vigorous health upon the future wellbeing of the race, the self-reliance which enables one to assert full rights, and in the capacity to maintain the struggle for subsistence. This difference justifies a difference in legislation, and upholds that which is designed to compensate for some of the burdens which rest upon her.[31]

We'll see how the paternalistic narrative that underlies *Muller* began to be erased over time, but first, a word or two on a few assumptions I'll make regarding trial practice and fact finding may prove helpful.

In the United States, most crimes are defined by state statute, and many such statutes are simply codifications of the common law. This is especially so with statutes pertaining to acts that have been considered crimes throughout history – for example, murder, as opposed to, say, wire fraud or Internet gambling. Thus, a person charged with a particular crime comes to trial under the terms of an indictment that identifies the acts allegedly committed and the statute(s) allegedly violated. Statutes also broadly lay out available defences, as well as the elements necessary to prove each defence. At trial, both the prosecution and the defence offer testimonial and physical evidence in support of or in opposition to the competing positions. At the close of evidence, the judge instructs the jury as to the law, and the jury retires to deliberate, weigh evidence, and (unless deadlocked) make a determination of guilt or non-guilt.

Plainly, this architecture offers many outcroppings upon which the various participants may hang narratives – a fact that has been well enough documented by others and that I will not belabour here.[32] Suffice it to say that all the actors at a trial have a story to tell – even the judge, who does so through rulings on the admissibility of evidence and in the selection and ordering of the jury charge. What is important for our purposes is *how* a jury processes the various competing narratives, constructs its own, and arrives at a decision that (at least in important cases) is subject to endorsement, qualification, or rejection by courts of appeal and that feeds back into the body of rules upon which it was based.

To illuminate and contextualize these points, we can refer to a couple of cases that are representative in several key respects. In *State v. Hundley*, the Kansas Supreme Court was presented with a homicide conviction involving a defendant who had failed in her effort to mount a defence based on proof that she suffered from what is now generally referred to as 'battered person syndrome.'[33] There was no factual dispute that the married life of Carl and Betty Hundley had been tumultuous. Throughout their ten-year marriage, Carl regularly abused Betty. The Court reported that 'he had knocked out several of her teeth, broken her nose at least five times, and threatened to cut her eyeballs out and her head off. Carl had kicked Betty down the stairs on numerous occasions and had repeatedly broken her ribs.'[34]

Betty, finally having enough, moved into a motel in Topeka, Kansas. This did not, however, break Carl's pattern of harassment, which culminated in the incident giving rise to his death:

> On January 13, 1983, the day of the shooting, Betty had seen Carl early in the day, at which time Carl told Betty he was going to come over and kill her. That night she heard a thumping on her motel door while she was in the bathroom. By the time Betty got out of the bathroom Carl had broken the door lock and entered the room. His entry was followed by violence [which the Court recounts in graphic detail] ... Even after that, Carl continued to threaten Betty. She was sobbing and afraid. He pounded a beer bottle on the night stand and threw a dollar bill toward the window, demanding she get him some cigarettes. Betty testified Carl had hit her with beer bottles many times in the past. Therefore, feeling threatened by the beer bottle, she went to her purse, pulled out the gun and demanded Carl leave. When he saw the gun, Carl laughed tauntingly and said, 'You are dead, bitch, now!' As he reached for the beer bottle, Betty shut her eyes and fired her gun. She fired it again and again. There were five spent shells in the gun when it was seized. At the time of the shooting the deceased had his back to Betty and was paying attention to the beer bottle. She was not physically blocked from going to the door.[35]

The Court emphasized that none of the facts were in dispute; the only issue on appeal was whether the trial court improperly instructed the jury as to the elements of self-defence. To facilitate our discussion of the Court's analysis of the facts as given, a brief aside regarding jury instructions is warranted.

Kansas, like most states, has developed 'pattern' jury instructions, which are to be used verbatim, absent unusual circumstances:

We highly encourage courts to follow the language found in the Pattern Instructions for Kansas (PIK) unless the facts of the case dictate otherwise. The uniform use of the PIK instruction language is a highly desirable goal, a goal which takes very little effort to effectuate. Use of the PIK instruction language helps to protect the rights of criminal defendants in our courts and significantly reduces the number of criminal appeals and issues raised in appeals of criminal cases.[36]

The motivations behind this rule are at least two: first, uniform instructions ensure a measure of invariance across judging subjects; and second, they make statutes (more) intelligible to lay juries. They are, thus, definitive statements of the law for most cases, and their practical authority is greater than that of the statutes from which they derive because they provide the sole standard against which jury members are to measure a defendant's conduct.[37]

One of the most frequent criticisms of pattern jury instructions is that 'they are too abstract,' by which these critics mean that 'because they are written generally to apply in all cases, it can be argued that that they do not apply effectively to the facts of any case in particular.'[38] Cast in these terms, we see that this is an instantiation of a larger theoretical debate – that is, whether legal decisions can be justified by reference to universal criteria.[39] I don't propose to resolve this debate, but I think I can show that a narrative account of jury instructions can deflect some particularist attacks on the universalist position.

The crowning feature of the Rule of Law is its rules of law. Indeed, as Jeremy Waldron puts it,

we should not describe a system of governance as a system of law unless it does the sort of thing that the Rule of Law celebrates – for example, unless it regulates and controls state power and resolves disputes among individuals and firms (and between individuals and firms and the state) using clear, general, stable norms, promulgated in advance so that they can be used as a basis on which individuals and firms can figure out what they owe to one another and to the state.[40]

In addition to this predictive benefit, clear, general, and stable norms bring regularity to adjudicative processes by providing yardsticks against which to measure particular conduct and to justify consequent remedies.[41] This is so because, as Neil MacCormick submits,

there is ... no justification without universalization; motivation needs no universalization; but explanation requires generalization. For particular facts – or particular motives – to be justifying reasons they have to be sub-sumable under a relevant principle of action universally stated, even if the universal is acknowledged to be defeasible.[42]

Against the universalist flow, particularists assert that though rules may deliver formal justice, substantive justice can never be ensured without overriding attention to the facts of each case. But is it fair to assume that cases – even difficult cases that present problems of clas-sification or novelty – suffer under a system of universal rules?[43] I think not, as revealed by an examination of how legal rules are *applied* in the jury system.

If we assume that juries attend to their instructions – and there is evidence that they try to – then they engage in a process akin to that of the normative syllogism that we have previously discussed.[44] (We will discuss the process in the next chapter in the context of fact con-struction and interpretation and in the final chapter in the context of legal and moral 'reasoning'). In other words, jury members take the rule embedded in each instruction, evaluate the evidence presented, and engage in a matching process to determine whether that evidence squares with the rule (to some appropriate standard such as 'beyond a reasonable doubt'). In *Hundley*, the question was not whether Betty's conduct matched the elements of some type of homicide; rather, the issue was whether all the facts and circumstances matched the rule allowing exceptions for self-defence, and, more important, whether the rule – as embodied in the jury instruction – required modification to incorporate Betty Hundley's situation, *her narrative*, if you will.

In Betty's case, the trial court had used the then standard PIK instruc-tion on self-defence, which read:

The defendant has claimed his conduct was justified as (self-defense) (the defense of another person).

   A person is justified in the use of force against an aggressor when and to the extent it appears to him and he reasonably believes that such con-duct is necessary to defend himself or another against such aggressor's immediate use of unlawful force. Such justification requires both a belief on the part of defendant and the existence of facts that would persuade a reasonable person to that belief.[45]

On appeal, Betty's counsel argued that the use of the word 'immediate' in the PIK instruction (rather than 'imminent,' as stated in the statute) prevented the jury from considering (even though it had been copiously presented at trial) the evidence concerning the long-term violence that Carl visited on Betty. For the Court, then, the question became 'what instruction should accompany this evidence in order to charge the jury with the proper manner in which such evidence should be considered?'[46] In other words, the Court wanted to ensure that Betty's status as a battered woman figured into the self-defence equation. And to do so, it undertook a somewhat strained analysis of the difference between 'immediate' and 'imminent':[47]

> Thus, the question is whether the instruction allows the jury to consider 'all the evidence' or whether the use of the word 'immediate' rather than 'imminent' precludes the jury's consideration of the prior abuse. 'Immediate' is defined in Webster's Third New International Dictionary (1961): 'Occurring, acting or accomplished without loss of time.' p. 1129. 'Imminent' is defined as: 'Ready to take place ... or impending.' p. 1130. Therefore, the time limitations in the use of the word 'immediate' are much stricter than those with the use of the word 'imminent.'[48]

Despite the appeal to semantics, the Court quickly showed its hand: Betty's ontological narrative coincided with a dark narrative that had remained hidden beneath social convention for centuries:[49]

> The issue is dramatized by the nature of this case. This is a textbook case of the battered wife, which is psychologically similar to hostage and prisoner of war cases. Betty Hundley had survived her husband's brutal beatings for ten years. Her bones had been broken, her teeth knocked out and repeated bruises inflicted, but she did not leave him. She called the police occasionally but would continue to stay with Carl Hundley. The mystery, as in all battered wife cases, is why she remained after the beatings. The answer to that question can only be gleaned from the compiled case histories of this malady. It is not a new phenomenon, having been recognized and justified since Old Testament times. It goes largely unreported, but is well documented. It is extremely widespread, estimated to affect between four and forty million women.[50]

From this historical synopsis, the Court generally concluded that 'battered women are terror-stricken people whose mental state is distorted and bears a marked resemblance to that of a hostage or a prisoner of war ... They become disturbed persons from the torture.'[51] And from this general conclusion, coupled with the specific facts of the case, the Court reasoned (1) that the objective component of the self-defence instruction should comprehend 'how a reasonably prudent battered wife would perceive Carl's demeanor' and (2) that '"immediate" in the instruction on self-defense places undue emphasis on the immediate action of the deceased, and obliterates the nature of the buildup of terror and fear which had been systematically created over a long period of time.'[52] This latter point remains something of a *non sequitur* (and freights a single word with a weighty narrative), but that simply underscores how generative the alignment of public and personal narratives proved to be in the case. In any event, the case had immediate – and unintended – consequences, once Betty Hundley's narrative had been absorbed into the PIK instructions and, thereby, was passed on to future juries.

In the wake of *Hundley*, courts began to give broad, 'battered woman' self-defence instructions, juries began to acquit defendants, and the Kansas Supreme Court found no errors in those acquittals.[53] This all changed with the arrival of the first 'burning bed' case (i.e., a case in which an abused spouse kills her husband while he is sleeping) at the Kansas Supreme Court. That case, *State v. Stewart*, presented background facts not unlike those presented in *Hundley*: a marriage troubled from the outset; a cruel, unpredictable, and physically abusive husband; attempted flights by the battered wife; ... and a gun.[54] At trial, the court gave the jury a standard self-defence instruction (duly modified to reflect the *Hundley* holding that imminence rather than immediacy was the proper standard for judging temporal proximity), but then added what we might call a *Hundley* tag: 'You must determine, from the viewpoint of the defendant's mental state, whether the defendant's belief in the need to defend herself was reasonable in light of her subjective impressions and the facts and circumstances known to her.'[55]

The Court was thus faced with two related questions: first, whether a person in Stewart's shoes should be entitled to a self-defence instruction *at all*; and second, whether the *Hundley* tag was an appropriate statement of the law of self-defence. It answered these questions by turn, holding first that

in order to instruct a jury on self-defense, there must be some showing of an imminent threat or a confrontational circumstance involving an overt act by an aggressor. There is no exception to this requirement where the defendant has suffered long-term domestic abuse and the victim is the abuser. In such cases, the issue is not whether the defendant believes homicide is the solution to past or future problems with the batterer, but rather whether circumstances surrounding the killing were sufficient to create a reasonable belief in the defendant that the use of deadly force was necessary.[56]

Given this holding, it was probably superfluous to consider the form and content of the self-defence instruction that the jury considered, but the Court did so anyway, apparently to emphasize two key points: that 'battered woman's syndrome' is not in itself a defence to murder (rather, evidence of the syndrome may be introduced in support of a defence of self-defence), and that the defence of self-defence has both objective and subjective elements:

We first use a subjective standard to determine whether the defendant sincerely and honestly believed it necessary to kill in order to defend. We then use an objective standard to determine whether defendant's belief was reasonable – specifically, whether a reasonable person in defendant's circumstances would have perceived self-defense as necessary. In *State v. Hundley* ... we stated that, in cases involving battered spouses, 'the objective test is how a reasonably prudent battered wife would perceive [the aggressor's] demeanor.'[57]

This turn to objectivity (a subject we will consider in greater detail near the end of the next chapter) is troublesome in no less than two respects. First, notions of objective reasonableness depend on notions of common sense. But as *Hundley*, *Stewart*, and a host of other cases make clear, there is no 'common sense' when it comes to battered women – they exist in a condition outside the ordinary juror's ability to know. Justice Herd (the author of the *Hundley* opinion) explicitly makes that point in dissenting from the *Stewart* majority.[58] Second, by removing a whole category of cases from the province of the jury, the Court effectively cut off (for now) the quasi-public part of the rule-building process upon which the *democratic* growth (again, more on that in the next chapter) of the American common law depends – namely, the testing of narratives in front of judges and juries.

As *Hundley* and *Stewart* show, legal rules develop through an accretive process, slowly absorbing and deflecting narratives on a case-by-case basis.[59] But is the influence of individual narratives ephemeral? Or do they become formally institutionalized? They do, at least with respect to pattern jury charges. We can plainly see this in the current version of the PIK pertaining to self-defence:

*PIK 54.17 Use of Force in Defense of a Person*
The defendant has claimed his conduct was justified as self defense. A person is justified in the use of force against an aggressor when and to the extent it appears to him and he reasonably believes that such conduct is necessary to defend himself against such aggressor's imminent use of unlawful force. Such justification requires both a belief on the part of defendant and the existence of facts that would persuade a reasonable person to that belief.

...

*Comments*
In State v. Hundley, 236 Kan. 461, the Court disapproved PIK 2d 54.17 in the use of 'immediate' in lieu of the statutory term 'imminent.' The Court held it to be reversible error to use the work [sic] immediate in the self-defense instruction in that it places undue emphasis on the immediate action of the aggressor whereas the nature of the buildup of terror and fear which has been going on over a period of time, particularly in battered spouse instances, may be most relevant. The word imminent would describe this defense more accurately, as the definition implies impending or near at hand, rather than immediate.

The existence of the battered woman syndrome in and of itself does not operate as a defense to murder. In order to instruct a jury on self-defense, there must be some showing of an imminent threat or a confrontational circumstances (sic) involving an overt act by an aggressor. State v. Stewart, 243 Kan. 639.[60]

Both Betty Hundley and Peggy Stewart's stories are fossilized – along with thousands of others – in the present rule of self-defence. Theirs are noteworthy only because we can still see them in the sediment, like the occasional leaf that is apparent between layers of limestone.[61] Others are mere traces, but their influence is still vital, even as they are buried deeper each day under a fresh layer of narratives, some compelling, some less so, some not at all.[62]

Thus conceived, jury instructions represent two things: the state of the law, and a collage of multiple individual narratives as they have been institutionalized. They are of course not permanent in either respect and can never be more than 'stabilized for now.'[63] But they nonetheless stand at an important theoretical crossroads – namely, a place where normative and narrative coherence meet. This is important because one could plausibly posit that these types of coherence are different in an exclusive sort of way – that is, a proper system of norms must be coherent in a snapshot sort of way (synchronically); a narrative must be coherent in a storybook sort of way (diachronically).[64] As Neil MacCormick suggests, however, 'this picture ... ignores the way in which legal doctrines and norms themselves develop through time.'[65] As a general example of this temporal development, MacCormick cites the feminist critique of self-defence doctrines in the context of domestic violence – in other words, the sort of situation that *Hundley* and *Stewart* so concretely represent. To amplify this theme, we can think of the current iteration of a jury instruction – and indeed of any legal rule – as the most complete to date version of what Ronald Dworkin has referred to as a 'chain novel.' Dworkin's analogy has not gone unchallenged, but it is nonetheless illuminating in many respects germane to our present discussion, and we therefore need to consider it.

## Law's Constraints: Generic or Precedential?

In *Law's Empire*, Dworkin develops an extended metaphor likening the development of the law to a multi-author serial novel – that is, one in which each chapter is authored by a different person.[66] The metaphor is imperfect[67] – most obviously because the novel is a relatively closed-ended form and the law is an open-ended one[68] – but in the main it captures a salient feature of the law: that it develops through a series of sequential narratives, most of which feature and are told by different actors. This narrative aspect is not the one most often discussed (at least not directly) in the back-and-forth as to whether the metaphor is actually functional or beside the point. Instead, the debate usually centres on whether the metaphor is descriptive of the constraining power of precedent. This question seems irresolvable at present[69] – at least to any reasonable degree of certainty – but I believe that the metaphor has a greater utility, one with which both chain and anti-chain commentators might agree. But before presenting that position, we must first sketch out Dworkin's thesis and that of his most ardent critic (on this point), Stanley Fish.[70]

'All those who have studied the law have at least an intuitive notion of precedent or stare decisis.'[71] This intuition is easy to articulate in the abstract: when a court has held that a principle of law is applicable to a certain set of facts, it will adhere to that principle, and apply it to all future cases where the facts are substantially the same.[72] But this definition is devilishly difficult to apply in concrete instances because determining whether facts are 'substantially the same' is not always easy. And though there is widespread disagreement as to *when and why* courts should treat like cases alike, there is, nonetheless, general agreement that courts *should* treat them alike absent unusual circumstances. That is, I think most would agree that 'objectivity' is a cardinal virtue of the Rule of Law and that any rational account of objectivity demands that judgments be invariant across judging subjects.[73] The rub comes when precedent is employed as the tool for ensuring invariance. Some argue that precedent is simply a mask behind which judicial manipulation takes place.[74] But others quite persuasively point to the predictability of outcome – and attendant systemic stability – that comes with 'coherence in interpretation of particular provisions over many cases.'[75] Were the situation otherwise, a legal system 'would be a sham if the law were subject to varying interpretation from case to case, for it would only be nominally the same law that applied to different cases with essentially similar features.'[76]

Dworkin casts his chain novel hypothesis in the foreground of the historical debates over the efficacy and desirability of a jurisprudence built on *stare decisis*. And his mission is, as Linquist and Cross have noted, both normative and descriptive.[77] As a description, Dworkin offers the metaphor to show how precedent constrains judges. Here is how Dworkin's ideal chain novel is produced: a group of coauthors agree each to write a separate chapter of a work. They draw lots to determine the order of writing, after which the

> lowest number writes the opening chapter of a novel, which he or she then sends to the next number who adds a chapter, with the understanding that he is adding a chapter to that novel rather than beginning a new one, and then sends the two chapters to the next number, and so on. Now every novelist but the first has the dual responsibilities of interpreting and creating because each must read all that has gone before in order to establish, in the interpretivist sense, what the novel so far created is. He or she must determine what the characters are 'really' like; what motives in fact guide them; what the point or theme of the developing novel is; how far some literary device or figure, consciously or unconsciously used, contributes to these, and whether it should be extended or refined or trimmed

or dropped in order to send the novel further in one direction rather than another.[78]

This conceit is apt, in Dworkin's view, because it is analogous to the development of the common law. Thus, just as the novelists become increasingly constrained as the plot thickens (because each new chapter must 'fit' with its predecessors in terms of plot, character, and style), common law judges become constrained by the build-up of precedent:

> Deciding hard cases at law is rather like this strange literary exercise. The similarity is most evident when judges consider and decide common-law cases; that is, when no statute figures centrally in the legal issue, and the argument turns on which rules or principles of law 'underlie' the related decisions of other judges in the past. Each judge is then like a novelist in the chain. He or she must read through what other judges in the past have written not simply to discover what these judges have said, or their state of mind when they said it, but to reach an opinion about what these judges have collectively *done*, in the way that each of our novelists formed an opinion about the collective novel so far written. Any judge forced to decide a lawsuit will find, if he looks in the appropriate books, records of many arguably similar cases decided over decades or even centuries past by many other judges of different styles and judicial and political philosophies, in periods of different orthodoxies of procedure and judicial convention. Each judge must regard himself, in deciding the new case before him, as a partner in a complex chain enterprise of which these innumerable decisions, structures, conventions, and practices are the history; it is his job to continue that history into the future through what he does on the day. He *must* interpret what has gone before because he has a responsibility to advance the enterprise in hand rather than strike out in some new direction of his own.[79]

Fish chides Dworkin for missing the point. That is, though Fish agrees that textual interpretation is always constrained, he vigorously dissents from Dworkin's location of precedent as the source of interpretive restraints. Instead, Fish identifies (without using the term) what rhetoricians call 'genre constraints' as the actual dampers on full interpretive licence. Thus, whereas Dworkin posits that successive writers become increasingly constrained by the text already produced, Fish argues that the first author is already constrained by the genre in which he or she has chosen to write:[80]

[Dworkin's] idea is that the first author is free because he is not obliged 'to read all that has gone before' and therefore doesn't have to decide what the characters are 'really' like, what motives guide them, and so on. But in fact the first author has surrendered his freedom … as soon as he commits himself to writing a novel, for he makes his decision under the same constraints that rule the decisions of his collaborators. He must decide, for example, how to begin the novel, but the decision is not 'free' because the very notion 'beginning a novel' exists only in the context of a set of practices that at once enables and limits the act of beginning … He is free to begin whatever kind of novel he decides to write, but he is constrained by the finite (although not unchanging) possibilities that are subsumed in the notions 'kind of novel' and 'beginning a novel.'[81]

Fish goes on to assert not only that the first novelist is generically constrained but also that the subsequent novelists are generically free. Indeed, the 'last author is as free … as is the first.'[82] This seems counterintuitive because one would 'think that the more information one has (the more history) the more directed will be one's interpretation.'[83] But Fish slips this knot (or at least tries to do so) by arguing that all information always comes in interpreted form and that, therefore, information/history cannot act as a check on interpretation.[84] For support, Fish resorts to a hypothetical debate among the serial novelists as to the specific subgenre to which they will contribute: where one sees a straightforward piece of realism, another sees a social satire, and yet another sees a comedy of manners. He is thus able to pin Dworkin with the weight of his own argument: 'If Dworkin's argument is to hold, that is, if the decisions he talks about are to be constrained, in a strong sense, by an already-in-place text, it must be possible to settle this disagreement by appealing to that text. But it is precisely because the text appears differently in the light of different assumptions as to what is its mode that there is a disagreement in the first place.'[85]

To some extent, Dworkin is the author of his own misfortune here. This is so because he deploys his metaphor as a description of how judges should resolve hard cases, which – by definition it would seem – arise against an unsettled historical record or extraordinary facts. The very reason that cases are 'hard' is that (1) the body of law to which a judge should refer is either so ambiguous or so vague on a particular point as to leave resolution of the exact legal question presented open to debate, or (2) the factual scenario presents problems of classification and categorization (e.g., a matter of first impression). Put in novelistic terms, hard cases are hard because the novel is not yet coherent – it is unfinished.[86] So just as no rational writer could come to pen the last chapter of *The Grapes of Wrath* thinking that the novel is a comedy of manners, no rational judge could come to an ordinary slip-and-fall case thinking that 'duty' is not an element of a negligence claim. The point here is that none of Fish's objections hold true in run-of-the-mill cases, in which the 'novel' is essentially complete and subject to only occasional revisions or glosses.[87] Typically, a lengthy series of cases covering a wide distribution of facts has already established legal rules (and their constituent elements that must be pled and proven) against which the facts of a particular case can be assessed. A judge has little latitude in this situation, and it matters not at all whether the reason is styled a genre restraint or a precedential restraint.[88]

## Novelizing Law

What gets lost in the Dworkin–Fish debate is the aptness of Dworkin's metaphor to how common law rules are built through narrative accretion over time. We have seen this process at work in self-defence jury instruction cases, but it may be useful to catch a novel-building exercise in mid-flow. I've chosen a simple example – one with a fairly circumscribed universe of case law available – for the sake of brevity; nonetheless, the principle at work holds across the board.

In the United States, many of the individual states have a 'savings statute' that preserves a plaintiff's right in certain circumstances to commence a lawsuit that would otherwise be time barred under an applicable statute of limitations. Generally, these statutes allow a plaintiff to file a lawsuit outside the limitations period if (1) he had previously commenced the suit within the limitations period and (2) that suit had been dismissed for reasons other than the merits. Kansas adopted such a statute in 1868; Oklahoma did so when it adopted the Kansas code of civil procedure, of which the Kansas savings statute was a part, shortly after achieving statehood in 1907.[89] Each state's version of the statute has been recodified and slightly amended over the years, but both largely maintain their original character.[90]

Fairly early on in the last century, courts began to face an unanticipated (probably) scenario – one in which a plaintiff timely filed a suit in state 'A,' had it dismissed for some non-substantive reason (such as lack of personal jurisdiction or improper venue), and then refiled it in state 'B' after the statute of limitations had run but within the period allowed under state B's savings statute. This presents the question whether a state's savings statute should apply to a case first filed in another state.

Oklahoma was the first of the two states to take up the question, holding in *Herron v. Miller* that Oklahoma's statute would not 'save' a case that had first been filed in another jurisdiction.[91] The very next year, Kansas, in *Jackson v. Prairie Oil & Gas*, approved – in dictum – of the rule announced in *Herron*.[92] There the matter rested for decades as a matter of little controversy; indeed, the *Herron* rule squared with 'the general rule among older cases' across the country.[93] This began to change after mid-century, though, as the American national narrative shifted from one based on rural roots (Jefferson's nation of small farmers) to one of widespread migration brought on by increasing industrialization. Thus, by the 1980s, courts were divided on the issue, and with increasing frequency they were finding 'no significant policy to be furthered by interpreting the statute to exclude actions filed outside' the forum state.[94] In short, a developing sense that there was a fundamental *interstate* right of access to the courts came to outweigh outmoded parochial concerns.[95]

As between Oklahoma and Kansas, Oklahoma was the first state to revisit the *Herron* rule. But with not even a nod to changing times, the Oklahoma Supreme Court simply announced – with a citation to *Herron* – that 'we adhere to the rule that the provisions of this section accrue only to actions filed within the State of Oklahoma.'[96] The Oklahoma Supreme Court continues to acknowledge this precedent.[97] The Kansas Supreme Court, on the other hand, has still not firmly resolved the issue, though it has signalled that it will adopt the modern view when called upon to do so. In the relevant case, *Goldsmith v. Learjet, Inc.*,[98] the Court noted as background for a related issue that the United States Court of Appeals for the Tenth Circuit already had predicted that the Kansas Supreme Court would extend the benefit of the Kansas savings statute to cases first filed in another state,[99] a holding that United States District Courts in Kansas have since followed.[100]

What we have, then, are two independent systems that have started from the same point yet have created 'novels' that stand in direct opposition. Kansas was able to move more quickly to bring its law into phase with the modern cultural narrative because it was not freighted with unequivocal precedent. Oklahoma has found itself constrained by previous chapters even though other courts have criticized its rulings and have themselves moved in the opposite direction.[101] This is not to say that Oklahoma is stuck with a novel that everyone hates. Plot twists – even reversals – are just as permitted within the legal genre as in the novelistic genre, so long as those twists make sense at that point in the chain. In fact, at least one Oklahoma Supreme Court justice has obliquely suggested that it is time write a new chapter.[102] He did this in two ways: first, by indicating that Oklahoma's rule had been strongly criticized and, second, by focusing attention on *Morris*, not *Herron*. This second point raises an interesting back-narrative that makes it all the more likely that *Morris* will one day be overruled. For that opinion was authored by Justice Nelson Corn, who was at the epicentre of a major Oklahoma Supreme Court scandal in the early 1960s. Justice Corn was convicted and imprisoned for evading federal income tax on bribes he had taken while sitting on the Supreme Court in the late 1950s (i.e., at about the time that *Morris* was decided).[103] And as all Oklahoma practitioners and jurists know, every case from that period bears the trace of the scandal; consequently, each lacks the persuasive force that would otherwise be its due.[104]

## Resisting Narratives: Keeping the Outside Out

There is probably no great dispute that law is a conservative institution. The cases we have just reviewed exemplify that. But in the context of our examination of how narratives can influence the law, what does this mean? One could simply posit that legal institutions will react more slowly to shifts in public narratives and move on, but that seems unsatisfactory. On the other hand, attempting to trace the ebb and flow of particular narratives across a range of social institutions is an exercise in history far beyond our present scope. There is a middle course, however, one that reveals traces of clashing narratives in the form of particular linguistic features and, more important, the speed with which various institutions bow to forces that represent a newly dominant narrative. What we find – consistent with our hypothesis – is that legal institutions prove more resistant to shifting narratives than do other institutions.

The sixteenth and seventeenth centuries were a period of great change in the relations between Scotland and England, marked on one end with relative independence between the parties and on the other with a relative unification. And though the period was punctuated with moments of great upheaval, the larger arc traces a gradual shift in political influence from Edinburgh to London. This is not to say that the Scottish national narrative was stamped out – it remains quite strong today – but the English current plainly overwhelmed certain Scottish institutions. One measure of Scottish institutional resilience can be found at the level of language, an area capably investigated by Amy Devitt in her language-based study of the period from 1520 to 1659.[105]

Devitt's methodology is one tied to genre, which she elsewhere describes as 'a nexus between an individual's actions and a socially defined context.'[106] With respect to her study of Scotland, she thus looks at particular types of writing associated with particular social contexts to determine whether, to what extent, and how rapidly standard Anglo-English forms superseded traditional Scots-English forms.[107] What she finds is that there was wide variation in the rate and depth of anglicization across contexts. Of particular interest are the variations between the genres associated with the two major institutions she studies: Church and State. Of signal importance is her observation that religious treatises anglicized quickly and almost completely, whereas public records (mostly legal documents) did so slowly and only partially. The explanation for these divergent phenomena is found in the institutional settings that gave rise to the generic writings under examination.

Religious treatises became rapidly anglicized for a number of reasons: they were directed to (and intended to persuade) both English and Scottish readers, they were aimed at a general audience, they were meant to be kept rather than discarded (i.e., they were more like books than newspapers), and they were expositions of a version of the Bible that was written in Anglo-English (a translation of the Geneva Bible). One might therefore expect public records to take a similar standardization turn, given that they, too, were highly formal, addressed a serious subject matter (legal affairs) and were intended for a general audience and for posterity. But as Devitt shows, this was not the case:

A fuller understanding of the situation offers a fuller understanding of the records' resistance. Anglo-English may have been becoming the new standard for the Scots, but Scots-English had been the standard for centuries ... The writers had no obligation to persuade their readers, but they did have an obligation to preserve the proceedings of the government. In addition to encouraging linguistic conservatism, the situation may have encouraged linguistic nationalism. These public records were, after all, national records: their purpose was to record the activities of groups which represented Scotland. As these groups were increasingly undermined by the political unification of Scotland and England, the perhaps unconscious nationalism of the authors, who were writing documents to preserve Scottish laws and actions, might have expressed itself quite readily in use of the Scottish language, in conformity with the Scots-English Standard.[108]

Devitt goes on to posit that the public records genre, which was largely legal in nature, itself afforded a degree of immunity to the otherwise pervasive influence of Anglo-English:[109]

> The genre itself was so well established as to have served as a constraint on writers of the genre, to have strengthened intertextuality. The Acts of the Privy Council and other national records had been written for centuries, though not always preserved. They constituted a long-standing and highly traditional genre. [A] genre can become a part of the situation itself if that genre becomes so conventionalized that certain formal characteristics are expected of all instances of the genre, whether appropriate or not. The national records had become so conventionalized. Long before Anglo-English became prestigious, the Scottish records had not only adopted the Scots-English language standard, but also developed their own expected style, full of established formats and traditional phrases ... The established convention of the genre thus constrained *any* change in the genre, including a change in usage. This effect of the tradition reveals itself especially in the traditional phrases, the stock phrases which seem to have maintained Scots-English forms even more strongly than the rest of the genre.[110]

All of this accords with Fish's account of the constraints inherent in the common law genre, and I think it in good part accounts for the lag we often sense in legal developments. But I don't want to stop right there, because I believe that a swerve back into narrative can help us develop a more comprehensive explanation of how law builds upon itself. That is not really the stretch it might seem at first blush, once we recall that narrative is itself a genre (or perhaps even a sort of meta-genre). In any event, I hope to show – by analogy to Devitt's linguistic data and arguments – that narratology offers a compelling institutional account of how and why legal systems react more slowly to shifts in public narratives and metanarratives than do institutions of popular culture.

For sociologists and social historians, 'it is a commonplace in the study of nationalism that the construction of national identity inevitably relies on the creation and use of narratives – part history, part myth – that imbue nations and nationalist projects with coherence and purpose.'[111] If this is so (and I think it is), how then can we use this fact to explain institutional resistance to *incoherent* influences of the sort we just observed in Devitt's study? For explanation, we should first turn to the specifics of the Scottish nationalism that Devitt notes and that others have explored across a broader historical topography, especially in the context of legal institutions.

Nineteenth-century Scotland provides an interesting case study because of its complicated narrative relationship with England. Many have likened this to a colonial relationship, but one with an almost defining twist: the colonization was effected via cultural levelling, not military conquest. And this came as something as a surprise, given that the 1707 Act of Union ostensibly reserved to the Scots sufficient autonomy within key cultural institutions to remain separate from but to gain equality with their southern neighbours:

> Had they not carefully set aside a space for difference and thus for equality rather than subservience within the Union by retaining their own law and religion? But by the beginning of the nineteenth century, the Scots began to realize that the London parliament was encroaching on their legal and religious sovereignty. As N.T. Phillipson writes: 'it became increasingly clear ... that assimilation was not something which could be sought in [the Scots'] own time and on their own terms ... Assimilation was a force for change which rendered existing institutions inefficient or even redundant.' He continues: 'lawyers [began] to think of assimilation in rather broad terms, as something capable of damaging the whole quality of national life.' The Scots, indeed, began to realize that through subtle encroachment upon and erasure of their Scottish difference, they had come to occupy a decidedly secondary, if not irrelevant position in the Union.[112]

This cultural erosion did not go unnoticed, but it accelerated at a time when Scotland began to enjoy the economic fruits of the Union – that is, at a time when Scotland came to be written into England's narrative of economic prosperity. This, coupled with the theme of constitutional evolution, fused to form what Hearn and the Scottish historian Michael Fry have identified as the classic 'whig' narrative. 'In this narrative, constitutionalism, democracy, and economic "improvement" – in other words, all things good – seemed to flow from England to Scotland and the empire, to the rest of the world. It is in many of its essentials the antecedent of modernization theory in the twentieth century.'[113] Hearn goes on to trace various iterations of and engraftments on the whig narrative up to the present, including a turn toward a decidedly Marxist vocabulary after the 1970s (e.g., adoption of Franz Fanon's anti-colonial voice). But his main point – one shared by other commentators as well – is that both individual Scots and Scottish institutions have found themselves trapped between clashing public narratives: the economic–whig narrative and nationalistic–Scots narrative.

Caroline McCracken-Flesher believes – a sentiment with which I concur – that Walter Scott offers a particularly good example of the national confusions that have plagued Scots ever since the border marked by the Tweed began to erode practically, if not jurisdictionally.[114] In fact, Scott's ontological narrative may fairly be said to embody the narrative clash to which I just adverted. On the one hand, Scott's writing brought him both regard in and a substantial livelihood from the English market. But on the other hand, Scott's novels are infused with distinctly Scottish historical subject matter, and – even more important for our discussion – Scott was both a practising lawyer and an official in the legal system at a time when it was coming under siege from the English parliament. McCracken-Flesher reports that 'during 1806–7, when Scott was Clerk to the Court of Session, Westminster started to impinge on its powers. And Scott actively, if hopelessly, resisted English incursions on Scottish law.'[115] I will return in a moment to McCracken-Flesher's choice of the adverb 'hopelessly' and focus on what she means by 'actively.' One of Scott's biographers, J.G. Lockhart, recounts that after a debate on proposed legislation in the Faculty of Advocates, Scott

> made a speech much longer than any he had ever before delivered in that assembly … It had a flow of energy of eloquence for which those who knew him best had been quite unprepared. When the meeting broke up … his reforming friends … complimented him on the rhetorical powers he had been displaying, and would willingly have treated the subject-matter of the discussion playfully. But his feelings had been moved to an extent far beyond their appreciation: he exclaimed, 'no, no – 't is no laughing matter; little by little, whatever your wishes may be, you will destroy and undermine, until nothing of what makes Scotland Scotland shall remain.' And so saying, he turned round to conceal his agitation – but not until Mr. Jeffrey saw tears gushing down his cheek – resting his head until he recovered himself on the wall of the Mound.[116]

Returning to the word 'hopelessly,' we may now ask whether that label is apt. Even if we concede that individual acts of resistance like Scott's often prove futile (but I wouldn't go so far as to say that they always do), what about the inherent power of legal institutions to resist incongruent extrasystemic narratives? In Devitt's linguistic study we saw this at work vis-à-vis language; now we may ask whether this holds for matters of substance. For proof, we can look to certain aspects of Scots law.

As noted above, it is well known that a condition of the Act of Union between England and Scotland was that the Scottish educational, legal, and religious systems would remain separate. And though the economic pressures represented by the whig narrative have diminished the practical import of this separation, that is not so across the full range of Scots law. For as Lindsay Farmer has illustrated,

> The criminal law ... has succeeded in remaining resolutely independent from its English neighbor. The more serious offences are still to be found in the common law not statute. There has been stubborn resistance to the idea of codifying the substantive law. The system has its own courts, rules of procedure and evidence, and even punishment. And, perhaps most significantly of all, unlike the civil law it is completely self-contained, there being no appeal to the House of Lords on criminal questions. This independence has not occurred accidentally but is rather the result of specific and deliberate resistance ...[117]

Farmer locates the source of this resistance, at least in significant part, in the Scottish national narrative of independence, of difference from England. For support, Farmer turns to Baron Hume, who explained in the introduction to his *Commentaries on the Law of Scotland Respecting Crimes* that he was motivated to write by 'the desire of rescuing the law of my native country from that state of declension in the esteem of some part of the public, into which, of late years, it seems to have been falling.'[118] As Farmer further demonstrates and wryly concludes,

> the cause of this falling esteem is clearly identified as 'those multiplied references to the criminal law of England.' He proceeds to devote some pages to an enumeration of the Scottish system, although as a firm supporter of political union he points out that this is not intended to disparage the English system. There is a slightly provocative edge to his declaration that he regards the English system as 'liberal and enlightened' due to the 'much greater number of dissolute and profligate people' and 'the greater progress ... of every sort of corruption.' The English courts, in other words, get more practice![119]

Farmer conducts his discussion in the context of what is often thought (but nearly as often disputed) as the defining characteristic of the Scottish criminal system: the power of the High Court to declare acts criminal. As one court put it nearly two hundred years ago, 'the genius of our law rests on a principle diametrically opposite to that of England; the Courts of criminal jurisdiction being authorized to punish crimes without positive enactment.'[120] Farmer is concerned – using the declaratory power of the High Court as a fundamental example – to show that Scottish criminal law rests on an 'invented tradition,' an 'imaginary past.'[121] For our purposes, it is immaterial whether the High Court does or should have declaratory power or whether Scottish lawyers have deluded themselves into basing their traditional beliefs and practices on fiction rather than fact. What *is* material, however, is that statements articulating differences between English and Scottish law 'represent part of a successful attempt to assert national identity through institutions such as law in the century following the Union with England. The very tangible economic benefits of the Union could be obtained, but some sense of Scottishness preserved.'[122] And though Farmer decries aspects of this conservative nationalism and its consequences, he nonetheless concedes the sustaining power of nationalistic public narratives once they set up behind institutional walls.[123]

None of this is unique to Scotland. I would argue that *all* legal institutions tend to preserve existing public narratives and to adopt new ones only slowly. This temporal lag carries the salutary consequence of reduced legal volatility, but it also leads to decisions that appear quaint or even downright silly. As an example we can examine how the law has dealt with one of the most potent metanarratives of last couple of hundred years – namely, the popular belief that 'scientific' evidence is evidence of truth. 'The idea that scientific inquiry is objective is unquestionably among the ruling ideas of our epoch, and it represents science as not serving the interests of a particular class, but a purely general interest in the understanding of nature. Indeed, the idea of scientific objectivity has often been invoked on behalf of the claim that the attitude of modern science is "the only rational, universally valid" one.'[124]

In the early 1940s the silent film star Charlie Chaplin found himself embroiled in a paternity suit.[125] Following commencement of the suit (and prior to birth of the child), Chaplin and the soon-to-be mother, Joan Berry, entered into a stipulation (agreed to by the child's guardian *ad litem* and approved by the superior court) under which Chaplin agreed to pay Berry's pre- and post-natal medical expenses and attorney's fees and Berry agreed

> [that she would] voluntarily submit said child after its birth to medical tests for the purpose of determining its paternity and that she would make herself and said child available at all times so that said tests could be made by competent medical experts; ... that one physician shall be named by defendant, one by the guardian ad litem, and the two so chosen shall select a third 'who shall be especially skilled in such matters, who shall make a blood test or other tests accepted by medical science for the purpose of proving and establishing paternity.'[126]

The parties further agreed that if two of the three physicians determined that Chaplin was not the father, plaintiff's attorneys would dismiss the suit or – upon presentation of a proper medical report from the two physicians – the court would dismiss the case with prejudice.

In keeping with what I think of as the Burns rule of contract ('The best-laid schemes o' mice an' men / Gang aft a-gley'), *all three* physicians concluded that Chaplin was not the father, but plaintiff's counsel refused to dismiss the case and two judges presiding over later stages of the matter declined to enforce the parties' stipulation.[127] The case then proceeded to trial, at which Joan Berry put on wholly circumstantial evidence of her child's paternity:

> She testified that she and defendant had had four acts of sexual intercourse at or about the date when, in the ordinary course of nature, the child must have been begotten ... Her testimony was corroborated by defendant's butler as to the fact that she arrived at defendant's home on the evening of December 23d and remained there until some time in the afternoon of December 24th, occupying either defendant's room or a room connected therewith by a bathroom, and that defendant was present in the room during at least a portion of the night of the 23d and in the morning of the 24th.[128]

Against this evidence, Chaplin offered considerable counter-circumstantial evidence, some of which offered other candidates for fatherhood and some of which tended to undermine Berry's credibility. But his principal argument was scientific: namely, that the blood tests proved he was not the father:

The qualifications, competency, and integrity of the physicians designated to make the blood tests are not questioned. After the tests were completed they made a report reading as follows:

Examination of the bloods of Charles Chaplin, Joan Berry and Carol Ann Berry give the following results.

|  | Group | Type |
| --- | --- | --- |
| Charles Chaplin | O | MN |
| Joan Berry | A | N |
| Carol Ann Berry | B | N |

Conclusion reached as the result of these blood grouping tests is that in accordance with the well accepted laws of heredity, the man, Charles Chaplin, cannot be the father of the child, Carol Ann Berry. The law of heredity which applies here is 'The agglutiongens A and B cannot appear in the blood of a child unless present in the blood of one or both parents.'

Two of the physicians testified at the trial that the report truly represented their findings from the tests made. They and one other physician testified that by reason of said tests defendant was not and could not have been the father of [Carol Ann]. *The report and the evidence of the physicians were not controverted by any scientific evidence.*[129]

Despite this uncontroverted scientific evidence, the jury determined that Chaplin was the father of Carol Ann Berry. On appeal, the Court conceded 'the immutability of the scientific law of blood grouping,' but held (based on an unfortunate precedent) that blood test evidence is merely 'expert opinion' and that 'the law makes no distinction between expert evidence and that of any other character.'[130] Thus the jury was entitled to valorize Joan Berry's circumstantial proof over the unrebutted scientific proof. In a concurring opinion, Justice McComb pointedly remarked how out of step the majority opinion was with the scientific metanarrative – indeed, with the metanarrative of Modernity itself – that had already come to dominate other corners of public discourse:

It is possible that in view of the advances made in the medical profession since the decision by the Supreme Court in the Arais case, the present court may see fit to review the rule announced in the previous decision and establish a rule of jurisprudence on this subject consonant with the principle uniformly recognized without question by the medical profession of the United States and Europe.

Ascertainment of the factual truth in the adjudication of any controversy is a consummation devoutly to be wished. Time was when the courts could rely only upon human testimony. But modern science brought new aids. The microscope, electricity, X-ray, psychology, psychiatry, chemistry, and many other scientific means and instrumentalities have revised the judicial guessing game of the past into an institution approaching accuracy in portraying the truth as to the actual fact where, in the pursuit of which, scientific devices may be applied. The chemical tests for learning the presence of poisons in the blood stream, application of the Roentgen ray in defining the fracture of a bone, the use of the microscope in acquiring exact knowledge of the authorship of documents, or the presence of bacteria or the prevalence of white corpuscles – all argue eloquently for a reliance upon scientific devices for ascertaining the truth. If the courts do not utilize these unimpeachable methods for acquiring accurate knowledge of the pertinent facts they will neglect the employment of available, potent agencies which serve to avoid miscarriages of justice.

In the case at bar a widely accepted scientific method of determining parentage was applied. Its result were definite. To reject the new and certain for the old and uncertain does not tend to promote improvement in the administration of justice.[131]

This conservative tendency in the law – this resistance to shifting higher-order narratives – does not, of course, mean that law is unresponsive to cultural change. It just means that there is a cycle that must be completed before changes can occur. First, a sufficient number of individual narratives must through their collective weight effect a change in higher-order narratives. By this I mean that a public narrative or metanarrative on a particular subject must absorb enough individual narratives to change the direction of the story. Sometimes this amounts to the wholesale displacement of a dominant narrative. By the time of *Berry v. Chaplin*, metanarrative change had already happened: Western culture had already seized on the idea of science as truth.[132] But that wasn't enough, because law's tipping point is higher than that of cultural narratives – put another way, the law's rate of narrative absorption is lower than that of the culture at large. So there is a second, critical, step in legal evolution – more individual narratives must work their way through the legal system before rules change.[133] To cast this in evidentiary terms, cultural narratives change on a 'preponderance' standard, whereas laws change on something higher – perhaps 'clear and convincing' or 'beyond a reasonable doubt.' We can see this process at work in any set of thematically related cases. Cases based on racial relations provide a particularly good example.

### Absorbing Narratives: Letting the Outside In

Slavery was legally institutionalized – albeit obliquely and euphemistically (the word 'slave' and its cognates appear nowhere) – in the United States Constitution.[134] This does not mean, however, that there was a clear consensus – an unambiguous public narrative, if you will – about the morality or practical desirability of slavery. In fact, much evidence suggests that the Constitution's drafters were so divided on the subject that that they could do little more than agree to disagree and await the emergence of a dominant view:

> The framers [dealt] with slavery by seeking, so far as possible, to take it out of the national political arena. They were unable in 1787 to settle the issue, one way or the other. They could not establish straightforward Constitutional guarantees against emancipation, as the South Carolinians desired, because many Northerners, and perhaps some Southerners, would not permit it. Nor could they give Congress power to regulate slavery in any way, much less abolish it, because Southerners refused to yield control over the institution. Realizing that it was utterly beyond their power to fashion a national consensus on slavery, or to 'govern' the issue in the absence of one, they had contented themselves with measures aimed at preventing friction over slavery between the states and sections. Thus, when it was decided to tie representation to population, it became necessary to set a date when the slave trade could be terminated, because of the relationship it now bore to the balance of political forces in the union. And when Pierce Butler raised the question of escaped slaves, the Convention was willing to oblige, because most Northerners were as reluctant for blacks to flee north as Southern slave owners were to lose their property. The fugitive-slave clause, like the slave-trade clause, was intended to remove a potential sore point between the states ...
>
> There is no evidence that any framer thought the Constitution contained power to abolish slavery. They all knew how deep the Southerners felt, and however much some of them may have regretted the hold that slavery had on the South, they were all fully sympathetic with the determination of the Deep Southerners to resist abolition in the present

circumstances … But there was no guarantee that powers of emancipa-
tion were forever denied to the federal government. The evidence there
is permits the conclusion that the future, with respect to possible public
action against slavery, was left open on purpose. [The] framers, as of 1787,
agreed unanimously to place the institution of slavery, as it existed within
the South, not 'in the course of ultimate extinction,' as Lincoln argued, but
beyond national regulation.[135]

Given the equivocal public stance toward slavery that we find institutionalized in the Constitution, it is thus not surprising that we see
developments in the public narrative over time. We can trace these
developments through case law, a forum in which shifting racial narratives have been regularly tested.

By the mid-nineteenth century, pressures from the North-South sectional conflict began to mount as the United States began to expand
westward, which raised the question whether slavery would be allowed
to expand along with it. Various political solutions had failed to ease
these pressures, and public sentiment increasingly leaned in favour of
'leaving it to the Supreme Court.'[136] The Court – which was the only
major branch of government that had not tried its hand at resolving the
conflict – itself came to accept the view that it could simply command
away the growing sectional rift.[137] This belief proved profoundly, dev-
astatingly wrong.

The Court entered the slavery fray in *Dred Scott v. Sanford*, which has
proved to be one of the most vilified decisions in Supreme Court history. The decision is wrong on many levels, but for our purposes the
Court's narrative blunders are the most instructive. The case arose from
the intersection of Dred Scott's personal narrative and the larger public
narrative that had yet to explain a nation divided both literally and
philosophically over slavery. Dred Scott, who had admittedly once been
a slave, brought a trespass suit in federal court against John Sanford. He
claimed that the federal court had 'diversity of citizenship' jurisdiction
over the suit because he was a citizen of Missouri and Sanford was a
citizen of New York.[138] In the early 1830s Scott's former owner took him
from Missouri to Illinois, where they resided for two years, then on
to Minnesota, which was at that time part of the Louisiana Territory.
Within about four years, they returned to Missouri and Scott was sold
to Sanford as a slave. During this period, slavery was legal in Missouri,
but prohibited in Illinois by state law and in the Louisiana Territory by
the Missouri Compromise.[139] Scott asserted that he became free by vir-

tue of his residence in two areas in which slavery was banned. Sanford countered that even if Scott were free, that did not make him a 'citizen' of Missouri and, therefore, the federal court had no jurisdiction to hear Scott's case. Moreover, merely residing in a free state or territory could not emancipate a slave in derogation of his or her owner's property rights upon returning to a slave-permitting state.

As we have seen, America was born in a state of narrative suspension, dangling between a commitment to social equality and the looming paradox of slavery. Chief Justice Roger Taney's majority opinion in *Dred Scott* misrepresents this past, claiming universality for a public narrative in which blacks figured only as members of a 'subordinate and inferior class of beings':

> It is difficult at this day to realize the state of public opinion in relation to that unfortunate race, which prevailed in the civilized and enlightened portions of the world at the time of the Declaration of Independence, and when the Constitution of the United States was framed and adopted. But the public history of every European nation displays it in a manner too plain to be mistaken.
>
> They had for more than a century before been regarded as beings of an inferior order, and altogether unfit to associate with the white race, either in social or political relations; and so far inferior, that they had no rights which the white man was bound to respect; and that the negro might justly and lawfully be reduced to slavery for his benefit. He was bought and sold, and treated as an ordinary article of merchandise and traffic, whenever a profit could be made by it. This opinion was at that time fixed and universal in the civilized portion of the white race. It was regarded as an axiom in morals as well as in politics, which no one thought of disputing, or supposed to be open to dispute; and men in every grade and position in society daily and habitually acted upon it in their private pursuits, as well as in matters of public concern, without doubting for a moment the correctness of this opinion.[140]

In dissent, Justice McLean demonstrated that Justice Taney's majority opinion rested on a false premise because slavery was not a universally recognized institution – even at the time that Constitution was adopted:

> There is no nation in Europe which considers itself bound to return to his master a fugitive slave, under the civil law or the law of nations. On the

contrary, the slave is held to be free where there is no treaty obligation, or compact in some other form, to return him to his master. The Roman law did not allow freedom to be sold. An ambassador or any other public functionary could not take a slave to France, Spain, or any other country of Europe, without emancipating him. A number of slaves escaped from a Florida plantation, and were received on board of ship by Admiral Cochrane; by the King's Bench, they were held to be free ...

The state of slavery is deemed to be a mere municipal regulation, founded upon and limited to the range of the territorial laws. This was fully recognised in Somersett's case, (Lafft's Rep., 1; 20 Howell's State Trials, 79,) which was decided before the American Revolution ...

No case in England appears to have been more thoroughly examined than that of Somersett ...

In giving the opinion of the court, Lord Mansfield said:

The state of slavery is of such a nature that it is incapable of being introduced on any reasons, moral or political, but only by positive law, which preserves its force long after the reasons, occasion, and time itself, from whence it was created, is erased from the memory; it is of a nature that nothing can be suffered to support it but positive law.[141]

This eviscerates Taney's only serious attempt at justification – viz., the 'originalist' appeal to the meaning of the Constitution when adopted.[142] Thus unmasked, we see Taney's opinion as nothing more than a raw and unanchored exercise of power, one consciously declining to endorse the ever strengthening narrative of America as a land of freedom. And I choose the word 'consciously' quite deliberately. For Taney acknowledges that public opinion has changed, even though he is not going to be the one to act on it: 'It is not the province of the court to decide upon the justice or injustice, the policy or impolicy of these laws. The decision of that question belonged to the political or law-making power; to those who formed the sovereignty and framed the Constitution.'[143]

A civil war, three Constitutional Amendments, and a host of enabling acts later, there was no longer doubt that blacks were legal persons entitled to the full range of Constitutional protections.[144] But what that range *entailed* was a different matter. *Plessy v. Ferguson*, which was decided nearly forty years after *Dred Scott*, showed how the narrative of difference had not been erased and could still trump the grand public narrative of America as a bastion of freedom and equality.[145] In 1890, Louisiana passed a statute requiring railways to

provide 'equal but separate accommodations for the white and colored races.' Criminal liability attached to a passenger of one race using
the facilities intended for the other race. Plessy, who claimed to be
seven-eighths white, was prosecuted for refusing to leave a 'white'
passenger car. The gravamen of Plessy's suit was that Louisiana's legislation could not be justified under even a minimal 'reasonableness'
standard.[146] But the majority disagreed, holding that anything negative about the law came not from the law itself but from the defective
construction that blacks placed on it!

> We consider the underlying fallacy of the plaintiff's argument to consist
> in the assumption that the enforced separation of the two races stamps
> the colored race with a badge of inferiority. If this be so, it is not by reason
> of anything found in the act, but solely because the colored race chooses
> to put that construction upon it. The argument necessarily assumes that
> if, as has been more than once the case, and is not unlikely to be so again,
> the colored race should become the dominant power in the state legisla-
> ture, and should enact a law in precisely similar terms, it would thereby
> relegate the white race to an inferior position. We imagine that the white
> race, at least, would not acquiesce in this assumption. The argument also
> assumes that social prejudices may be overcome by legislation, and that
> equal rights cannot be secured to the negro except by an enforced com-
> mingling of the two races. We cannot accept this proposition. If the two
> races are to meet upon terms of social equality, it must be the result of nat-
> ural affinities, a mutual appreciation of each other's merits, and a volun-
> tary consent of individuals ... Legislation is powerless to eradicate racial
> instincts, or to abolish distinctions based upon physical differences, and
> the attempt to do so can only result in accentuating the difficulties of the
> present situation. If the civil and political rights of both races be equal, one
> cannot be inferior to the other civilly or politically. If one race be inferior
> to the other socially, the constitution of the United States cannot put them
> upon the same plane.[147]

In dissent, Justice Harlan pounced on the sophistry underlying the
majority's pronouncements, as well as on the sharp disconnect between
those pronouncements and the notions of liberty and equality that animated the adoption of the Civil War Amendments:

> It was said in argument that the statute of Louisiana does not discrimi-
> nate against either race, but prescribes a rule applicable alike to white and

colored citizens. But this argument does not meet the difficulty. Every one knows that the statute in question had its origin in the purpose, not so much to exclude white persons from railroad cars occupied by blacks, as to exclude colored people from coaches occupied by or assigned to white persons ... But in view of the constitution, in the eye of the law, there is in this country no superior, dominant, ruling class of citizens. There is no caste here. Our constitution is color-blind, and neither knows nor tolerates classes among citizens. In respect of civil rights, all citizens are equal before the law. The humblest is the peer of the most powerful.[148]

Going further, he presciently observed that *Plessy* would stand to feed narratives of 'race hatred' and give government sanction to 'more or less brutal and irritating' encroachments upon 'the admitted rights of colored citizens.' This would in turn, he argued, 'create and perpetuate a feeling of distrust between these races' because it rests 'on the ground that colored citizens are so inferior and degraded that they cannot be allowed to sit in public coaches occupied by white citizens.'[149] Thus, states must be debarred from attempts to turn back the pages of history to the antebellum period when the national narrative accepted not just social inequality but slavery itself:

> The sure guaranty of the peace and security of each race is the clear, distinct, unconditional recognition by our governments, national and state, of every right that inheres in civil freedom, and of the equality before the law of all citizens of the United States, without regard to race. State enactments regulating the enjoyment of civil rights upon the basis of race, and cunningly devised to defeat legitimate results of the war, under the pretense of recognizing equality of rights, can have no other result than to render permanent peace impossible, and to keep alive a conflict of races, the continuance of which must do harm to all concerned.[150]

It took another fifty-plus years for the Supreme Court to undo the separate-but-equal mischief wrought by *Plessy* and its progeny. That happened in *Brown v. Board of Education of Topeka*, a case in which the plaintiffs challenged the constitutionality of state laws permitting schools segregated by race.[151] That case is important because it (mostly) closes the narrative loop opened in *Dred Scott* and refashioned in *Plessy*, but in our context it is more important *how* the Court did so than *why*.[152] To recall the majority opinions in the two earlier cases, the justices there took flat-footed, monolithic positions about what the respective framers had in mind when they drafted the Constitution and the Civil War

Amendments. Justice Warren, writing for a unanimous Court, started from the premise that the historical record surrounding adoption of the Fourteenth Amendment was generally 'inconclusive' and – because of a developing public narrative concerning the importance of public education – largely irrelevant:

> The most avid proponents of the post-War Amendments undoubtedly intended them to remove all legal distinctions among 'all persons born or naturalized in the United States.' Their opponents, just as certainly, were antagonistic to both the letter and the spirit of the Amendments and wished them to have the most limited effect. What others in Congress and the state legislatures had in mind cannot be determined with any degree of certainty ... An additional reason for the inconclusive nature of the Amendment's history, with respect to segregated schools, is the status of public education at that time ... Education of Negroes was almost nonexistent, and practically all of the race were illiterate ... Today, education is perhaps the most important function of state and local governments ... It is the very foundation of good citizenship. Today it is a principal instrument in awakening the child to cultural values, in preparing him for later professional training, and in helping him to adjust normally to his environment. In these days, it is doubtful that any child may reasonably be expected to succeed in life if he is denied the opportunity of an education. Such considerations apply with added force to children in grade and high schools. To separate them from others of similar age and qualifications solely because of their race generates a feeling of inferiority as to their status in the community that may affect their hearts and minds in a way unlikely ever to be undone.[153]

For support, the Court turned not to the particular narratives of the individual plaintiffs, but to a growing body of sociological evidence, especially that growing out of the work of Kenneth Clark.[154] This tacitly signals, I think, that the Court accepted that the public racial narrative had tipped decidedly in favour of Constitutional standards that would support broad social equality for blacks.[155] In other words, the national race narrative had been revised – even reconstructed – in a way that ultimately leveraged the *Plessy*-era legal narrative into sync with the evolved public narrative.[156]

## What Law Can Learn from Literature (and History)

Now that we have seen the process of narrative evolution at work within the law, it behooves us to explain it. As I mentioned before, legal narratives are not different in kind from other types of narratives; to the degree they *are* different, it is only because they are made according to a particular set of conventions. Ian Watt has made this point in examining the contours of the 'realistic' novel:

> Here, however we are concerned with a much more limited conception, with the extent to which the analogy with philosophical realism helps to isolate and define the distinctive narrative mode of the novel. This, it has been suggested, is the sum of literary techniques whereby the novel's imitation of human life follows the procedures adopted by philosophical realism in its attempt to ascertain and report the truth. These procedures are by no means confined to philosophy: they tend, in fact, to be followed whenever the relation to reality of any report of an event is being investigated. The novel's mode of imitating reality may therefore be equally well summarised in terms of the procedures of another group of specialists in epistemology, the jury in a court of law. Their expectations, and those of the novel reader coincide in many ways: both want to know 'all the particulars' of a given case – the time and place of the occurrence; both must be satisfied as to the identities of the parties concerned, and will refuse to accept evidence about anyone called Sir Toby Belch or Mr. Badman – still less about a Chloe who has no surname and is 'common as the air'; and they also expect the witnesses to tell the story 'in his own words.' The jury, in fact, takes the 'circumstantial view of life', which T.H. Green found to be the characteristic outlook of the novel.[157]

Now whether particular narrative conventions actually serve the ends of truth is a topic we must defer for a moment. But for now, suffice it to say that Watt sees it as an open question: 'Formal realism is, of course, like the rules of evidence, only a convention; and there is no reason why the report on human life which is presented by it should be in fact any truer than those presented through the very different conventions of other literary genres.'[158]

To get us closer to the question of 'truth' and what that might mean when we speak of legal narratives, Paul Veyne's description of how history is (re)constructed seems an apt analogy. In his view,

> History is an account of events: all else flows from that. Since it is a direct account, it does not revive, any more than the novel does. The actual experience, as it comes from the hands of the historian, is not that of the actors;

it is a narration, so it can eliminate certain erroneous problems. Like the novel, history sorts, simplifies, organizes, fits a century into a page. This synthesis of the account is not less spontaneous than that of our memory when we call to mind the last ten years through which we have lived. To speculate on the interval that always separates the actual experience and the recollection of the event would simply bring us to see that Waterloo was not the same thing for a veteran of the Old Guard and for a field marshal; that the battle can be related in the first or third person; that it can be spoken of as a battle, as an English victory, or as a French defeat; that from the start one can drop a hint of the outcome or appear to discover it. These speculations can produce amusing experiments in aesthetics; to the historian, they are the discovery of a limit.[159]

History is a synthesis and a condensation; furthermore, it is driven by *perspective:* it is not unmediated 'fact.' And this is so even for direct actors, whose memories and perceptions are never more than partial and are subject to distortion, even delusion:

That limit is that in no case is what historians call an event grasped directly and fully; it is always grasped incompletely and laterally, through documents or statements, let us say through *tekmeria*, traces, impressions. Even if I am a contemporary and a witness of Waterloo, even if I am the principal actor and Napoleon in person, I shall have only a perspective of what historians will call the event of Waterloo; I shall be able to leave to posterity only my statement, which, if it reaches them, they will call an impression. Even if I were Bismarck deciding to send the Ems dispatch, my own interpretation of the event would perhaps not be the same as that of my friends, my confessor, my regular historian, and my psychoanalyst, who may have their own version of my decision and think they know better than I do what it was I wanted. In essence, history is knowledge through documents. Thus, historical narration goes beyond all documents, since none of them can be the event; it is not a documentary photomontage, and does show the past 'live, as if you were there.'[160]

In law, this means we must attend closely to how narratives are constructed. In even a simple case – a minor fender bender at an intersection – we can never 'know' whether the traffic light was red or green when the cars crashed. The best we can do is fashion a narrative reconstruction of the event, one that sorts, sifts, and synthesizes the competing narratives offered by the actors and witnesses, along with physical evidence and any accompanying expert testimony interpreting that evidence. In difficult cases, this involves both choosing among competing narratives and building a coherent adjudicative narrative from among narrative fragments – that is, a narrative that will stand to justify the ultimate decision in a case. For instruction and for an extended rumination on what it means to find 'facts,' we now turn to Robert Browning's *The Ring and the Book*.[161]

In June 1860, Robert Browning bought an 'old yellow book' at a flea market in Florence. This book was actually a collection of legal materials (briefs, letters, and the like) pertaining to a late-seventeenth-century trial of an Arentine nobleman/churchman for the murder of his young wife and her parents. Over the next few years, Browning fashioned this raw material – through a process that warrants closer examination – into the twelve dramatic monologues (by ten different speakers) that collectively constitute his monumental poem.

The basic story behind *The Ring and the Book* is fairly simple. In 1693, Guido Franceschini, a nobleman who had had a disappointing career in the Church, married a thirteen-year-old girl, Francesca Pompilia, who had been raised in Rome by her ostensible parents (more on that is coming), a couple named Comparini (Pietro and Violante). After the marriage, which was unhappy from the start, the Comparini visited Guido's palace in Arezzo, which they found much poorer than expected. Because Guido had misrepresented his financial condition at the time of the marriage, they brought suit against him in Rome for the return of Pompilia's dowry. As grounds, the Comparini argued that Pompilia was really the daughter of a prostitute, from whom Violante had purchased the infant Pompilia to satisfy a condition precedent (having a child) to the vesting of an inheritance. As a result of this suit, the marriage deteriorated further and Guido became intolerable. Pompilia sought relief from local authorities, to no avail, and she eventually made an escape with the help of a young canon, Giuseppe Caponsacchi. Guido gave chase and overtook the fleeing couple about fifteen miles from Rome, at Castelnuovo. The couple were subsequently tried at Rome: Caponsacchi was banished to Civita Vecchia for three years; Pompilia was sent to a convent. But because Pompilia was pregnant, she was soon returned to the Comparini. Several months later, she gave birth to a boy, Gaetano. Shortly after Gaetano's birth, Guido and four henchmen gained entrance to the Comparini home by claiming to bear a message from Caponsacchi and then murdered the Comparini and left Pompilia for dead with twenty-two stab wounds, from which she died four days later. Guido and his cohorts were captured, charged with murder, and tried.

In the criminal trial, Guido did not claim that he had not committed the acts charged; rather, he argued that a husband should be allowed to kill his adulterous wife and those who aided her. Guido's justification defence thus called upon the court to pass judgment on the relationship between Pompilia and Caponsacchi (which was never fully resolved in the earlier proceeding), as well as the conduct and motivations of everyone involved. Ultimately, the court decided against Guido and condemned him to death by beheading. But Guido, who held minor orders in the Church, appealed to Pope Innocent XII to set aside his sentence under canon law. The Pope declined to intervene, and Guido was executed on 22 February 1698. Quickly thereafter, the court ruled Pompilia innocent and declared Gaetano the legal heir to her property.

When we look at specifics in a minute, we will see that Browning took this basic set of facts, passed them through the lens of his own imagination, and projected them into a work of art. Book I, whose narrator is something of a stand-in for Browning, is a general introduction. In Book II, 'Half-Rome,' the speaker is an older man with his own matrimonial difficulties; he takes up Guido's cause. The speaker in Book III, 'The Other Half-Rome,' is a young man with obvious sympathies for Pompilia. The narrator of Book IV, 'Tertium Quid,' strives for a neutral tone and to balance the arguments put forth by the two speakers immediately preceding him. Book V, Guido's first of two monologues, comes close on the heels of the murder. He is speaking to his judges and defends himself though a series of thinly disguised appeals to shared values and experiences. The narration of Book VI, which Caponsacchi delivers, is full of grief for Pompilia, hatred for Guido, and scorn for the judges, who – after all – had treated the earlier proceeding with juvenile humour. Book VII is 'Pompilia,' a deathbed confession in which she struggles to make sense of all that has happened to her. Books VIII and IX belong to the two lawyers, Dominus Hyacinthus de Arcangelis and Juris Doctor Johannes-Baptista Bottinius, the former representing Guido, and the latter prosecuting him. After the relatively lighthearted interlude of the two lawyers, the Pope takes centre stage and renders a damning judgment on Guido. In Book XI, Guido is given a chance to say his last words. He appears in a form much different from that of his previous monologue, this time showing not solicitousness but unvarnished bitterness and hatred.

Book XII, 'The Book and the Ring,' closes the cycle of narratives with the reappearance of the speaker from Book I. Its closing observations about the relationship between 'facts' and 'meaning' are critical to an understanding of the work as whole and – indeed – all narrative reconstruction: 'So write a book shall mean beyond the facts, / Suffice the eye and save the soul beside.'[162]

In confessing that he wants to get 'beyond the facts,' Browning draws our attention to the fictional, constructed aspect of his work. This construction offers a single space within which the full panoply of legal actors and observers can appear simultaneously. Thus, unlike the typical legal encounter, we have access to the historically situated thoughts of three outside observers, two lawyers, the victim, the chief witness, the accused, and the judge, all bookended with the commentary of a temporally unbounded narrator. As a technique, this drops us into a complex narrative stream, what Marie Hockenhull Smith calls (in an analysis of one of Walter Scott's novels, *The Heart of Midlothian*) 'a kind of narrative cubism.'[163] This lays bare for us, then, the posts and lintels of the poem and allows us to see the integration of the different discourses that have informed and have been informed by the murder and trial. As such, the account is 'what Bakhtin calls a heteroglossia, all the many voices brought into dialogue with one another.'[164] In *The Ring and the Book*, as in *The Heart of Midlothian*, 'the interest is in the plurality of relations (in both senses) which make up the experience of law.' And this 'knot of narratives' entangles both actors and observers, including us. For the very structure of Browning's poem reminds us not only of the fact that perspective influences interpretation but also that our readerly perspective is not as independent as we might like to think:

> [E]ven as thus by step and step
> I led you from the level of to-day
> Up to the summit of long ago,
> Here, whence I point you the wide prospect round –
> Let me, by like steps, slope you back to smooth,
> Land you on mother-earth, no whit the worse [...][165]

Thus forewarned of the limitations on the independence of our own perceptions, we can push on through the poem. But full-blown explication of this enormous work would capsize us, so we must content ourselves with an examination of just a few key 'facts' that we can assess from multiple perspectives. In Book I, the narrator alerts us to the fundamental – yet unstable – relationship between fact and narrative. He finds the 'old yellow Book,' which he characterizes as 'pure crude fact,' and becomes so transfixed by it that in the time it took to walk home from the market he 'had mastered the contents, knew the whole truth.'[166] From the outset, though, we know that Browning is up to something more than merely 'reporting' the 'facts.' For he describes to us the work of the goldsmith, who blends gold (fact) with an alloy (artistic imagination) to make the gold workable, then removes the alloy to reveal a finished ring (the work of art):

> That trick is, the artificer melts up wax
> With honey, so to speak; he mingles gold
> With gold's alloy, and, duly tempering both,
> Effects a manageable mass, then works:
> But his work ended, once the thing a ring,
> Oh, there's repristination! Just a spirt
> O' the proper fiery acid o'er its face,
> And forth the alloy unfastened flies in fume;
> While, self-sufficient now, the shape remains,
> The rondure brave, the lilied loveliness,
> Gold as it was, is, shall be evermore:
> Prime nature with an added artistry –
> No carat lost, and you have gained a ring.[167]

This fact-plus-artistry-equals-ring formula that Browning establishes is worth testing a bit to see how well it generalizes to and explains (if at all) the formation of the adjudicative narratives we have been examining so far. Along the way, we will of necessity need to consider what 'facts' are, what 'truth' is, and how those concepts subsist within (and are perhaps only derivable from) a narrative framework. Browning is at some labour to characterize his source material as 'fact' and his own work as 'truth' – or at least 'fact' of a different order. Of the Old Yellow Book, he says:

> Now, as the ingot, ere the ring was forged,
> Lay gold, (beseech you, hold that figure fast!)
> So, in this book lay absolutely truth,
> Fanciless fact, the documents indeed,
> Primary lawyer-pleadings for, against,

The aforesaid Five; real summed-up circumstance
Adduced in proof of these on either side,
Put forth and printed, as the practice was [...][168]

Here, Browning clearly overstates the purity of the facts set forth in the Old Yellow Book – after all, the documents making up that compendium were *authored*, which necessarily means that 'what really happened' has been interpreted – but I think Browning knows this. His claim is that there are different modes of interpretation and that the one he practises may swerve closer to 'truth' than others. He stakes this claim by first defending his process against the common charge of art-as-fiction:

Do you tell the story, now, in off-hand style,
Straight from the book? Or simply here and there,
(The while you vault it through the loose and large)
Hang to a hint? Or is there book at all,
And don't you deal in poetry, make-believe,
And the white lies it sounds like?'
                                         Yes and no!
From the book, yes; thence bit by bit I dug
The lingot truth, that memorable day,
Assayed and knew my piecemeal gain was gold, –
Yes; but from something else surpassing that,
Something of mine which, mixed up with the mass,
Made it bear hammer and be firm to file.
Fancy with fact is just one fact the more;
To wit that fancy has informed, transpierced,
Thridded and so thrown fast the facts else free,
As right through ring and ring runs the djereed
And binds the loose, one bar without break.[169]

Browning sees his mission as one mimetic on – if somewhat paler by comparison than – the Creation: 'Man ... / Repeats God's process in man's due degree, / Attaining man's proportionate result, – / Creates, no, but resuscitates, perhaps.'[170] Thus anticipating Veyne, he sees this process of recuperation as constituting *a* truth, one potentially closer to *the* truth than that revealed in the dry facts ossified in the pages of the Old Yellow Book. This is so, he argues, because temporal distance – in the right hands – can manufacture an interpretation richer than that delivered by the direct observation of the senses, 'Which take at best imperfect cognizance, / Since, how heart moves brain, and how both move hand, / What mortal ever in entirety saw?'[171] This is of course counterintuitive and counter to trial practice (e.g., the rule against hearsay and the 'best evidence' rule), so Browning pauses to take a gentle satiric swipe at our common pre- (mis?)conceptions:

> Then, since a Trial ensued, a touch o' the same
> To sober us, flustered with frothy talk,
> And teach our common sense its helplessness.
> For why deal simply with divining-rod,
> Scrape where we fancy secret sources flow,
> And ignore law, the recognized machine,
> Elaborate display of pipe and wheel
> Framed to unchoke, pump up and pour apace
> Truth till a flowery foam shall wash the world?
> The patent truth-extracting process, – ha?[172]

Though legal fact finding is not always as painful as a trip to the dentist, Browning makes a fair point, the same one that Cardozo made when attacking 'mechanical jurisprudence' in *Hynes*. That is, things get lost when we come to look on the law as a machine, whether this touches on injustice in an individual case or a class of cases, or on the opportunity to explore the subtleties and complexities of human motivation.[173] To guard against this, Browning counsels us to reach beyond a 'single-minded' approach to interpretation; he suggests, indeed, that acts can only be understood through a multiplicity of perspectives – through the clash of narratives we earlier considered through the work of Bankowski and Nussbaum.[174] To explore this fully, we would need to explicate his poem line by line, which, as I have mentioned before, would plainly engulf our discussion. As an alternative, I propose that we look at two types of fact finding that take place in the poem: *what*-facts and *why*-facts. As a specific example of the former, we will look at the question of whether Pompilia sent the letters to Caponsacchi that stand as evidence of an adulterous affair; of the latter, we will look at Guido's stated reason for the murders – that he killed as a matter of honour.

Whether Pompilia was able to write is one of the dominant issues in the Old Yellow Book, for the answer to that question has the potential to eviscerate the most damaging evidence of an affair between Pompilia and Caponsacchi: the love letters that Guido claimed to have found when he caught up with the fleeing couple at Castelnuovo.[175] Half-Rome, the pro-Guido narrator of Book II, is the first to take up the issue of the letters. He believes that 'the case was clear' and rendered so by the 'love-letters':

> Mad prose, mad verse, fears, hopes, triumph, despair,
> Avowal, disclaimer, plans, dates, names, – was nought
> Wanting to prove, if proof consoles at all,
> That this had been but the fifth act o' the piece
> Whereof the due proemium, months ago
> These playwrights had put forth, and ever since
> Matured the middle, added 'neath his nose.[176]

Nor, for two reasons, is Half-Rome swayed by the assertion that Pompilia was illiterate and, therefore, could neither have written letters to Caponsacchi nor read letters received from him. First, he finds it difficult to reconcile Pompilia's claim to illiteracy with her admission that she received letters from Caponsacchi. Second, he finds it equally damning that Caponsacchi admits receiving letters he believed to be from Pompilia.[177] At a minimum, then, Half-Rome – who by no coincidence has suspicions about his own wife's fidelity – concludes that the letters would have justified Guido in killing the couple on the road to Rome.[178]

Other Half-Rome, a young man with romantic tendencies, takes Pompilia's part. For him, something in the 'tale' of a long-standing affair rings false. He, like Half-Rome, has reasons for thinking the way he does. First, Pompilia has been consistent in her denials:

> For her part,
> Pompilia quietly constantly avers
> She never penned a letter in her life
> Nor to the Canon nor any other man,
> Being incompetent to write and read [...][179]

Second, he finds the admitted 'romance-book' character of Pompilia's version of the story credible because 'she avers this with calm mouth / Dying [...],'[180] which squares with the common belief that statements made upon imminent death are truthful. (This belief is institutionalized in the rule of evidence that privileges deathbed statements over ordinary instances of hearsay.) Third, Other Half-Rome sees Caponsacchi's admission (when a flat denial would have served him better) of having sent letters to Pompilia as evidence of general veracity. Fourth, and most important, Other Half-Rome believes there is unequivocal evidence that Guido had earlier forged a letter from Pompilia to his brother, so one can safely assume he acted in conformity with his past conduct and did the same with the letters he allegedly 'found' at the inn:

> The ins and outs o' the rooms were searched: he found
> Or showed for found the abominable prize –
> Love-letters from his wife who cannot write,
> Love-letters in reply o' the priest – thank God! –
> Who can write and confront his character
> With this, and prove the false thing forged throughout:
> Spitting whereat, he needs must spatter whom
> But Guido's self? – that forged and falsified
> One letter called Pompilia's, past dispute:
> Then why not these to make sure still more sure?[181]

As pure partisans, both Half-Rome and Other Half-Rome construct factual conclusions from unspecified source material (including, presumably, gossip) to suit their larger sympathies, pro-Guido and pro-Pompilia. They thus make no reasoned analysis of *all* the evidence, perhaps because they stand to bear no real consequences for overstating their respective cases. By contrast, the prosecutor, Johannes-Baptista Bottinius (the Fisc), takes care to argue no more than necessary from the (admittedly equivocal) evidence because he need not take the unreserved position that Pompilia could not have written the letters to disable Guido's claim of justification. That is, he need only show that even if Pompilia did write the letters, she did so with a motive that was sufficiently pure. Thus the Fisc first suggests that Guido forged the letters and planted them on the couple at Castelnuovo and then offers good reason why the letters were excusable even if she wrote them:

> Grant the tale
> O' the husband, which is false, were proved and true
> To the letter – or the letters, I should say,
> Abominations he professed to find
> And fix upon Pompilia and the priest, –
> Allow them hers – for even though she could not write, [...]
> So she, though hunger after fellowship,

May well have learned, though late, to play the scribe ...
Concede she wrote (which were preposterous)
This and the other epistle, – what of it?
Where does the figment touch her candid fame?
Being in peril of her life – 'my life,
Not an hour's purchase,' as the letter runs, –
And having but one stay in this extreme,
Out of the wide world but a single friend –
What could she other than resort to him,
And how with any hope resort but thus? [...]
From all which I deduce – the lady here
Was bound to proffer nothing short of love
To the priest whose service it was to save her [...]
                                        Licit end
Enough was found in mere escape from death,
To legalize our means illicit else
Of feigned love, false allurement, fancied fact.[182]

This throws into sharp relief the difference between advocacy and judgment. The advocate's job is to cast evidence in the light most favourable to his case and in a way that satisfies his burden of proof. His goal is thus to present evidence in a way that enhances the chance that the finder of fact will actually find facts that support his claim or defeat those of his opponent. The judge (or jury, as the case may be), in contrast, has a more difficult task: she must consider the full range of evidence, weigh it, contextualize it, and then narrate it in a way that justifies the ultimate decision. This does not mean, however, that she can resolve every point of ambiguity or contradiction. The best she can do is to tell the best story possible. In *The Ring and the Book*, that role falls to the Pope.

Guido's case arrives at the office of the Pope with a nearly complete record. All the principal players have spoken (save Guido for the second time). With respect to the letters, therefore, Guido, Caponsacchi, and Pompilia have each given their testimony. To briefly recap: Guido sticks to the story he had told in the proceeding leading to Caponsacchi's three-year banishment and Pompilia's confinement: viz., he caught them together at Castelnuovo and found the letters on them.[183] Caponsacchi tells a more nuanced tale. He says he knew from the start that the supposed letters from Pompilia were but a 'transparent trick' of Guido's. He also learned that she was illiterate, that Guido had forged letters in Caponsacchi's hand, and that the messenger ('She who brought letters from who could not write') and principal witness in Guido's favour was a common prostitute and thus not credible.[184] In the main, Pompilia's deathbed rendition of the facts coincides with Caponsacchi's, amplifying and in no way undermining it. If anything, her plainspoken version underscores the insidious nature of Guido's scheme.[185]

The Pope begins his analysis from the raw evidentiary record, which he finds deficient in itself (a mere semblance or shadow of fact), but from which the truth is 'evolvable':

> I have worn through this sombre wintry day,
> With winter in my soul beyond the world's,
> Over these dismalest of documents
> Which drew night down on me ere eve befell, –
> Pleadings and counter-pleadings, figure of fact
> Besides fact's self […]
> Truth, nowhere, lies yet everywhere in these –
> Not absolutely in a portion, yet
> Evolvable from the whole: evolved at last
> Painfully, held tenaciously by me.[186]

With respect to the letters, the Pope ultimately deems them forgeries, not because of any physical evidence but because the idea of an adulterous affair between Pompilia and Caponsacchi doesn't hang together with the rest of the evidence – it makes the story incoherent:

> Hence this consummate lie, this love-intrigue,
> Unmanly simulation of a sin,
> With a place and time and circumstance to suit –
> These letters false beyond all forgery –
> Not just handwriting and mere authorship,
> But false to body and soul they figure forth –
> As though the man had cut out shape and shape
> From fancies of that other Aretine,
> To paste below – incorporate the filth
> With cherub faces on a missal-page![187]

If pinning down physical facts (e.g., whether Pompilia wrote any of the letters) is a daunting task, then reaching conclusions about psychological facts (e.g., Guido's motive) is doubly difficult. Guido's initial position, which is echoed in the monologues of Half Rome and Guido's lawyer, is that the murders were a matter *honoris causa*.[188] The Pope, however, locates Guido's motives elsewhere: 'All is the lust for money: to get gold, – / Why, lie, rob, if it must be, murder!'[189] In so recognizing this in Guido, the Pope bars him access to the mitigating cloak of honourable vengeance:

> So plans he,
> Always subordinating (note the point!)
> Revenge, the manlier sin, to interest
> The meaner, – would pluck pang forth, but unclench
> No gripe in the act, let fall no money-piece.[190]

In divining Guido's animating force and intent – and those of the other actors, for that matter – the Pope relies on the experience of a lifetime ('eyes grow[n] sharp by use'), not on any particular analytical method. This experience leads him to 'find the truth.'[191] As Robert Langbaum explains it, 'the Pope does not weigh argument against argument, fact against fact, but cuts right through the facts to a sympathetic apprehension of the motives and essential moral qualities behind the deeds.'[192] I don't disagree with this assessment, but I think we can sharpen it even further by recontextualizing it within our earlier discussion of particulars and universals. What the Pope achieves, I submit, is a proper balance between the particular facts presented in the pleadings and the universal rule to which Guido seeks resort (justifiable homicide). That is, Guido's ontological narrative – which embodies an unbroken pattern of acts driven by greed – is not subsumable under the then existing rule justifying homicide in cases of adultery. Neither the physical facts (e.g., Guido killed not just Pompilia but her parents as well; he killed not by himself or in the heat of passion but after cold reflection and with four hirelings) nor the psychological facts (e.g., Guido was motivated by avarice) fit within the set of 'honour killing' narratives that had been reduced to a universally stated rule.

If there is a single lesson to be learned from *The Ring and the Book*, it is that multiple narrative perspectives can aid the search for truth. Some commentators have suggested that truth can be 'induced' from a multiplicity of viewpoints.[193] I would not go quite so far, but I do believe that Browning's poem shows us that – given a large enough range of narrative viewpoints – there is something of a narrative inevitability to the final version of the story (i.e., the findings of fact supporting a judgment), at least when the author of that version carefully attends to both particulars and universals.

Over the course of this chapter, we have seen how narratives become rules and how narratives compete with one another to become or remain institutionalized. In the next chapter, we will elaborate on this idea of a 'narrative marketplace' and explore how that marketplace contributes not just to the development of the law but to laws and institutions congenial to democracy.

# 3 Law, Narrative, and Democracy

In the previous chapters, we explored how narratives influence laws and the institutions in which they are housed. Now it is time to explore the other half of the equation I established at the outset – that is, how legal systems that are generally receptive to narratives facilitate the development of democracy. As the following discussion will show, narrative receptivity is a condition precedent to the development and maintenance of at least some democratic institutions. And this is so, I think, because narrative is one of the tools with which complex societies harmonize the overlapping – sometimes competing – drives of democracy and the Rule of Law.[1] To anchor the line of reasoning to which this conclusion is tied, I need to explain what I mean by 'democracy' and 'Rule of Law,' both of which are disputed terms.[2]

Democracy, in its most basic formulation, could mean something quite narrow, something like 'majority rule.'[3] So conceived, a democracy might have little to do with the Rule of Law, as we will presently describe it, because all decisions of a 'legal' nature could be made ad hoc, retrospectively, and with wide variance. But this is not what we have in mind when we think of democracy. Instead, we have in mind constitutional democracies in which – no matter the precise form of government – there is a baseline expectation of universal and equal suffrage, majority rule, and competing political parties, as well as a broad range of legally enforceable civil rights that inure to the benefit of all members of the society (not the least of which are members of identifiable minorities). This set of characteristics – especially with respect to the latter point – begins to define what Ronald Dworkin calls the 'partnership view' of democracy.[4] The partnership view assumes (because it depends on more than unenforceable statements of aspirations) responsive and accountable institutions, and it thus hints at a nexus between democracy and law.[5] To comprehend this nexus, we must have a common understanding of the features of the Rule of Law, given that most would agree that 'the rule of law is among the essential pillars upon which any high-quality democracy rests.'[6]

## The Rule of Law and Its Limits

'Rule of Law' (like its partial cognates *Rechtsstaat* and état de droit)[7] in its most basic articulation means that a state is accountable to and exercises its power according to law.[8] In an often cited definition from the nineteenth century, A.V. Dicey established a three-part test for the Rule of Law: 'the absolute predominance of regular law, so that the government has no arbitrary authority over the citizen; the equal subjection of all (including officials) to the ordinary law administered by the ordinary courts; and the fact that the citizen's personal freedoms are formulated and protected by the ordinary law rather than by abstract constitutional declarations.'[9] This, I think, is the conception of the Rule of Law in which Thomas More places his faith in Robert Bolt's *A Man for All Seasons*, as this exchange between More and William Roper illustrates:

MORE: The law, Roper, the law. I know what's legal not what's right. And I'll stick to what's legal.

ROPER: Then you set man's law above God's!

MORE: No, far below; but let me draw your attention to a fact – I'm *not* God. The currents and eddies of right and wrong, which you find such plain sailing, I can't navigate. I'm no voyager. But in the thickets of the law, oh, there I'm a forester. I doubt if there's a man alive who could follow me there, thank God.

ROPER: [Y]ou'd give the Devil benefit of law!

MORE: Yes. What would you do? Cut a great road through the law to get after the devil?

ROPER: I'd cut down every law in England to do that!

MORE: Oh? And when the last law was down, and the Devil turned round on you – where would you hide, Roper, the laws all being flat? This country's planted thick with laws from coast to coast – man's laws, not God's – and if you cut them down – and you're just the man to do it – d'you really think you could stand upright in the winds that would blow then? Yes, I'd give the Devil benefit of law, for my own safety's sake.

ROPER: I have long suspected this; this is the golden calf; the law's your
   god.
MORE: Oh, Roper, you're a fool, God's my god ... But I find him rather
   too subtle ... I don't know where he is nor what he wants.[10]

But the sort of naked faith in legal rules that More espouses (even
admitting that a system of rules is preferable to a Hobbesian state of
nature or the whims of a Tudor monarch) does not go quite far enough
to modern eyes. *Something* is missing, but it's not always immediately
clear what that something is. A literary counterfactual should aid us in
the task of conceptualizing (at least part of) the problem.

Herman Melville's *Billy Budd, Sailor (An Inside Narrative)* well illustrates that the Rule of Law has limits in a society that strives for more
than rote, formal 'justice.'[11] The story ultimately teaches that justice cannot be communicated by rules alone: a receptiveness to fully rounded
narratives is equally important. And it is an insistence on narrative
completeness that I would like us to consider more closely. For it is the
rare case indeed that neatly grades from black to white – the 'whole
story' is usually much more complicated, as *Billy Budd* illustrates.

The plot of the novella is straightforward. A twenty-one-year-old
sailor, Billy Budd, is impressed from a merchant ship, the *Rights of
Man*, onto an English warship, the *Bellipotent*. Billy is an incarnation
of a stock nautical character, the Handsome Sailor. Wherever he goes,
others adore him and are improved just by making his acquaintance,
though his mere presence drives men of a certain type to an inner fury.
As Billy's superior on the *Rights* explains to the lieutenant of the *Bellipotent*: 'Before I shipped that young fellow, my forecastle was a rat-pit
of quarrels ... But Billy came; and it was like a Catholic priest striking
peace in an Irish shindy. Not that he preached to them or said or did
anything in particular; but a virtue went out of him, sugaring the sour
ones. They took to him like hornets to treacle; all but the buffer of the
gang, the big shaggy chap with the fire-red whiskers [who is finally
won over after Billy gives him "a terrible drubbing"].'[12] This pattern
repeats itself on the *Bellipotent*, where Billy is generally beloved, save
by Claggart, the malevolent master-at-arms.

Billy's involuntary enlistment into the *Bellipotent* comes in the summer of 1797, just weeks after the infamous Nore and Spithead muti-
nies and at a time when fears that the French Revolution will spread
to Great Britain still linger. 'To the British Empire the Nore Mutiny was
what a strike in the fire brigade would be to London threatened by gen-

eral arson.'[13] Accordingly, British naval officers are on heightened alert for signs of discontent among their crews. It is this sensitivity to revolt that Claggart is able to exploit, as we shall soon see. But first, it will be helpful to detour for a word or two on the dramatis personae.

Much of the novella is cloaked in allegory, albeit undermined in some respects by ambiguity.[14] Billy is presented as a Christ and Adam figure, but an invisible defect mars his perfection: under stress, he is unable to speak. Claggart, on the other hand, is more or less flatly portrayed as evil (though looking 'like a man of high quality'), variously described as 'the direct reverse of a saint,' 'depraved,' a 'madman,' and 'the scorpion for which the Creator alone is responsible.' The ship's captain, Edward Fairfax Vere, whose name suggests truth, is, even more than Billy, of a divided nature.[15] He is a 'sailor of distinction even in a time prolific of renowned seamen,' but he oscillates between 'a certain dreaminess of mood' and the rigorous nature of a 'martinet.' Billy soon finds himself ensnared in the gap between Claggart's 'antipathy spontaneous and profound' and Vere's 'queer streak of the pedantic.'

After surreptitiously visiting various minor plagues on Billy via his subordinates, Claggart ups the ante and accuses Billy of conspiring to mutiny. Vere is unimpressed with Claggart's tale, finding it in sharp discord with his own impression of Billy and Claggart himself lacking in credibility. Vere thus determines to investigate the issue in as private a manner as possible and summons Billy to his cabin to confront Claggart and his accusation. Billy, upon hearing Claggart out, is – in keeping with his vocal defect – dumbstruck. Vere, sensing the nature of Billy's difficulty, attempts to soothe him and encourages him to take his time in responding: 'Contrary to the effect intended, these words so fatherly in tone, doubtless touching Billy's heart to the quick, prompted yet more violent efforts at utterance – efforts soon ending for the time in confirming the paralysis, and bringing to his a face an expression which was as a crucifixion to behold. The next instant, quick as the flame from a discharged cannon at night, his right arm shot out, and Claggart dropped to the deck.'[16] The single blow kills Claggart; within seconds his body is like 'a dead snake.' Vere immediately summons the ship's surgeon, who confirms that Claggart is dead, and then sends the surgeon to inform the ship's other senior officers (with a 'charge ... to keep the matter to themselves') of the death and of his intent to call a drumhead court.

From the outset of the story, we have been preconditioned to know that 'justice' on a warship will be different from justice in other contexts. When Billy departs the merchant ship for the *Bellipotent*, he cries out (without irony on his part, but otherwise dripping it), 'And good-bye to you too, old *Rights-of-Man*.'[17] Now whether this justice should be delivered swiftly and in secret is another matter, as the surgeon and other officers conclude. 'As to the drumhead court, it struck the surgeon as impolitic, if nothing more. The thing to do, he thought, was to place Billy Budd in confinement, and in a way dictated by usage, and postpone further action in so extraordinary a case to such time as they should rejoin the squadron, and then refer it to the admiral.'[18] Vere thinks otherwise, 'feeling that unless quick action was taken on it, the deed of [Billy], so soon as it should be known on the gun decks, would tend to awaken any slumbering embers of the Nore among the crew, a sense of the urgency of the case overruled in Captain Vere every other consideration.'[19]

Vere thus immediately calls the drumhead court, knowing full well that (at least under *his* interpretation of it) the martial code under which Billy is to be judged supplants ordinary notions of blame and responsibility: 'In a legal view the apparent victim of the tragedy was he who had sought to victimize a man blameless; and the indisputable deed of the latter, navally regarded, constituted the most heinous of military crimes. Yet more. The essential right and wrong involved in the matter, the clearer that might be, so much the worse for the responsibility of a loyal sea commander, inasmuch as he was not authorized to determine the matter on that primitive basis.'[20] Given this framework, the only facts relevant to Billy's trial are those directly tied to Billy's act of striking Claggart. On this point, there is no dispute: Vere 'concisely narrated all that had led up to the catastrophe,' and Billy confirms the accuracy of Vere's account: 'Captain Vere tells the truth. It is just as Captain Vere says, but it is not as the master-at-arms said.' Answering further, Billy states that he had no intent to harm Claggart: 'No, there was no malice between us. I never bore malice against the master-at-arms. I am sorry that he is dead. I did not mean to kill him. Could I have used my tongue I would not have struck him. But he foully lied to my face and in presence of my captain, and I had to say something, and I could only say it with a blow, God help me!'[21] To this Vere responds, 'I believe you, my man.' But Billy's *moral* justification in killing Claggart is not a *legal* justification in this context. For as Vere counsels the members of the court: 'Quite aside from any conceivable motive actuating the master-at-arms, and irrespective of the provocation to the blow, a martial court must needs in the present case confine its attention to the blow's consequence, which consequence justly is to be deemed not otherwise than as the striker's deed.'[22] Vere understands, nonetheless, that this rule runs counter to 'natural justice,' which would not permit the 'summary and shameful death [of] a fellow creature innocent before God, and whom we feel to be so.'[23] And Vere even concedes that Billy's plea that he 'proposed neither mutiny nor homicide' would elsewhere prove a good defence: 'before a court less arbitrary and more merciful than a martial one, that plea would largely extenuate. At the Last Assizes it shall acquit.'[24] Why not here?

The answer is twofold – part interpretive, part narrative. First, mitigation of Billy's penalty in the face of a clear rule would lead to interpretation by the crew, which could perhaps foment mutiny and thereby undermine the very purpose of the code. Hence, Vere feels an institutional compulsion to block interpretation of Billy's story beyond the level of act-and-consequence.[25] Second, as Vere explains to the other officers, the Mutiny Act 'resembles in spirit the thing from which it derives – War.' By this he means, I think, that warfare and its adjuncts are carried out under a public narrative very different from the ones that order general civil society: 'In receiving our commissions we in the most important regards ceased to be natural free agents. When war is declared are we the commissioned fighters previously consulted? We fight at command. If our judgments approve the war, that is but coincidence. So in other particulars. So now.'[26] This martial narrative commands complete hegemony. Because it is hermetic, it does not allow other narratives – public or private – to infect it. In practice, this means that martial judges must leave their interpretative predilections at the bench. In other words, the judge's interpretation of the facts is irrelevant to the extent that it extends beyond the narrowest sphere. Narrative completeness is no virtue in this context.

In narrative terms, *Billy Budd* is about the consequences of individual and systemic narrative failure. Billy is a failed narrator (he can't tell his story); the system of martial law makes judges into failed narratees (they can't listen). We find all this disquieting, above all – perhaps – because it cuts off what we see as an essential characteristic of judging and, therefore, of justice. I'm thinking here of what Zenon Bankowski and others have referred to as 'attention,' which requires, among other things, listening before judging.[27] Put differently, I think we expect justice to consist of law and narrative in somewhat equal measures.[28] When we find the balance lacking, we get the same sense of dissatisfaction that we feel when we consider the fate of Billy. Of course the circumstances are neither so extreme nor the consequences so dire in the quotidian world, but if we attend closely to cases that strike us 'unfair,' or 'unreasonable,' or 'unjust,' I think we will very often find a judgment that was made without due consideration for 'the whole story.'[29]

## Toward a Democratic Rule of Law

As *Billy Budd* exemplifies, laws and the institutions that faithfully execute those laws are not alone sufficient to ensure a society that we would consider just, fair, or democratic. And this is so beyond the military context within which Melville places his narrative. For as Guillermo O'Donnell posits (drawing examples from Latin American countries), 'an act that is formally according to law may nonetheless entail the application of a rule that is invidiously discriminatory or violates basic rights.'[30] Indeed, totalitarian regimes often pay rough homage to some cramped vision of the Rule of Law.[31] These types of deficiencies in the narrow Dicey articulation of the Rule of Law have called others to offer further definitional refinements, a task attempted by several notable theorists, including Lon Fuller, Joseph Raz, and – more recently – Neil MacCormick. Fuller, in his characteristic fashion, presents his criteria through parables, one of the most famous of which is 'The Problem of the Grudge Informer.'[32] In this hypothetical narrative, a dictatorship has been overthrown. Under that regime, there was a legal system, but it encouraged the use of state power to settle old scores. Now, there is an appetite among the liberated citizenry to dispense a bit of vigilante justice against the 'grudge informers.' Fuller leaves it to the reader to determine how to handle the problem: viz., how presently to treat acts that were legal under a displaced regime. To show the complexity of this type of situation, to suggest a possible way to address it, and to blunt the force of easy, knee-jerk solutions to it,[33] Fuller also offers the tale of King Rex, whose 'laws' were waylaid along eight different routes:

> The first and most obvious lies in a failure to achieve rules at all, so that every issue must be decided on an ad hoc basis. The other routes are: (2) a failure to publicize, or at least to make available to the affected party, the rules he is expected to observe; (3) the abuse of retroactive legislation, which cannot itself guide action, but undercuts the integrity of rules prospective in effect, since it puts them under the threat of retrospective

change; (4) a failure to make rules understandable; (5) the enactment of contradictory rules or (6) rules that require conduct beyond the powers of the affected party; (7) introducing such frequent changes in the rules that the subject cannot orient his action by them; and, finally, (8) a failure to achieve congruence between the rules as announced and their actual administration.[34]

Most commentators – including Fuller himself – have recast this list of 'don'ts' into a list of 'dos,' which holds that laws must be general, promulgated, prospective, understandable, consistent, performable, continuous, and congruently administered.

Fuller's set of eight is not universally accepted, of course. Raz, for instance, places as much emphasis on the architecture of the state that interprets and applies laws as on the laws themselves:

> 1. All laws should be prospective, open, and clear; 2. Laws should be relatively stable; 3. The making of particular laws ... must be guided by open, stable, clear, and general rules; 4. The independence of the judiciary must be guaranteed; 5. The principles of natural justice must be observed (i.e., open and fair hearing and absence of bias); 6. The courts should have review powers ... to ensure conformity to the rule of law; 7. The courts should be easily accessible; 8. The discretion of crime preventing agencies should not be allowed to pervert the law.[35]

This emphasis on state actors and institutions takes us closer to what we would expect from a legal system in a democratic regime, but we have still not closed the circle. What remains to consider is how we con-ceptualize a *democratic* Rule of Law.[36] MacCormick gets to the nub of the matter (i.e., to the *Billy Budd* problem) when he suggests:

> If the Rule of Law is to be actually a protection against arbitrary interven-tion in people's lives, it seems clear that it is not in practice enough to demand that the operative facts did on some occasion actually happen or obtain. It is necessary that some specific and challengeable accusation or averment of relevant facts be made to the individual threatened with action. This in turn must be supported by evidence in an open proceeding in which the party charged may contest each item of evidence both one at a time and in the cumulative effect of the totality of items adduced, and may offer relevant counter-evidence as she/he chooses. Moreover, it must also be possible to challenge the relevancy of the legal accusation or claim.

Such a challenge is to the effect that, whatever may be the facts of the matter, the legal materials that supposedly warrant the assertion of a rule governing the case do not warrant it at all in the alleged, or the actually proven, state of the facts.[37]

If we take this as a challenge, how do we answer it? In other words, how do we craft a system that respects the Rule of Law yet adequately responds to our democratic sensibilities?

There are many points of entry into this inquiry, perhaps none more convenient than Jürgen Habermas's discourse theory of law and democracy – a concept set forth in his *Between Facts and Norms*. His argument is difficult to capsulize, but we know that Habermas links the informal sources of democracy with the formal decision-making institutions that any complex society needs for the Rule of Law to flourish. In this scheme, the constitutional state is the mechanism that converts the citizenry's democratic desires into legitimate administrative activity: law 'represents ... the medium for transforming communicative power into administrative power.' This perspective helps us account for the various principles and institutions of the constitutional state, 'such as the separation of powers, majority rule, statutory controls on administration, and so forth.'[38]

Habermas also carefully links the Rule of Law to the democratic process. In his view, 'laws are legitimate if (1) they are agreed to in a fair and open participatory process, (2) citizens agree to each law in the sense of continued cooperation, and (3) this process makes the public deliberation of the majority the source of sovereign power.'[39] Laws so conceived preserve democracy by resisting the twin bureaucratic urges to totalize and to decide increasing numbers of issues outside the public sphere.[40] This makes sense as an abstraction and partially explains the formation of statutory law, but one may ask how these standards apply to a system that is not wholly code driven and, even then, how individual wills figure in the 'participatory process.'[41] In other words, how do citizens participate in a democracy other than by casting a ballot every few years? In a discussion of constitutional provisions born of revolution, Habermas marks a trail that should seem familiar to us:

As we have seen, by generalizing and abstracting from the adjudication of cases, legal theory gains distance without giving up the participant perspective as such. By contrast, the objectifying gaze of the historian focuses on the social contexts in which the law, as a system of action, is embedded – and from which the implicit background assumptions of adjudication and contemporary legal doctrine are nourished ... In some prominent places, the text of the law itself reveals these implicit diagnoses of the times, for example, in the 'bill of rights' section of constitutions that have emerged from political upheavals or revolutions. In contrast to the professionally formulated or developed law of legal scholars, even the style and wording of these declarations display an emphatic statement of will from citizens who are reacting to concrete experiences of repression and humiliation. Most articles in a bill of rights resonate with a suffered injustice that is negated word for word, as it were.[42]

In speaking of 'concrete experiences' and so forth, I think Habermas is allowing that the 'discourse' that is central to his conception of law and democracy may take a narrative shape. And in certain key respects, I would go so far as to say that this is often the case. For examples, we can circle back around to certain of the Fuller–Raz–MacCormick criteria, and place them in the context of what we have learned from Habermas, O'Donnell, and others about democratic institutions. Specifically, I have in mind the common emphasis on access to and administration of the legal system, not just laws themselves. That is, laws are by themselves insufficient to establish either the Rule of Law or democracy: in addition, courts, legislatures, and administrative agencies must be *accessible* – and in a meaningful way.

For contrast to the ideal, we can look to Franz Kafka's short story 'Before the Law,' which is something of a parable of the antiseptic, unresponsive law of the early modern bureaucratic state.[43] The story is very brief: a man from the country comes seeking entry to the law, but a gatekeeper bars him entrance. After the gatekeeper tells him that 'it is possible' that he will one day be admitted, the man decides to wait by the side of the gate, not wishing to challenge the fierce gatekeeper or the increasingly powerful gatekeepers to be found at subsequent steps inside. He waits 'for days and years,' spending everything he brought with him in the vain attempt to gain entrance. Finally, he grows weak with age and asks the gatekeeper one last question: 'Everyone strives to reach the Law,' says the man, 'so how does it happen that for all these many years no one but myself has ever begged for admittance?' The gatekeeper sees that the man is already dying and, to reach his diminishing sense of hearing, he shouts at him, 'No one else could ever be admitted here, since this gate was made only for you. I am now going to shut it.'

This image of the law can be read in a number of ways, from the fairly literal to the highly metaphorical. For instance, the infinite regress of gatekeepers could represent the law's maddening procedural hurdles, the man's status as a 'country-man' could say something about the status before the law of outsiders in general, or – more interestingly – the seeming impenetrability of the law could stand for the need to mediate it, to *interpret* it. I'll say more on this latter point in a minute, but for now I want to focus on the literal fact that the man from the country never got to tell his story (whatever it was – Kafka doesn't say). And that – the ability to hear, adjudicate, and legislate from narratives – is a hallmark of all truly democratic regimes, as even proponents of 'minimalist' democracy (like Judge Posner) would likely concede.[44] It thus remains for us to identify – and begin to map the features of – institutions whose democratic missions are facilitated by narrative interaction.

A modern constitutional democracy is a system of dizzying complexity. Within such a system, law – as Habermas would have it – has come to play a central role for no reason other than that older, simpler orders have been overwhelmed. As Michel Rosenfeld explains:

> Habermas conceives of law functionally, as filling gaps 'in social orders whose integrative capacities are overtaxed.' In our increasingly complex societies, the common cultural traditions, beliefs, practices and normative assumptions, which emerge from what Habermas calls the 'lifeworld' of a historically situated social group, can no longer furnish comprehensive normative justification for all the existing modes of social interaction. At the same time, such interactions are increasingly mediated through largely autonomous systems, like the market economy and the administrative bureaucracy of the state, which largely escape control by social actors who depend on them … Under these circumstances, Habermas maintains that law is the only legitimate means for society-wide normative integration, a 'hinge between system and lifeworld.'[45]

What this implies is that the health of a democracy depends on more or less continuous acts of mediation, balancing, and adjustment. Absent these acts, a disjunction develops between system and lifeworld, and the system becomes a Kafkaesque edifice unto itself. How, then, does a viable democracy maintain a proper system/lifeworld flow through law?

## The Jury as a Structural Safeguard of Democracy

As we have already seen, both low-order and high-order narratives – when they align – can create new laws (recall *The Jungle* and the Meat Inspection Act) or reconfigure old ones (recall *Hundley* and the law of self-defence). Is there a democratic angle to this process? I think there is – or at least there can be. But first, we must state the problem that narrative solves. In a representative democracy like that of the United States, individual citizens play virtually no direct role in government other than to exercise (or mostly not) the right to vote. High offices tend to be held by members of a highly educated political elite (the last four presidents have been graduates of Columbia, Harvard, and/or Yale), a situation exacerbated by a system of campaign finance that favours the entrenched elites. As Posner puts it, American political figures 'are by no means ordinary men and women but instead belong to an elite of intelligence, cunning, connections, charisma, and other attributes that enable them to present themselves to the public plausibly as "the best."'[46] If we juxtapose this with Posner's discussion of the 'elite' conception of democracy, which views the American electorate as 'ignorant and apathetic,' then what is there in the system to brake a slide to oligarchy?[47] The answer: a legal system receptive to the narratives of even the 'ignorant and apathetic.'

In the United States, courts serve at least two important and related democratic functions: (1) ensuring the legal rights and liberties of ordinary citizens, oppressed minorities, and others, and (2) making the other branches of government 'horizontally' accountable for their acts.[48] Federal courts enjoy a large degree of independence from the other branches of government, given the life tenure of judges and the wide range of powers granted under Article III of the Constitution.[49] Many state court judges also enjoy a fair amount of insulation from day-to-day political jostling through lengthy terms and 'appointment and retention' rather than 'election' systems. On its face, this scheme is countermajoritarian – and thus in one sense anti-democratic – but it guards against one of democracy's greatest pitfalls: the 'tyranny of the majority.' Its net effect, then, is – paradoxically – to preserve democratic values through non-majoritarian means.

Though judges are of course drawn from the same pool of elites as other officials (a problem we will discuss in a moment), judges can stand against the tide in ways that elected officials never could. This gives them the freedom to police and protect core democratic values that executives and legislatures may be unable or unwilling to police and protect (or, in some cases, may be willing to infringe).[50] We can see this in cases like *Brown v. Board of Education*. But that aspect of the courts is not my main concern here. For as I suggested in the last chapter, the jury system has an institutionalized, democratizing influence on the law, one that we can now explore more deeply.

Notwithstanding the significant check that an independent judiciary places on its fellow branches of government, it does nothing to ameliorate the rule-by-elites phenomenon that is in some ways a natural consequence of the architecture established in the pre-amendment Constitution. For as Michael Parenti suggests: 'Whatever conjectures we might make about the motivations of the Framers, the more important task is to judge the end product of their efforts. And the Constitution they fashioned tells us a good deal about their objectives. It was and still is largely an elitist document, more concerned with the securing of property interests than with personal liberties.'[51] The Constitution did not end, however, with the Constitution-proper: the Bill of Rights was soon appended. And though these amendments did not 'democratize' the federal bench, they did significantly ensure broad participation in the legal system itself. This was so in two respects. First, broad rights to speak were institutionalized.[52] These rights ensure that – unlike Kafka's man from the country – all persons have an opportunity to tell their stories and seek 'a redress of grievances.' Second – and even more important, I think – specific rights to hear and be heard were also institutionalized, none more important than the expansion to civil cases of the right to trial by jury.[53] These rights have been amplified in the civil context by prohibitions against re-examination of jury findings and in the criminal context by the bar against double jeopardy.[54] What this means in practice is that lay juries have enormous power in particular (especially criminal) cases, cases that can in turn have universalizing consequences. We earlier saw this at work in *Stewart*, in which the appeal's only impact was on *future* cases because Peggy Stewart had been acquitted and therefore could not be retried, even though the appellate court found that her acquittal was improper. It remains for us to consider the broader social implications of the jury's institutionalized role in the democratic constitutional order.[55]

The notion that juries serve a democratic purpose is not new. Alexander Hamilton saw trial by jury (at least in criminal cases) as one of few points upon which there was general agreement among the Founders, albeit for slightly different – but altogether democratic – reasons:

> The friends and adversaries of the plan of the convention, if they agree in nothing else, concur at least in the value they set upon the trial by jury; or if there is any difference between them it consists in this: the former regard it as a valuable safeguard to liberty; the latter represent it as the very palladium of free government. For my own part, the more the operation of the institution has fallen under my observation, the more reason I have discovered for holding it in high estimation; and it would be altogether superfluous to examine to what extent it deserves to be esteemed useful or essential in a representative republic, or how much more merit it may be entitled to as a defense against the oppressions of an hereditary monarch, than as a barrier to the tyranny of popular magistrates in a popular government. Discussions of this kind would be more curious than beneficial, as all are satisfied of the utility of the institution, and of its friendly aspect to liberty.[56]

By the mid-nineteenth century, Alexis de Tocqueville was able to observe that the American jury system had 'political' and 'educational' dimensions that might be more important than the obvious one (viz., deciding individual cases). Indeed, he believed that the jury system was as 'direct and extreme a consequence of the dogma of the sovereignty of the people as universal suffrage.'[57] For support, he cited instances in which absolute monarchs (Napoleon and the Tudors) had destroyed or weakened the jury system as a means of consolidating their power. Given this history, Tocqueville asserted that it begged the question to concern oneself with issues of juror qualification and such, because that type of inquiry would focus on the administrative function of juries and thereby overlook the jury system's larger institutional roles:

> When the question is from what elements the list of jurors should be composed, discussion is limited to the enlightenment and capacities of those to be chosen, as if one was concerned with a purely judicial institution. But, in my view, that is really the least important aspect of the matter; the jury is above all a political institution; it should be regarded as one form of the sovereignty of the people; when the sovereignty of the people is discarded, it too should be completely rejected; otherwise it should be made to harmonize with the other laws establishing that sovereignty. The jury is part of the nation responsible for the execution of the laws, as the legisla-

ture assemblies are the part with the duty of making them; for society to be governed in a settled and uniform matter, it is essential that the jury lists should expand or shrink with the lists of voters. This aspect of the matter, in my opinion, should always be the lawgivers' main preoccupation. All the rest is, so to say, frills.[58]

No less important than this 'political' function is what Tocqueville describes as the broad participatory function that jury service affords, which inculcates in the citizenry democratic values, respect for judicial decisions, personal responsibility, a sense of shared governance, and an equitable turn of mind.[59] In short, jury service – particularly civil jury service – has 'a great influence on national character,' even though Tocqueville is ultimately unsure whether 'a jury is useful to the litigants'![60] This 'influence' that Tocqueville identifies is but another name for 'education.' In the United States, 'ordinary' citizens have virtually no opportunities to participate directly in the workings of the government. Jury service is a notable exception, one allowing an important interface between specialized elites and a cross-section of the citizenry: 'It should be regarded as a free school which is always open and in which each juror learns his rights, comes into daily contact with the best educated and most-enlightened members of the upper classes, and is given practical lessons in the law, lessons which the advocate's efforts, the judge's advice, and also the very passions of the litigants bring within his mental grasp.'[61] To this education Tocqueville attributes as a consequence the 'practical intelligence and the political good sense of the Americans.' Some wags would claim that this is a condition contrary to fact, but we need not accept it to endorse Tocqueville's larger point: 'The jury is both the most efficient way of establishing the people's rule and the most efficient way of teaching them how to rule.'[62]

The idea of the jury as a cauldron into which elites and non-elites are stirred as part of the democratic recipe is attractive, but it calls for greater scrutiny than Tocqueville provides. What is missing is a theoretical account of how lay jurors impact particular cases in ways that impact universal rules in democratic ways. For that account, I want to return to an issue noted but not discussed in the last chapter: Stanley Fish's concept of 'interpretive communities.'

## The Democratic Role of Interpretive Communities

Many theories of interpretation privilege text over reader. Those theories hold that a text has a single meaning (or at most a finite set of mean-ings) that is there for a reader to ferret out. Interpretations that do not accord with this meaning are – in polite scholarly discourse – labelled 'extratextual' or – in less polite discourse, in descending order – 'erro-neous,' 'lame,' or 'stupid.' The apotheosis of literary interpretation of this mode came packaged in the form of American 'New Criticism,' which called for the 'close reading' of texts.[63] This phrase, 'close read-ing,' is pregnant with meaning. It means much more than that a critic should read a text carefully and completely. In fact, I think the phrase is something of a misnomer because it implies a methodology built on *focus* (attending only to the words on a page) when it operates by a process of *exclusion* (disregarding everything not on the page).[64] This method rescued literary criticism from a great deal of precious and trivial biographical criticism.[65] (To this day, I remember a fellow gradu-ate student who was studying Fitzgerald's novels complaining of the reams of paper he had to wade through to get past books and articles that stopped and started with commentary of the Scott-got-drunk-and-did-such-and-such type.) But the rescue came at a price: namely, texts became reified and divorced from both authors and readers.

There is no school of legal interpretation that is perfectly analogous to New Criticism, though there are certainly 'textualists' who believe that interpretation of constitutional and statutory provisions should be performed within their four corners, as well as 'originalists' who seek to interpret such provisions in light of their intent and meaning when drafted. We will soon look more carefully at legal interpretation, but for now it is enough to showcase the position of Justice Antonin Scalia of the United States Supreme Court:

> How upsetting it is, that so many of our citizens (good people, not lawless ones, on both sides of this abortion issue, and on various sides of other issues as well) think that we Justices should properly take into account their views, as though we were not engaged in ascertaining an objective law but in determining some kind of social consensus. The Court would profit, I think, from giving less attention to the *fact* of this distressing phenomenon, and more attention to the *cause* of it. That cause permeates today's opinion: a new mode of constitutional adjudication that relies not upon text and traditional practice to determine the law, but upon what the Court calls 'reasoned judgment,' which turns out to be nothing but philosophical predilection and moral intuition ... What makes all this relevant to the bothersome application of 'political pressure' against the

Court are the twin facts that the American people love democracy and the American people are not fools. As long as this Court thought (and the people thought) that we Justices were doing essentially lawyers' work up here – *reading text and discerning our society's traditional understanding of that text* – the public pretty much left us alone. Texts and traditions are facts to study, not convictions to demonstrate about. But if in reality our process of constitutional adjudication consists primarily of making value judgments ... then a free and intelligent people's attitude towards us can be expected to be (*ought* to be) quite different.[66]

In contradistinction to text-based interpretive theories, other theories privilege the reader, holding that all texts contain lacunae that only readers can fill. For purposes of concision, I'm going to refer to reader-based theories under the generic label 'reader response theory,' but there are a multitude of theoretical strands at issue, a good part of which cannot be so easily bundled. As a point of departure, we should at least nod to the 'reception' theory of Hans Robert Jauss, who elaborates on Edmund Husserl's idea that reality is understood through 'horizons,' yokes it to Thomas Kuhn's observation that scientific facts are generated by dominant paradigms, and takes it to the level of technique through application of Hans Georg Gadamer's philosophical hermeneutics.[67] Jauss's central point is that – contrary to the central tenet of New Criticism – texts are interpreted differently over time: 'A literary work is not an object which stands by itself and which offers the same face to each reader in each period. It is not a monument which reveals its timeless essence in a monologue.'[68] We can see this at the macrolevel as the literary fortunes of writers rise and fall over time[69] and at the microlevel as the meanings of words and phrases change. This explains why, for example, Shakespeare's plays must be heavily annotated and why the following quotations make no immediate sense to many modern readers (for those playing along at home, the answers are in the footnote):

- 'Mice, rats and such small *deer*.' (*King Lear*)
- 'Thy head is as full of quarrels as an egg is full of *meat*.' (*Romeo and Juliet*)
- 'I'll make a ghost of him who *lets* me.' (*Hamlet*)
- 'I dreamt a dream *tonight*.' (*Romeo and Juliet*)
- 'Doth she not count her blest ... that we have wrought so worthy a gentleman to be her *bride*?' (*Romeo and Juliet*)
- 'My ships are safely come to *road*.' (*Merchant of Venice*)

- 'Heaps of pearl, inestimable stones, *unvalued* jewels, all scattered in the bottom of the sea.' (*Richard III*)
- And in a meta-example: 'O Captain! God's light, these villains will make the word as odious as the word *occupy*, which was an excellent word before it was ill-used.' (*2 Henry IV*).[70]

Other reader-response theorists – while agreeing with Jauss that texts have no predetermined meanings – have pushed interpretive responsibility even further into the domain of the reader. Wolfgang Iser, for example, submits that a text is a 'network of response-inviting structures' that encourages certain 'implied' readings. But each 'actual' reader brings an 'existing stock of experience' that necessarily colours her interpretation.[71] Umberto Eco, who approaches the subject from a semiotic angle, argues that texts tend to construct two 'Model Readers': a 'semantic' reader who 'wants to know what happens,' and a 'semiotic' reader who 'wants to know how what happens has been narrated.'[72] The common thread winding through Jauss, Iser, and Eco is that the perceiver is at least as important as the perceived, which suggests that valid interpretations may exist across a spectrum (which is not to say across infinity). To illustrate this process, let's examine Wittgenstein's famed duck–rabbit puzzle.

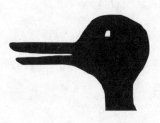

Is it a duck looking left or a rabbit looking right?[73] The answer is, of course, that it depends on who is looking at the picture. Everyone has an immediate take on it, (usually) one way or the other, and when informed of the other possible interpretation, everyone I've ever shown it to says something like, 'Oh, yeah, I can see that, but I still think it's a [duck or rabbit].' But I have never had someone say that the picture is of a trout stream, a lawnmower, or a Gothic cathedral, though I have had an occasional person identify a particular species of duck or something more general, like 'a bird.' I don't want to make too much of any of this, however, because this is an example that is designed to be ambiguous and, consequently, is far different from most interpretive dilemmas faced in the legal context. But before turning to Fish's particular take on reader-response theory, I want to round out our preliminary discussion by considering one poetic example and one legal example. Since I already referred to Robert Burns's 'To a Mouse' in the last chapter, I'll start with it:

WEE, sleekit, cow'rin, tim'rous beastie,
O, what a panic's in thy breastie!
Thou need na start awa sae hasty,
   Wi' bickering brattle!
I wad be laith to rin an' chase thee,             5
   Wi' murd'ring pattle!
I'm truly sorry man's dominion,
Has broken Nature's social union,
An' justifies that ill opinion,
   Which makes thee startle             10
At me, thy poor, earth-born companion,
   An' fellow-mortal!
I doubt na, whiles, but thou may thieve;
What then? poor beastie, thou maun live!
A daimen icker in a thrave             15
   'S a sma' request:
I'll get a blessin wi' the lave,
   An' never miss't!
Thy wee bit housie, too, in ruin!
It's silly wa's the win's are strewin!         20
An' naething, now, to big a new ane,
   O' foggage green!
An' bleak December's winds ensuin,
   Baith snell an' keen!
Thou saw the fields laid bare an' waste,     25
An' weary winter comin fast,
An' cozie here, beneath the blast,
   Thou thought to dwell –
Till crash! The cruel coulter past
   Out thro' thy cell.             30
That wee bit heap o' leaves an' stibble,
Has cost thee mony a weary nibble!

Now thou's turn'd out, for a' thy trouble,
  But house or hald,
To thole the winter's sleety dribble,                          35
  An' cranreuch cauld!
But Mousie, thou art no thy lane,
In proving foresight may be vain:
The best-laid schemes o' mice an' men
  Gang aft agley,                                   40
An' lea'e us nought but grief an' pain,
  For promis'd joy!
Still thou art blest, compar'd wi' me
The present only toucheth thee:
But, Och! I backward cast my e'e.                    45
  On prospects drear!
An' forward, tho' I canna see,
  I guess an' fear!

This poem, in scarcely four dozen lines, fairly represents a range of problems common to both legal and literary interpretation. The first, and most obvious, difficulty is the language, which is recognizable as English but full of Scots-English forms that are no longer in everyday use. Thus, to understand the poem on a basic linguistic level, one must either (1) know the dialect, or (2) have a secondary source at hand (e.g., a glossed or footnoted text). The second, and more interesting, difficulty is figuring out what the poem means, given that an absolutely literal reading takes us only so far – and not very far at that (assuming that even the sharpest of Scottish mice do not understand any English, be it Scots or Anglo). So the first textual gap that the reader must fill is to identify the addressee (typically referred to in reader-response litera-ture as the 'narratee.')

Ostensibly, the speaker is addressing a mouse whose nest he had turned up with a plough in November 1785. If we leave aside certain basic issues – such as whether the speaker is Burns himself[74] or a char-acter created for dramatic effect (cf. Browning's narrators) – we see that the poem breaks into three sections, each of which has a different tone and sense of urgency. The first section – which is the longest, running from lines 1 to 36 – recounts the actual events and expresses the poet's sorrow for frightening the mouse and destroying her nest and, more generally, for man's breaking of nature's grand social bond that once connected all creatures great and small. In the penultimate stanza (ll. 37

to 42), the poet shifts from a tone of regret to one of empathy – something like: 'Mouse, my friend, I know how you feel – you're not the only one to have had your hopes dashed.' And by the final stanza (ll. 43 to 48), the order is reversed: by comparison, the mouse has it good because she always lives in the present, with no sense of past disappointments and trepidation at what may come.

As readers, we're left to wonder what the progression of the poem is supposed to mean. Is it a statement of the human condition? The penultimate stanza is general in scope, speaking of 'men' and 'us,' which hints at something larger than a personal dilemma. But could it be something more idiosyncratic, perhaps a statement of personal disappointment? The final stanza has five personal references (I/my/me), which suggests an individual discouragement. Does any of this turn on the fact that the poet is a *poet* stuck behind a plough on a dreary November day? Reader-response theorists would tell us that we can't answer these questions with reference solely to the text – the reader must engage the text to produce meaning. Take the last question I posed. Is that even an important point? Why did I raise it? Would every reader raise it? Did I raise it because it made me remember feeding cattle on bitter January mornings, picking up hay in oppressive July heat, and a host of other things I would rather not have been doing as a boy on the Great Plains of western Kansas? Perhaps. I can't say because I can't stand outside myself as a neutral observer.[75] But I can say that I feel a sense of partnership every time I read this poem and mull it over. And that, I think, is what response theory tries to conceptualize.

Legal texts raise analogous issues. Nowhere is this more true than with respect to the United States Constitution, which is now more than two hundred years old. The problem is essentially a conflict between the original meaning of particular Constitutional provisions and contemporary mores. This issue typically arises in one of two ways: either a practice that was clearly permissible at the time the Constitution was adopted is now condemned, or vice versa. For example, much current litigation involves the Eighth Amendment's prohibition of 'cruel and unusual punishments.' The United States Supreme Court recently held that neither mildly retarded nor minor convicted murderers can be executed because that would constitute a 'cruel and unusual' punishment.[76] In both cases, the Court followed a similar course of reasoning:

The prohibition against 'cruel and unusual punishments,' like other expansive language in the Constitution, must be interpreted according to its text, by considering history, tradition, and precedent, and with due regard for its purpose and function in the constitutional design. To implement this framework we have established the propriety and affirmed the necessity of referring to 'the evolving standards of decency that mark the progress of a maturing society' to determine which punishments are so disproportionate as to be cruel and unusual.[77]

What is most interesting in this formulation is that it first pretends to a textualist interpretive mode (note the references to 'text,' 'history,' 'tradition,' 'precedent') but then sweeps that mode aside in favour of an *ex post facto* one that substitutes current 'standards of decency' for the original meaning of the phrase 'cruel and unusual punishments.' To be clear, there was no dispute that the phrase, when drafted, would not have barred the execution of sixteen- or seventeen-year-old minors. Indeed, the Court had held – only a decade and a half before – that 'cruel and unusual punishments' did *not* include the execution of minors (at least above a certain age) within its meaning.[78] Setting aside whether a Supreme Court opinion is the best vehicle for enacting constitutional changes in a democracy (there are good arguments on either side of the issue), there is no doubt that cases like *Roper* demonstrate that modern readers of the Constitution are in some sense 'making' its meaning. And that is the point that reader-response theorists have been making all along.

Stanley Fish's contribution to this debate has been to posit that the textualists and the receptionists are both right (or both wrong, I suppose). For Fish, constraints on textual interpretation do not reside solely within the text (they are not self-constraints) but at the same time a reader's interpretive licence is not unconstrained.[79] How do we explain this paradox? In *Is There a Text in This Class?* Fish sets out to show that

it is interpretive communities, rather than either the text or the reader, that produce meanings and are responsible for the emergence of formal features. Interpretive communities are made up of those who share interpretive strategies not for reading but for writing texts, for constituting their properties. In other words these strategies exist prior to the act of reading and therefore determine the shape of what is read rather than, as is usually assumed, the other way around.[80]

The point here is that we are all members of (many) interpretive communities, each of which authorizes only certain ways of seeing – of fact finding, if you will. We will examine the consequences of Fish's theory in a legal context more closely in a bit, but for now, I want to look at the process more generally.

Susan Glaspell's one-act play *Trifles* (also published as a short story, 'A Jury of Her Peers') opens in the gloomy and disordered kitchen of a Nebraska farmhouse of a century ago. The owner of the farm, John Wright, has been murdered – strangled – and his wife has been taken into custody. Five characters occupy the stage as the curtain rises: County Attorney Henderson, Sheriff Peters and his wife, and two neighbours, Mr and Mrs Hale. Mr Hale had stopped by the farmhouse the day before and found Mrs Wright sitting in the kitchen looking 'queer.' She told him that Mr Wright had 'died of a rope around his neck' and that she didn't know who did it because – though she slept in the same bed – she 'sleep[s] sound.' Because of that story's incredibility, Mrs Wright has been arrested and held for murder. From the opening lines, though, we sense that this will be a story less about murder than about gender. Glaspell first puts this in spatial terms, showing how the men set about to discover clues upon which they can construct a story of Mrs Wright's guilt: 'what was needed for the case was a motive; something to show anger, or – sudden feeling.'[81] But they take up this task from a decidedly masculine point of view, looking only at the immediate crime scene and masculine spaces like the barn:

> COUNTY ATTORNEY: [*Looking around*] I guess we'll go upstairs first – and then out to the barn and around there. [*To the* Sheriff] You're convinced that there was nothing important here – nothing that would point to any motive.
> SHERIFF: Nothing here but kitchen things.[82]

The men denigrate everything feminine, unable to see feminine artefacts as anything other than 'trifles.' But these 'trifles' hold the key to the mystery, to the *narrative*:

> MRS. PETERS: She was piecing a quilt.
> MRS. HALE: … I wonder if she was goin' to quilt it or just knot it?
> SHERIFF: They wonder if she was going to quilt it or just knot it!
> [*The men laugh, the women look abashed.*]
> MRS. HALE: [*resentfully*] I don't know as there's anything so strange, our

takin' up our time with little things while we're waiting for them to get the evidence. I don't see as it's anything to laugh about ... Mrs. Peters, look at this one. Here, this is the one she was working on, and look at the sewing! All the rest of it has been so nice and even. And look at this! It's all over the place! Why, it looks as if she didn't know what she was about!

[*After she has said this, they look at each other, then start to glance back at the door. After an instant Mrs. Hale has pulled at a knot and ripped the sewing.*]

MRS. PETERS: Oh, what are you doing, Mrs. Hale?

MRS. HALE: Just pulling out a stitch or two that's not sewed very good. [*Threading a needle*]. Bad sewing always made me fidgety.

* * *

MRS. PETERS: Why, here's a birdcage. Did she have a bird, Mrs. Hale?

MRS. HALE: Why, I don't know whether she did or not – I've not been here for so long. There was a man around last year selling canaries cheap, but I don't know as she took one; maybe she did. She used to sing real pretty herself.

MRS. PETERS: Seems funny to think of a bird here. But she must have had one, or why should she have a cage? I wonder what happened to it?

MRS. HALE: I s'pose maybe the cat got it.

MRS. PETERS: No, she didn't have a cat. She's got that feeling some people have about cats – being afraid of them. My cat got in her room, and she was real upset and asked me to take it out ... Why, look at this door. It's broke. One hinge is pulled apart.

MRS. HALE: Looks as if someone must have been rough with it.

MRS. PETERS: Why, yes.

MRS. HALE: I wish if they're going to find any evidence they'd be about it. I don't like this place ... Did you know John Wright, Mrs. Peters?

MRS. PETERS: Not to know him; I've seen him in town. They say he was a good man.

MRS. HALE: Yes – good; he didn't drink, and kept his word as well as most, I guess, and paid his debts. But he was a hard man, Mrs. Peters. Just to pass the time of day with him. [*Shivers.*] Like a raw wind that gets to the bone ... I should think she would 'a wanted a bird. But what do you suppose went with it?

MRS. PETERS: I don't know, unless it got sick and died.

[*She reaches over and swings the broken door, swings it again; both women watch it.*]

MRS. HALE: She – come to think of it, she was kind of like a bird herself – real sweet and pretty, but kind of timid and – fluttery. How – she – did

– change … Tell you what, Mrs. Peters, why don't you take the quilt in with you? It might take up her mind.

MRS. PETERS: Why, I think that's a real nice idea, Mrs. Hale. There couldn't possibly be any objection to it, could there? Now, just what would I take? I wonder if her patches are in here – and her things.

[*They look in the sewing basket.*]

MRS. HALE: Here's some red. I expect this got sewing things in it [*Brings out a fancy box.*] What a pretty box. Looks like something somebody would give you. Maybe her scissors are in here. [*Opens box. Suddenly puts her hand to her nose.*] Why – [*Mrs. Peters bends nearer, then turns her face away.*] There's something wrapped up in this piece of silk … Oh, Mrs. Peters – it's –

MRS. PETERS: It's the bird.

MRS. HALE: But, Mrs. Peters – look at it. Its neck! Look at its neck! It's all – other side to.

MRS. PETERS: Somebody – wrung – its neck.

[*Their eyes meet. A look of growing comprehension of horror. Steps are heard outside. Mrs. Hale slips box under quilt pieces, and sinks into her chair …*]

MRS. HALE: She liked the bird. She was going to bury it in that pretty box.

MRS. PETERS: When I was a girl – my kitten – there was a boy took a hatchet, and before my eyes – and before I could get there – If they hadn't held me back, I would have – [*Catches herself, looks upstairs, where steps are heard, falters weakly.*] – hurt him.[83]

MRS. HALE: I wonder how it would seem never to have had any children around. No, Wright wouldn't like the bird – a thing that sang. She used to sing. He killed that, too.

MRS. PETERS: We don't know who killed the bird.

MRS. HALE: I knew John Wright …

MRS. PETERS: We don't know who killed him. We don't *know*.

MRS. HALE: If there'd been years and years of nothing, then a bird to sing to you, it would be awful – still, after the bird was still …

MRS. PETERS: My, it's a good thing the men couldn't hear us. Wouldn't they just laugh! Getting all stirred up over a little thing like a – dead canary. As if that could have anything to do with – with – wouldn't they laugh!

MRS. HALE: Maybe they would – maybe they wouldn't. [*Mrs. Hale soon hides the canary and its box.*][84]

The men end the play as they began it: literally and figuratively clueless. They are so trapped within their masculinity that they cannot read the signs that are so obvious to the women. In other words, they cannot construct a text – a coherent narrative – that will make sense of the crime. As a result, the murderer will likely go free, as the County Attorney predicts: 'No, Peters, it's all perfectly clear except a reason for doing it. But you know juries when it comes to women. If there was some definite thing. Something to show – something to make a story about – a thing that would connect up with this strange way of doing it – .'[85] The women, on the other hand, have not only solved the murder but have justified it to their own satisfaction as well. In other words, as the play's final line ironically suggests, they have tied up all the loose ends:

COUNTY ATTORNEY: [*Facetiously*] Well, Henry, at least we found out that she was not going to quilt it. She was going to – what is it you call it, ladies!

MRS. HALE: [*Her hand against her pocket*] We call it – knot it, Mr. Henderson.[86]

*Trifles* teaches us that membership in an interpretive community in some sense controls what types of evidence we can find and what types of narrative we can construct to explain a terminal fact. The consequences of this are profound, as we will now see in the context of trials. As I mentioned before, most legal actors are members of an educational and social elite. In nearly all cases in the United States, judges and counsel are lawyers, which normally implies at least seven years of higher education, including – most important – three years of law school. Law school culture differs in many ways from other graduate education (and even other professional training), in that its primary mission is to teach students to what is often referred to as 'think like a lawyer.' As a result of this training, which Philip Kissam has likened (echoing Michel Foucault) to a 'discipline,' lawyers accede to membership in a specialized interpretive community.[87] (We'll discuss why and how this happens in the next chapter.)

But lawyers are not the only interpreters in the judicial system. Juries, which only rarely include lawyers, are an important, if imperfect, counterweight. Different mythologies have grown up around jury practice, so I think it is probably worth a moment to map out some borders. Over the course of American history, pressure from two sources conspired to push jury membership away from elite interpretive communities and into the hands of the laity: a belief that juries should represent a cross-section of society, and a suspicion that certain types of jurors might be too knowledgeable and too sophisticated to be impartial. Both these positions are important to our discussion of interpretive communities, so we need to consider each in greater detail. First, the notion that a jury should represent a cross-section of society is of much more recent vintage than is typically assumed. Indeed, not much more than fifty years ago, federal courts still impanelled 'blue ribbon' juries. According to Jeffrey Abramson, 'the theory was that justice required above average levels of intelligence, morality, and integrity. In place of random selection, therefore, jury commissioners typically solicited the names "of men of recognized intelligence and probity" from notables or "key men" of the community.'[88] In short, jurors were often drawn from the group of cultural elites of which lawyers were a subset.

Congress swept this system aside with the 1968 Jury Selection and Service Act, which declared that it would henceforth be 'the policy of the United States that all litigants in Federal courts entitled to a trial by jury shall have the right to grand and petit juries selected at random from a fair cross section of the community.'[89] The Supreme Court soon extended this policy to state courts as a matter of constitutional law.[90] As an immediate consequence, the 'elite,' all-white jury disappeared, replaced by one more (though not perfectly) representative of the community at large.[91] In some ways, this movement mirrored the larger cultural movement that has successively extended the democratic franchise to larger and larger groups. But the secondary consequences of replacing elite jurors with truly lay jurors have been profound. This is so because, as we will soon see, members of non-elite interpretive communities sometimes evaluate trial narratives in ways that seem extratextual to members of the elite, legal interpretive community. In thinking this through, we must therefore ask whether interpretive perspective (necessarily) comes at the expense of interpretive expertise.

We can now turn to the second force that has served to level the interpretive sophistication of jurors – the passion for 'impartiality.'[92] *Jurors should be impartial.* As stated, I don't think that this proposition would draw much fire. But if we begin to unpack the word 'impartial,' we see connotations that probably should be viewed as problematic. On the one hand, the term means things that could be labelled as universal virtues, things like 'unbiased,' 'not prejudiced,' and 'evenhanded.' On the other hand, though, impartiality too often gets defined as 'ignorance.'[93] As Abramson notes, it is this view of impartiality that Mark Twain burlesques to great effect in *Roughing It* when he charges that 'the jury system puts a ban upon intelligence and honesty, and a premium upon ignorance, stupidity and perjury.'[94] To illustrate this point, Twain tells the story of a particular jury trial:

> I remember one of those sorrowful farces, in Virginia, which we call a jury trial. A noted desperado killed Mr. B., a good citizen, in the most wanton and cold-blooded way. Of course the papers were full of it, and all men capable of reading, read about it. And of course all men not deaf and dumb and idiotic, talked about it. A jury-list was made out, and Mr. B. L., a prominent banker and a valued citizen, was questioned precisely as he would have been questioned in any court in America:
>
> > 'Have you heard of this homicide?'
> > 'Yes.'
> > 'Have you held conversations upon the subject?'
> > 'Yes.'
> > 'Have you formed or expressed opinions about it?'
> > 'Yes.'
> > 'Have you read the newspaper accounts of it?'
> > 'Yes.'
> > 'We do not want you.'
>
> A minister, intelligent, esteemed, and greatly respected; a merchant of high character and known probity; a mining superintendent of intelligence and unblemished reputation; a quartz mill owner of excellent standing, were all questioned in the same way, and all set aside. Each said the public talk and the newspaper reports had not so biased his mind but that sworn testimony would overthrow his previously formed opinions and enable him to render a verdict without prejudice and in accordance with the facts. But of course such men could not be trusted with the case. Ignoramuses alone could mete out unsullied justice.
>
> When the peremptory challenges were all exhausted, a jury of twelve men was impaneled – a jury who swore they had neither heard, read, talked about nor expressed an opinion concerning a murder which the very cattle in the corrals, the Indians in the sage-brush and the stones in the streets were cognizant of! It was a jury composed of two desperadoes, two low beer-house politicians, three bar-keepers, two ranchmen who could not read, and three dull, stupid, human donkeys! It actually came out afterward, that one of these latter thought that incest and arson were the same thing.

The verdict rendered by this jury was, Not Guilty. What else could one expect?[95]

The logic fault underlying this type of jury selection is that it equates knowledge with bias. I think that Abramson is exactly right to state that cases in which the parties go to extraordinary lengths to find ignorant jurors 'illustrate what we might call a process of deselecting well-informed citizens, as if civic engagement, concern for the issues on trial, and interest in reading the papers were enemies of fair-mindedness.'[96] It remains to be seen whether this prejudice against the well informed can have a salutary social impact. It certainly may (assuming that juries are not packed with absolute dolts), but – in any event – I think that we can learn a great deal from studying the ways in which non-elite jurors interpret trial narratives and construct narratives that justify (to themselves) verdicts in particular cases. The results are sometimes surprising – most often, I think, when and because jurors are members of minority interpretive communities that are under the sway of ontological and public narratives very different from those of the mainstream majority. (I don't mean 'minority' simply in the racial and ethnic sense, though that is certainly an important part of it.) And as we will see in the examples that follow, particular cases can have universal consequences.

### A Study in Contrasts: The Rodney King and O.J. Simpson Juries

In keeping with many of the cases we have reviewed to this point, controversial jury verdicts pop up more often than not in cases with a strong racial undercurrent. Perhaps nothing can illustrate this principle better than a comparison of the famed Rodney King and O.J. Simpson trials, both of which took place at about the same time and in about the same place. It is the second 'about' that I want us to keep in mind as we consider those two cases. For as I think the cases bear out, a difference of a few miles between actual communities can represent a manifold gulf between interpretive communities.

Most of the salient facts of the Rodney King case were never in dispute. King, a recent parolee, and two friends were cruising one of Los Angeles's freeways on a Saturday night 'looking for some action.'[97] At some point, King tried to elude a California Highway Patrol car, leading the officers – who were soon joined by, among others, several officers of the Los Angeles Police Department – on a high-speed chase through the Los Angeles hills. After the police forced the car to a halt, King 'came out of the car mugging and dancing a little jig.'[98] He did not immediately submit to the officers, and the confrontation between him and the officers escalated. A crowd began to gather, one member of which, George Holliday, turned a videocamera on the scene. What Holliday's video captured was a large black man on the ground, closely ringed by four police officers. While one officer shot him with Taser darts, the others struck him with their batons and kicked him. The officers then pulled him around with the wires from an electric harpoon, with which they ultimately tied him. Throughout the eighty-one-second video, the officers can be heard yelling at King, who at least twice can be seen getting to his hands and knees. The video also shows a number of other officers looking on but neither intervening nor participating. Throughout the incident, King's two companions lay stretched out in a prone position, watched by two officers.

Within a couple of days, Holliday's video had made its way onto the national news. Politicians, civil rights activists, and ordinary citizens immediately expressed outrage at what appeared to be an open-and-shut case of police brutality. In accordance with this tide of public opinion, the Los Angeles district attorney quickly convened a grand jury, which even more quickly found that there was sufficient evidence to indict the four officers for criminal assault and use of excessive force. The four officers did not, however, crumple in the face of the indictments. Rather, they went on the offensive, successfully challenging both the original judge assigned to the case and then – most important for our purposes – the Los Angeles venue for which the trial was slated (on the ground that pretrial publicity made a fair trial impossible in Los Angeles).

Simi Valley, the Los Angeles suburb to which the trial was transferred, is a bedroom community about thirty-five miles northwest of downtown Los Angeles. At the time of trial, the area was 'predominantly white, middle-class, and native-born,' with 'a well-earned local reputation as a bastion of law and order, family values, and conservative political views.'[99] Not surprisingly, then, the court seated a jury that reflected the population of Simi Valley (which was less than 2 per cent black): ten whites, one Asian, and one Hispanic. Moreover, the jury shared significant attributes of the defendants:

The majority of the jury (nine of twelve) had served in the military or been employed in the defense industry. Five men had served in the Navy, and two women had been in the armed forces. There were over two thousand police families living in the Simi Valley area, and one of the jurors was the brother of a retired police sergeant. Three members of the jury were members of the National Rifle Association. This was a jury who would resonate to the themes of law and order, to protect and serve, to support the local police.[100]

All trials involve the competing personal narratives of the primary actors, as well as the larger cultural narratives that frame them. In the *King* case, this meant that the jury's task was, for the most part, to interpret the 'text' of the video and determine whether it represented the story of a 'gentle giant' wrongfully attacked by goonish LAPD officers or that of a feral 'gorilla in the mist' who presented a danger not only to the officers on call that night but to society as well.[101] To some degree, the interpretive die was cast when the prosecution made the tactical decision not to call Rodney King to the stand, which meant that the defendants were able to give an essentially unrebutted interpretation of the damning videotape. A benign interpretation of the tape was first supported by an unbroken line of testimony implying not only that had King been drunk that night, but also that he was 'dusted' (i.e., under the influence of PCP, a drug known to make users superaggressive and violent). But the most powerful evidence turned out to be the tape itself, which the defence cleverly 'renarrated' through the use of slow motion, no sound, and a frame-by-frame analysis.[102] This renarration was supplemented by expert testimony, which – as critical race theorists Kimberle Crenshaw and Gary Peller posit – served to recontextualize the incident within recognized and appropriate police procedure:

> The defense attorneys … had frame-by-frame stills made of each video, which were mounted on clean white illustration board, and then used as a basis for questions to 'experts' on prisoner restraint … Once the video was broken up like this, each still picture could then be reweaved into a different narrative about the restraint of King, one in which each blow to King represented, not beating one of the 'gorillas in the mist,' but a police-approved technique of restraint complete with technical names for each baton strike (or 'stroke').[103]

In their closing arguments, the defence lawyers were tasked with ensuring that the deconstructed version of the videotape would be accepted as 'what really happened' and that it would thus be interpreted in a way tending to support verdicts of not guilty. In other words, they had to make sure that their narrative version of the facts plausibly fitted within a higher-order narrative shared by the jurors. They did this in two related ways, one particular, one general. First, they dehumanized King by referring to him with a thinly veiled racial vocabulary: 'bull,' 'bear,' and – with no little irony – 'gorilla.' Second, they repeatedly reminded the jury of 'the "thin blue line" that separates law-abiding citizens from criminals, that separates "civilization from chaos," and, by inference, that separates middle-class suburbs from the inner-city jungle.'[104] All of this was calculated to summon white, conservative fears of marauding inner-city blacks overrunning the suburbs and, as Gibbs puts it, 'destroying their way of life.'[105]

This tactic proved successful: the jury – after only six hours of deliberation – acquitted three of the four officers of all charges and found the fourth guilty of only one count of use of excessive force. In some sense, this outcome was – if not inevitable – something that the jury was predisposed to render. Why? The jurors were not just members of a geographic community; they were members of an *interpretive* community. In other words, the jury members were constrained to read the video in the context of their own shared values and experiences. Thus, as Gibbs astutely observes:

> They had processed the infamous videotape according to their own interactions with the police, which was the only way that they were able to make sense of what they saw and what they heard. Just as Rodney King's thoughts, feelings, and actions had been irrevocably shaped by his experiences as a black man in America, so too had these jurors' thoughts, feelings, and actions been shaped by their very different sets of experiences. They were all – the victim, the defendants, the jurors, and the judge – captives of their past racial history in the American society.[106]

Of course these actors – though the principal ones in the trial itself – were not the only people to read and interpret the video, as subsequent events soon showed. Within hours, violence erupted in South Central Los Angeles; the riots lasted for four days. The verdict in Simi Valley clearly triggered these riots, but they were representative of greater social ills. In fact, many black Angelinos saw the King videotape as a commonplace example of police brutality practised against members of their minority community and the verdict as a majority exoneration of those practices. The riots were, then – as John Mack, president of the Los Angeles Urban League, explained – 'a manifestation of a whole lot of things – injustice in the criminal justice system, reaction to the rampant police brutality that is so blatant in our community, particularly in relation to young African-American males. It was an expression, an acting-out of the have-nots.'[107] Put differently, it answered the rhetorical question that Langston Hughes poses at the end of 'Harlem': 'What happens to a dream deferred? / Does it dry up like a raisin in the sun? ... / Or does it explode?[108] I'll come back to the consequences of the sort of social combustion generated by friction between interpretive communities, but another example – this one based on a jury that mirrored a very different community from the one in Simi Valley – will round out the context of our discussion.

Just a couple of years after the King beating trial, another racially charged case captured headlines across the country. Football star cum general celebrity O.J. Simpson was charged with murdering his ex-wife, Nicole Brown Simpson, and her friend, Ronald Goldman, outside her West Los Angeles condominium. There was a mountain of circumstantial evidence against Simpson, much of it based on scientific evidence (blood and other forensic evidence linking Simpson to the crime) of the type that is routinely sufficient to convict less famous and less affluent defendants. But as a counterweight, the defence's 'Dream Team' (which included Johnnie Cochran, Robert Shapiro, F. Lee Bailey, Alan Dershowitz, Barry Scheck, and Peter Neufeld) was able to construct a compelling narrative built on evidence of police bungling, racism, and cover-ups.[109] And all this was presented to a jury that was very different from the Simi Valley jury that heard the King beating case: nine blacks (eight of whom were women), two white women, and one Hispanic man.[110]

From the outset, the Simpson trial was infused with a racial subtext, a subtext deeply informed by the narrative that grew out of the King beating case: 'jury consultants on both sides considered a person's race to be an important indicator of preconceptions about the case. The defense expert Jo-Ellan Dimitrius compiled survey results showing that the Rodney King episode had increased distrust of the police among all demographic groups in Los Angeles, but that African Americans were off the chart.'[111] Thus, the defence lawyers were charged with a fairly narrow mission: give the predominantly African-American jury a credible narrative upon which the jury members could hang their predilection to doubt the bona fides of the LAPD. As Abramson explains,

The key here was to disturb the jury with a story that begins with arresting officers jumping to the conclusion that Simpson must be guilty from the moment they learn the murdered woman is his ex-wife. So certain are the officers that they do not bother to conduct a thorough search. Maybe they make it easy on themselves by planting evidence to frame a man they presume guilty.[112]

This narrative proved controlling: the jury found Simpson not guilty in less than four hours, despite the nine-month trial and correspondingly lengthy trial transcript (running some 45,000 pages).

As with the King beating verdict, public reaction to the Simpson trial and subsequent verdict was sharply divided along racial lines.[113] An overwhelming number of whites found the notion of a police conspiracy against Simpson preposterous; a corresponding percentage of blacks saw the verdict as a legitimate expression of reasonable doubt, especially in light of the LAPD's treatment of Simpson in particular and African Americans in general.[114] As subsequent events were to show, each group's position had merit: in 1997 Simpson was found responsible for the deaths of his ex-wife and Ronald Goldman in civil suits brought by the Goldman and Brown families; the so-called 'Rampart division' scandals of the late 1990s revealed widespread corruption (including evidence planting and perjury) in the LAPD's anti-gang unit.[115] But most of us who followed the case even slightly remember the divide in terms of the endlessly looped television footage of law students' reactions at mostly black Howard University (jubilation) juxtaposed with that of mostly white students at another school (sombre mourning).[116] Abramson is right, I think, in holding that this 'juxtaposition of cheers and tears showed that the trial of O. J. Simpson had ceased to be a murder case. Somewhere along the line, the trial turned into a political event.'[117]

What this signals is the volatility that ensues when large swaths of the population belong to interpretive communities so vastly different that they cannot read ordinary events in the same way. At the interpretive level – the one that takes place at trial and in the jury room – the jurors must reconstruct the evidence they have heard in a way that is not just internally coherent but externally coherent with the larger cultural narratives they embrace. Patrick Hogan explains how this process works as a matter of cognitive science.[118] First, a jury is bombarded with a host of fragmentary and decontextualized 'discourse.'

In the Simpson case, the jurors heard months of testimony and viewed dozens of exhibits. From the prosecution side, for instance, they learned about bloody gloves found at the murder scene and behind Simpson's estate that resembled gloves he had previously worn and about footprints at the crime scene that were made by unusual shoes that Simpson was known to have owned, as well as that Simpson had previously beaten his wife and had 'dreamed' about killing her. From the defence side, the jury members learned that the blood evidence may have been tainted, that the police could not explain why they entered Simpson's estate without a warrant, and that one of the key prosecution witnesses was a racist and a liar. Second, from this dis-jointed 'discourse' the jury had to create a 'story,' just as a reader of a literary text would:

> In life as in art we only have the discontinuous, partially disordered frag-ments of experience. We are in much the same cognitive situation in the two cases. Unsurprisingly, then, we follow the same cognitive procedures. Specifically, given an array of fragments, we construct agents, objects, action, events, and causal sequences, hoping we 'get the story straight.' Here, as elsewhere, the human mind proceeds in the same way, whether it is dealing with nature or with art.[119]

Drawing on insights of narratologists David Bordwell and Richard Gerrig, Hogan explains that we transmute discourse into narrative through the agency of a cognitive *tertium quid* that he calls 'proce-dural schemas.'[120] These schemas are 'cognitive structures of action,' by which he refers to the way in which the mind works and is struc-tured. 'They allow us to do everything from walk to play music. In the case of narrative, they allow us to construct the story from the dis-course.'[121] Most important for us, these structures are at least partly subjective, idiosyncratic, and experience based. For example, if I hear someone say the word 'pet,' my mind usually summons up the word 'dog' and – depending on the context – the name and images of my childhood dog, a sable collie named Laddie, or one of our two current dogs, dachshunds named Sallie Ann and Senior. Someone else's mind would have a different cognitive structure and consequent lexical links, links that might not make a first-order connection between 'pet' and 'dog' – perhaps 'cat' instead. This is not to suggest, however, that the range is open-ended – very few people, I think, would immedi-ately connect 'pet' with 'giraffe' and even fewer (I hope) with 'vacuum cleaner' or 'nuclear reactor.' But we must bear in mind that interpretive narratives (narratives constructed to make sense of raw data or competing narratives) are always partly a function of the interpreter's experience:

> [Narrative] construction involves, first of all, the application of a vast wealth of information – prominently including an array of representational schemas – from our experience in the real world. Speaking of literary narrative, Gerrig points out that 'readers … must construct … situation models, which integrate information from the text with broader real-world knowledge.' Indeed, we evidently follow 'a *principle of minimal departure*,' according to which we assume maximum continuity between the real world and the world of fiction. In other words, we basically assume that the world of the story is identical with the world of our lived experience except in those specific cases where there is a direct contradiction from the narrative.[122]

To put this in the context of the Simpson case, the jury members were required to draw upon the world of their 'lived experience' to determine, for instance, whether the infamous bloody gloves fit better within a narrative in which (a) Simpson dropped the gloves in his haste to flee the crime scene and surreptitiously re-enter his estate without detection, or in which (b) overzealous and racist LAPD officers planted the gloves to enhance the possibility of convicting a suspect they had already deemed guilty. Similarly, the jurors in the King beating case were asked to decide whether the infamous video showed an out-of-control 'gorilla' who refused to be subdued or out-of-control police officers having sport with a hapless 'gentle giant.' Gibbs concludes, in conceptual agreement with Hogan's cognitive theory of narrative interpretation, that each of these juries was constrained by its respective community to interpret the facts as it did:

> There is a famous principle in psychology that governs the way all human beings process new information – the principle of cognitive dissonance. This principle states that people more easily assimilate information that fits in with or is consistent with their prior knowledge, beliefs, and experiences and will tend to reject information that is not consistent with their prior understanding of the world. Thus the jurors in Simi Valley were *inclined to believe* the police officers' defense because it was consistent with their prior experiences and beliefs about the police. In

contrast, the jurors in the Simpson case were *inclined to disbelieve* the testimony of the police because of their prior experiences and beliefs about police misconduct. In both cases, these jurors viewed the evidence, processed it, and evaluated it in terms of their own worldview and personal experiences.[123]

This fits neatly within the framework of Fish's theory of interpretive community, which – at bottom – is as much an account of interpretive *disagreement* as of agreement.[124] For as Fish explains, if one believes in single determinate meanings, then 'disagreement can only be a theological error. The truth lies plainly in view, available to anyone who has eyes to see; but some readers choose not to see it and perversely substitute their own meanings for the meanings that texts obviously bear.'[125] This belief is rooted in the more general belief that disagreements can be resolved by reference to 'facts.' But this line of argument is circular: as Eagleton observes, 'an interpretation on which everyone is likely to agree is one way of defining a fact.'[126] Thus, in the context of the Simpson case, it does little good for one side or the other to point to the gloves as a dispositive 'fact' because, reverting to Fish, 'not everyone believes the same thing or, to be more precise, not everyone's perceptions are a function of the same set of beliefs, and so there will not be one but many standard stories in which the world will be differently constituted, with different facts, values, ways of arguing, evidentiary procedures, and so on.'[127] So where one person may see a 'cause' or a 'motive,' another person may see a *non sequitur*.[128]

To extend this point a little, I think we can fairly conclude that belief in different public narratives can produce different facts. As we have seen in the King beating case (and to a lesser extent in the Simpson case), different public narratives, when they come into contact with one another, can produce explosive results. Oddly enough, though, pro-democratic consequences can flow from volcanic social eruption. And I think that the jury system both facilitates the exchange and ameliorates possible consequences. What I mean is this: Most institutional processes take place behind a veneer of relatively genteel discourse, in which representatives of 'The People' rarely say (or even know) what their constituents are actually thinking. Institutional actors speak in what Yeats called 'polite meaningless words' that conceal more than they reveal.[129] Juries and their verdicts, by contrast, often disclose how relatively insular groups see the world. The truth thereby unmasked can be ugly, but it can also facilitate institutional change more quickly than

would otherwise be possible. The reaction to the King beating verdict
is a perfect example. Prior to the South Central riots and the Simpson
acquittal, there was little public discourse about racism in the LAPD.
All that changed after the disturbances. This came at a high price, of
course, but perhaps not as high as it might have been had the grievances of the minority communities in Los Angeles continued to fester.
After all, a riot is better than a revolution.

## Is Jury Nullification Democratic and within the Rule of Law?

Before leaving juries and turning in earnest to a theory of democratic
legal interpretation, I want to consider one additional pro-democratic
aspect of the jury system. Though both the King beating case and the
Simpson case have been labelled as instances of 'jury nullification,'
that label is not apt. Nullification occurs when a jury declines to follow the law as instructed.[130] In the Simpson case, for instance, the jury
did not simply decide not to enforce the California law against murder; rather, it found that the State of California had not met its burden
of proof for the reasons we just examined.[131] To illustrate this contrast,
a brief look at *United States v. Marion Barry* will be helpful.[132]

In 1990, Marion Barry, an African American, was the mayor of the
District of Columbia, the population of which was about two-thirds
black.[133] He was enormously popular in the black community, but
rumours of drug use and 'chasing women' continuously swirled
around him. One day in January of that year, Rasheeda Moore, an
old friend of the mayor, contacted him and let him know she was in
town for a short visit. Later that day, Barry dropped by her hotel and
invited her to meet him in the lobby for a drink. Moore suggested
instead that he join her in her room, which he did. The two talked for
a while, and at some point Moore produced crack cocaine and a pipe,
which Barry eventually smoked (after first declining). FBI agents and
DC police officers then burst into the room and arrested Barry, who
learned that Moore was an informant and that their entire encounter
had been videotaped. Barry was later charged with over a dozen criminal counts. These charges included conspiracy to possess cocaine,
possession of cocaine, and perjury for lying to the grand jury that had
investigated him.

After his arrest and indictment, Barry publicly declared that he was
the victim of a racist prosecution. At trial, the jury apparently agreed,
finding Barry guilty of only one misdemeanour charge of cocaine

possession, while acquitting him on another and deadlocking on the remaining twelve. Among the charges on which the jury refused to convict was one based on the videotaped FBI sting operation. The trial judge (a white male) subsequently stated that he had 'never seen a stronger Government case' and that the evidence of Barry's guilt was 'overwhelming' on nearly all of the thirteen counts on which the jury acquitted or deadlocked.[134] The judge singled out four jurors for particular blame, finding that each had lied during jury selection to gain a seat and use that seat to acquit. As a matter of policy, the judge concluded, 'the jury is not a minidemocracy or a minilegislature. They are not to go back and do right as they see fit. That's anarchy. They are supposed to follow the law.'[135]

But is this right? Must a jury always follow the law? To be clear, the Barry case was not one in which the jurors reached an interpretation of the evidence that seemed out of step with that of a dominant interpretive community. Rather, it was a straightforward case of jury nullification – that is, there was no doubt that Barry had been caught smoking crack, so the jury's verdict could only be explained as a refusal to apply the law as instructed. Now of course the root cause of nullification is the same as for interpretive anomalies – jury members under the sway of a public narrative different from that of the mainstream. The difference can be described as one of conscious intent. A Simpson-type juror votes to acquit because he or she privileges certain evidence and discounts other evidence as a matter of interpretive belief. A Barry-type juror willingly votes to acquit even though he or she believes that the defendant committed the acts charged; that juror is voting his or her conscience, making a political statement, or showing mercy.[136] But the decision to cut against the grain is intentional, purposeful, and knowing. Not surprisingly, it is this obvious, flagrant disregard for the law as instructed that gives some critics of nullification the most pause. That concern, though valid, is nonetheless often counterbalanced and is in some sense misplaced.

When a jury nullifies, many observers – like the Barry judge – decry the act as an affront to the Rule of Law, civil society, and the judicial process. That is true enough in the sense that the jury disobeyed the instruction of a properly appointed judicial official. But the criticism is also too broad, because our judicial system – our rules of law – grant juries that power, at least in certain circumstances. We find that tacitly in the Constitution's Fifth Amendment, which – by virtue of the double jeopardy clause – prohibits appellate reversal of or retrial after an acquittal verdict.[137] There is historical support as well, stretching from the seminal *Bushell's Case*, in which the English Court of Common Pleas held that a juror in a criminal trial could not be fined for acquitting against the will of a judge,[138] to early state constitutions, which specifically provided that 'the jury shall be judges of law, as well as fact.'[139] And even today, two state constitutions allow criminal juries to decide matters of law *and* fact, thus rendering a court's instructions merely advisory.[140] I don't mean to suggest that jury nullification is favoured – it plainly is not – but it is not, as the Barry judge would have it, anti-constitutional.

I also don't mean to suggest that jury nullification is an ideal or even a clear net positive.[141] To confirm that fact, we need only recall that many all-white juries acquitted clearly guilty whites of crimes against blacks and civil rights workers in the 1950s and 1960s. But it does showcase narrative dissonance between communities in a way that can spark important reforms and give a democratic voice to socially hidden narratives. (After all, the Southern misadventures galvanized the movement to seek racial equality across the board.) To some extent, then, juries are of greater systemic importance as a source of information (concerning, for instance, the popular temper or particular community disaffection) than as a source of individual adjudication. Ultimately, with Abramson, I agree that nullification carries risks, but that these risks are part and parcel of the democratic enterprise:

> Questions about the law's justice or the wisdom of enforcing it against a particular defendant can and should not be avoided in any system designed to leave law's final enforcement to the people. If jurors may never properly decide that the specifics of a case make it unwise or trivial to enforce the law, if jurors may never balk at enforcing laws they believe are fundamentally unjust, then juries become the rubber stamp of legislatures and judges, not independent sources of democratic judgment.[142]

As Abramson goes on to suggest, 'to permit juries to show mercy by not enforcing the law in a given case is hardly to destroy the fabric of a society under law.' In fact, the jury system, as I just observed, is in some sense a feedback loop built into the larger legal system, a way – to refer back to Bankowski's remark – 'to let the outside in.'[143] And in so doing, a jury – by showing mercy in an individual case – can ennoble the entire system, as Portia concludes in *The Merchant of Venice*:

The quality of mercy is not strain'd.
It droppeth as the gentle rain from heaven
Upon the place beneath. It is twice blest:
It blesseth him that gives and him that takes.
'Tis mightiest in the mightiest; it becomes
The throned monarch better than his crown.
His scepter shows the force of temporal power,
The attribute to awe and majesty
Wherein doth sit the dread and fear of kings;
It is an attribute of God himself;
And earthly power doth then show likest God's
When mercy seasons justice.[144]

## Some Thoughts on Democratic Interpretation

Thus far, we have looked principally at how juries evaluate and reconstruct narratives and how that process serves democratic ends. Now I want to look at how judges perform a cognate process when interpreting and applying legal rules and to take some steps toward defining a theory of interpretation that is equally democratic (or at least less antidemocratic than some of the alternatives). What we find, as Bolt's Thomas More believed, is that legal interpretation *is* in some ways different from 'ordinary' interpretation: 'The world must construe according to its wits. This Court must construe according to the law.'[145] But what we also find is that these differences are neither absolute nor even largely exclusive of each other.

As I have already shown, some statutes and common law rules are particular narratives universally stated. These particular narratives take hold only when they accord with a higher-order narrative. Developments in the law can thus take place when (1) an especially compelling particular narrative is aired (2) in the presence of a higher-order narrative that makes the individual narrative both plausible and worthy of universalization and institutionalization. We saw this in the case of Betty Hundley: her personal story squared with a larger feminist narrative that had only recently displaced a sexist narrative. It was thus time to change the rules that were an instantiation of that displaced narrative.[146] Sometimes this narrative provenance is obvious, sometimes not. But the narrative is always there, if only as a trace. Part of the task of judging is, I think, a duty to interpret and apply rules with an eye to the narratives – both large and small – that gave rise to those rules.

This may require some digging – perhaps even imaginative reconstruction in some cases – but the exercise is necessary because it ensures that public opinion (as embodied in public narratives) is *considered*, even if that opinion is ultimately rejected for good reasons on the facts of a particular case.[147]

Before going further, we need to return to the question of what the process of *judicial* interpretation means – that is, whether that process is meaningfully different from the process of a juror interpreting the competing narratives presented at a trial, or of a literary scholar interpreting a novel or poem to which she has devoted a lifetime of study, or of me reading the morning newspaper with our dogs yapping in the background. The answer to this comes in two parts. First, judges are (what Karl Llewellyn dubbed) 'law-conditioned officials,' which means that they are members of a specially trained professional community, one that is taught to make fine-grained distinctions, to revere precedent, to be attuned to issues of causation, and to consider consequences of various legal strategies (including interpretation).[148] Then, too, judges must make difficult decisions, decisions with (sometimes) enormous consequences. (As far as I know, no one has ever suffered anything more than embarrassment for offering a discredited reading of *Moby Dick*.) But second, judges are members of other interpretive communities: each has a different basket of religious beliefs, political inclinations, moral standards, life experiences, and – as practitioners can readily confirm – abilities and temperaments. Thus, while a judge will by training know how to read a precedent more or less broadly or narrowly or to reason by way of a syllogism, how he or she chooses to do so in any given case may depend as much on extralegal influences as on legal training.[149]

When we follow this extralegal trail to its source, what we find is a *desire* for law, or – perhaps more accurately – a desire for social conditions that are (perhaps) available only in the presence of law. Regarding this point, Stanley Fish suggests that 'law emerges because people desire predictability, stability, equal protection, the reign of justice, etc., and because they want to believe that it is possible to secure these things by instituting a set of impartial procedures.'[150] In arguing for a 'pragmatic' theory of adjudication, Judge Posner emphasizes the need for these procedures to (at least appear to) preserve these values:

> The significance of the slogan that judges are to find rather than make law is merely as a reminder that aggressive judicial lawmaking is likely to undermine important systemic values. It is difficult to plan one's activities

if the judges are at any moment to veer in a new direction; and judges who become too caught up in the essentially political role of making new policies are apt to lose their neutrality and become partisans. We might even note a tension between two of the components of the rule of law, impartiality and predictability. Partial judges may be all too predictable. Impartial judges are predictable only if their discretion is circumscribed, either by precise and detailed rules laid down by a legislature or by a commitment to deciding cases in accordance with precedent, which is how the common law is stabilized.[151]

This need to circumscribe judicial authority is typically justified by an appeal to objectivity, by which legal theorists mean a number of things. As I mentioned before, some commentators think that legal objectivity is achievable; others think that the enterprise is doomed before it starts. The naysayers argue that objectivity is merely a cultural fiction or a manifestation of a reigning ideology or a blindness to the arbitrary nature of language or the mask of a powerful hierarchy or, most simply, a human delusion.[152] The yeasayers put their faith in the Enlightenment position that, as Peter Railton puts it, 'objectivity follows automatically once we proceed rationally.'[153] Of course there is a looming contradiction here: viz., how can an internal and thus inherently subjective process always yield objective results?[154] This question calls us to further ask what legal actors mean by objectivity and whether this concept bears on the narrative theory we have been developing.

Robert Nozick suggests a contrast: 'Something is objective when (or to the extent that) it is determined in its character by the features of an object; it is subjective when it is determined in its character by states such as consciousness, emotions, and desires that are intrinsic to being a subject.'[155] Science offers a familiar starting point for further elaboration. In that domain, most believers in objectivity propose a tripartite touchstone for discerning the objectivity of a scientific process:

- objective inquiry is value-free;
- objective inquiry is not biased by factual or theoretical preconceptions, e.g., it does not adopt a theory until the evidence is in, and it refuses to interpret evidence in light of the theory at issue; and
- objective inquiry uses procedures that are intersubjective and independent of particular individuals or circumstances – for example, its experiments are reproducible, its methods are determinate, its

criteria are effective, and it makes no essential use of introspective or subjectively privileged evidence in theory assessment.[156]

Of the criteria embedded in this type of conceptual or procedural framework (three of which can be summed up as accessibility from different angles, intersubjectivity, and independence), Nozick would emphasize the fourth, 'invariance,' by which he means that an objective fact is one that is invariant under various transformations (e.g., Einstein's Special Theory, which holds that all physical laws are the same for all observers at rest).[157] Nozick places emphasis on this spot because he believes that invariance is the most fundamental characteristic of an objective scientific truth.

This is all well and good in the world of beakers, pipettes, and their high-tech successors, but how do these standards help us achieve objective answers to legal and ethical questions? The answer is, I'm afraid, far from clear. For as Posner and Fish have argued, scientific objectivity in law is only 'sometimes attainable,' and the only way 'to kick legal objectivity up a notch … is to make the courts and legislatures more homogeneous, culturally and politically.'[158] This sort of judicial and legislative caste system would hardly serve democratic ends, and even then, it seems to me, the procedures employed would be narrowly formalistic, which – as we saw in *Hynes* – can lead to results that are legally justified yet unjust in a popular sense. This is not to suggest, however, that I think that all legal decision making is or should be ad hoc or that replicable results are not achievable in the vast majority of cases. But I do think we should guard against formalisms that do nothing more than glue a veneer of objectivity over essentially political decisions in difficult cases that turn on questions of interpretation.

Central to all textual interpretation is the question of language: What do these words *mean*? As I've already said, this question is of critical importance in law, because the consequences of one interpretation over another can quite literally (though rarely) have life-or-death consequences, or – less dramatically – because language is the medium through which the law works. Judge Posner observes with respect to this latter point that

a systemic value that requires particular emphasis is the importance of preserving language as an effective medium of communication. If judges did not generally interpret contracts and statutes in accordance with the ordinary meaning of the sentences appearing in those texts, certainty of legal obligation would be seriously undermined. For judges in run-of-the-mill contract and statutory cases to subordinate this consideration to weighing of case-specific consequences would therefore be unpragmatic, although it would be equally unpragmatic to refuse to consider case-specific consequences altogether just because the language of the contract or statute in issue seemed clear on its face ... The existence of [doctrines allowing departure from literal meaning] shows, by the way, that interpretation can be a good deal more complicated and uncertain than deduction, contrary to the view of those legal formalists who equate interpretation to deduction in an attempt to show that the language of a contract or a statute provides a sure guide to 'objective' adjudication ... Despite these qualifications, most contract and statutory cases are decided quickly and easily on the basis of the 'plain meaning' of the relevant texts.[159]

As Posner correctly indicates, many commentators equate the 'plain meaning rule' with 'objectivity,' thus identifying a fruitful line of investigation of the latter through the former. The plain meaning rule tends, at least in theory, to create uniformity in legal outcomes by constraining judges' interpretations of statutes and constitutional provisions to the literal meaning of the words used in the text at issue.[160] One of the earliest modern commentators on the rule speculated that 'the plain meaning rule seems to have been intended, originally, to rule out the traditional judicial doctrine of "the equity of the statute," a doctrine which justified alterations in the literal meaning of statutory language to avoid results which, in the opinion of an interpreting judge, were unfair or inequitable.'[161] In its contemporary application, however, the rule is most commonly invoked to bar extrinsic evidence of a text's meaning (e.g., legislative materials such as committee reports or social norms at the time of adoption).[162] There is nothing inherently suspicious in assigning presumptive validity to plain meaning interpretations: to the contrary, as Neil MacCormick persuasively argues, judicial respect for literal textual meaning serves democratic ends by forcing legislators to draft with clarity.[163] The problem is thus not with the general rule; rather, it is with resort to the general rule in those specific cases that are ill suited to a 'quick look' mode of interpretation.

A couple of examples are perhaps the best way of demonstrating how strict textualism can lead to results that are – if not absurd – undesirable. In *Caminetti v. United States*, the Supreme Court was called upon to decide whether the Mann Act, which criminalized the interstate transportation of women 'for the purpose of prostitution or debauchery or for any other immoral purpose' applied to the exploits of a young college man who drove a young woman across a state line on the way to a tavern at which they were to spend the night.[164] There was no dispute as to whether the two had sexual relations (no question of what 'is' is), but it was equally undisputed that there was no commercial transaction. It is clear from the legislative history of the Mann Act that it was not intended to apply to the scenario I just outlined. Indeed, the Mann Act is entitled 'The White Slave Traffic Act,' and Representative Mann, the bill's author, had assured members of the House – in response to this very line of questioning – that it was aimed solely at 'vice as a business.'[165] Nonetheless, a majority of the Supreme Court found that the statute was 'plain and unambiguous' and that the conduct at issue fit within the statute's 'other immoral purpose' proviso, no matter the actual intent of the legislature. What the Court missed was the misalignment between the higher-order narrative that gave rise to and is embedded in the Mann Act ('white slavery'/interstate prostitution) and the particular facts of the case (a college lark/extramarital but non-commercial sex). In other words, this case is another example of what we earlier discussed as narrative misclassification: liability should only attach when the particular narrative on trial is like the many particulars (the tales of abuse and exploitation of individual women) that conjoined to form the public narrative (against the white slave trade) that in turn gave rise to the universal rule against participating in the business of interstate prostitution.

At times, courts are so concerned with appearing objective that they shoehorn fairly obvious political or moral decisions into the plain meaning framework, often with destabilizing consequences. *Bowers v. Hardwick* is a good example.[166] Hardwick 'was charged with violating the Georgia statute criminalizing sodomy by committing that act with another adult male in the bedroom of respondent's home.'[167] Hardwick challenged the statute on several constitutional grounds, and the United States Supreme Court granted a petition for *certiorari* to consider whether the Georgia statute violated the fundamental rights of homosexuals. Justice White, writing for the majority, reframed this issue in a way that permitted an ultimate 'plain meaning' determination: 'The issue presented is whether the Federal Constitution confers a fundamental right upon homosexuals to engage in sodomy.'[168]

With the issue so constructed, Justice White was able to take a literalist approach, one loath to 'announcing rights not readily identifiable in the Constitution's text' or to '[making new] constitutional law having little or no cognizable roots in the language or design of the Constitution.'[169] The holding of the case was thus not surprising, given the narrowness of the task that Justice White set for himself – namely, to thumb through the Constitution and a few cases construing it looking for the words 'right to homosexual sodomy' and, finding none, to consider the matter at an end. But as Drucilla Cornell ably shows in a deconstructive reading of the opinion, Justice White misread the historical narrative at issue:

> The result for White is that 'fundamental liberties' should be limited to those that are 'deeply rooted in the Nation's history and tradition.' For Justice White, as we have also seen, the evidence that the right to engage in 'homosexual sodomy' is not a fundamental liberty is the 'fact' that at the time the fourteenth amendment was passed, all but five of the thirty-seven states in the union had criminal sodomy laws and that most states continue to have such laws. In his dissent, Blackmun vehemently rejects the appeal to the *fact* of the existence of anti-sodomy criminal statutes as a basis for continuing the prohibition, and the denial of a right, characterized by Blackmun not as the right to engage in homosexual sodomy but as 'the right to be let alone.' Quoting Justice Holmes, Blackmun reminds us that: 'It is revolting to have no better reason for a rule of law than that so it was laid down in the time of Henry IV. It is still more revolting if the grounds upon which it was laid down have vanished long since, and the rule simply persists from blind imitation of the past.'[170]

Cornell of course recognizes that 'a legal system if it is *to be* just must also promise universality, the fair application of the rules.'[171] And this calls up yet again the twin faces of justice, one looking to the particular, the other to the universal. As a result, Cornell notes, 'we have what for Derrida is the first aporia of justice, the *epokhe* [suspension] of the rule.' At this impasse a judge has not only an obligation to state the law but to *judge* it:

> In short, for a decision to be just and responsible, it must, in its proper moment if there is one, be both regulated and without regulation: it must conserve the law and also destroy it or suspend it enough to have to rein-

vent it in each case, rejustify it, at least reinvent it in the reaffirmation and the new and free confirmation of its principle.[172]

In Cornell's view, then, 'Justice White failed to meet his responsibility precisely because he replaced description with judgment, and indeed, a description of state laws a hundred years past, and in very different social and political circumstances.'[173]

What Cornell is getting at here is that public narratives concerning both homosexuals in specific and privacy rights in general had changed over the course of several generations (recall that high-order narratives are always already in the process of revision, subsumption, or replacement). Therefore, judging Hardwick's conduct under a statute animated by an outmoded narrative was unjust. Justice White was (wilfully?) blind to these new narratives, and this blindness had negative consequences for the democratic rule of law, if one assumes that predictability and stability are virtues. For within two decades, the Court admitted its mistake in *Bowers*, and overruled it.[174]

Cases like *Caminetti* and *Bowers* teach us that the very instruments of objectivity can be turned against it. It is a laudable aim of the law to establish procedures that insulate litigants from bias or whimsy. But we must remain mindful that formalisms are of limited utility in hard cases. We must arm ourselves not just for quotidian cases (i.e., the types of cases in which the facts and law are not credibly in dispute and in which, therefore, a mechanical jurisprudence can be expected to work fairly well), but for the more subtle, marginal ones as well. When setting out to divine the 'plain meaning' of a complicated text, an interpreter would be well advised to heed Hotspur's admonitory rejoinder to Glendower in *Henry IV*:

GLENDOWER: I can call spirits from the vasty deep.
HOTSPUR: Why so can I, or so can any man,
   But will they come when you do call for them?[175]

By way of conclusion, I return to the image of law presented in Kafka's 'Before the Law.' Law both produces and receives narratives; thus, narrative failures of the sort we have examined in the course of our various discussions can happen just as easily from the institutional side of the equation as from the human side. In his well-known reading of Kafka's story, Jacques Derrida suggests that the man from the country is trapped in what might be called a literary dilemma, which means that his failure to enter the law may have been a failure of his own making – a readerly failure, if you will:

There is no literature without a work, without an absolutely singular performance, and this necessary irreplaceability again recalls what the man from the country asks when the singular crosses the universal, when the categorical engages the idiomatic, as a literature always must. The man from the country had difficulty in grasping that an entrance was singular or unique when it should have been universal, as in truth it was. He had difficulty with literature.[176]

# 4 Narrative as Democratic Reasoning*

Humans act according to both reason and emotion. One of the oldest and most recurring questions in human inquiry is, thus, whether the former stands on equal ground with the latter. David Hume thought not (reason is 'the slave of the passions'); Immanuel Kant thought otherwise and devoted much of his later energy to explaining reason – whether 'pure' (logic, mathematics, etc.) or 'practical' (law, morality, etc.) – on its own terms. In *Practical Reason in Law and Morality*, Neil MacCormick takes up the challenge posed by these contradictory positions and undertakes to answer the question, 'Can reason be practical?'[1] He answers that question in the affirmative and goes on to examine the points of convergence and divergence between practical reason in the context of morals and in the context of law. This suggests the existence of a possible gap between moral reasoning (which everyone practises) and legal reasoning (which only members of the guild – or those trained to think like them – practise) that calls for description and explanation, here in light of the narrative theory we have developed.

## The Narrative Shape of Deliberation

M.J. Detmold has made the very practical point that 'Law is practical. Legal reasoning is practical reasoning.'[2] By this he means to draw our attention to the fact that a central purpose of a legal system is to make decisions, to hand down *judgments* in particular cases – not to make abstract conclusions. If this is right (and I think it is), the process of judgment has at least two phases. As MacCormick puts it, 'deliberative reasoning precedes decision.'[3] It's what goes into the deliberative stew that I now want us to consider in some detail.

From our earlier discussion of jury decision making, we learned that juries operate under the influence of the interpretive communities to which their members belong. One way to describe their decision making process is as 'lay practical reasoning' (as opposed to what some observers have posited as the 'legal reasoning' undertaken by lawyers and judges).[4] Without attempting to resolve the theoretical disagreements that abound over the issue of whether there are, in fact, different stripes of reasoning (or whether practical reasoning can lead, for example, to one answer in the moral arena, to another in the legal), I want to touch at least briefly on the issue and show the *democratic* importance of narrative context to reasoning, however defined.

In his seminal *Legal Reasoning and Legal Theory*, MacCormick considered at great length the case of *Donoghue v. Stevenson* and used it as a running example.[5] He returned to the case thirty years later in *Practical Reason in Law and Morality*, this time looking at the case through two lenses, one coloured by law, the other by morals, with both shaped by a broader historical context. This is the famous snail-in-the-soda-bottle case that pushed products liability in Scots law from a well-marked high road onto a byway that was mostly unstaked. A few facts, loosely drawn from MacCormick's analysis of the case, will aid our discussion.

One Sunday in late August of 1928, May Donoghue set out from the east end of Glasgow's city centre and, with a friend, rode an electric tram car to the nearby town of Paisley. At the end of the day, the pair wound up in a cafe, at which the friend bought each of them a refreshment. May chose an 'ice drink,' which is composed of a scoop of ice cream in a drinking glass over which a soft drink is poured (something akin to a root beer float). The cafe's proprietor brought May a glass with ice cream in it, along with a bottle of ginger beer, from which he poured some of the contents. May took a few sips of the concoction and in due course poured more of the ginger beer over it. As she attended to this task, the remains of a decomposing snail floated out of the bottle and onto her ice cream. The snail had theretofore been out of view because the ginger-beer bottle was opaque (a necessity caused by the then-practice of brewing ginger beer in the bottle, which left an unsightly yeast residue at the bottom). The ginger beer container bore the name of a local bottler, David Stevenson.

May took what MacCormick describes as a 'nasty turn' upon seeing the snail, which ultimately led to a bout of gastro-enteritis, a hospital stay, and the loss of several weeks' work as a shop clerk. She then consulted a lawyer, who sued Stevenson under the theory that Stevenson (as a manufacturer) owed her (as a consumer) a duty of care and that he had breached it. As factual support, May's counsel alleged that Stevenson's bottle storehouse was unsanitary and bore visible signs of snail trails. Stevenson, for his part, denied that the bottle described in the pleadings was his and averred that he had never used bottles of that type (namely, with a metal cap and adhesive label).

At this point, MacCormick goes beyond the pleadings and observes a custom of the bottling trade in Scotland. When the dispute arose in the 1920s, there was a penny deposit on every bottle sold in Scotland, the purpose of which was to motivate consumers to return empty bottles to retailers. Bottle exchanges provided the means for returning bottles embossed with a manufacturer's name to that manufacturer for reuse. But the system was voluntary, and there was no ready legal obstacle to prevent a manufacturer (large or small) from putting his own preparations in someone else's bottles. Had the case gone to trial, then, Stevenson might well have had a good defence to May's claim. Thus, MacCormick notes, 'the facts recited belong to the class of alleged rather than to that of proven facts.'[6]

With these 'facts' set on their marks, MacCormick strides onto the stage to examine them first in moral and then in legal terms. In the role of an 'impartial spectator,'[7] he finds the moral question easy enough:

> We can all imagine, with a quiver of revulsion, pouring a drink from an opaque bottle and discovering the contents to have been contaminated by animal remains like those of a snail or a small mouse. The kind of gastric illness that could result from such an event is familiar to us, as are the pain and debilitation attending it, with resultant unfitness for work.[8]

Our sensibilities are not offended by holding Stevenson liable in this situation, even though he did not act deliberately to harm May or any other consumer. After all, Stevenson was operating a commercial enterprise for gain, and that enterprise involved the mass production of goods that carried obvious risks to consumer health that only he – as the manufacturer – was situated to prevent, especially given that his products were not subject to inspection prior to consumption. So, MacCormick concludes, an impartial spectator would find it difficult to view Stevenson's side of the case sympathetically, absent compelling evidence that the bottle at issue was not his or had been used by another manufacturer or that the snail did not in fact exist. 'Being aware of the sentiments and emotions and physical events in this case, the impartial spectator would conclude that a poor woman suffering illness and loss in this way was owed some compensation by the one person who, by due care, could have prevented it from happening.'[9]

The legal case was not so easily resolved when it came up for decision, for several reasons. First among them was that negligence theories had not been fully institutionalized at the time. Negligence depends on identifying parties that owe duties to other parties, and the law had not yet settled on a method for handling disputes between parties with no direct dealings, a scenario that became more and more common after the Industrial Revolution and its methods of mass production and distribution. Should a manufacturer essentially insure all risk of harm traceable to its products? Or should – in a case like *Donoghue v. Stevenson* – the consumer be required to sue (on a contract/warranty theory) the retailer from whom she purchased, who could in turn sue the manufacturer for indemnity? These and other questions (e.g., Would a plague of bogus claims arise? Who would bear litigation costs?) were open at the time. Ultimately, though there was deep disagreement among the various judges who participated in the multiple stages of the case, the majority came down in favour of a rule placing a duty of care on manufacturers and allowing direct consumer actions against manufacturers who breach that duty.

MacCormick's overarching aim is to show that the moral and legal solutions to a Donoghue/Stevenson-type problem run close to each other (and that the legal solution must be considered against the background of a moral question), but that they are not coincident. The course of reasoning that we followed above to arrive at the moral conclusion is germane to a course of legal reasoning, but good legal reasoning must also exhibit 'three principal desiderata':

- Coherence: the ruling in the instant case should square with some broader principle that makes sense of the relevant body of law in the light of a reasonable evaluation of it;
- Consistency: the ruling must not contradict any binding established rule of law; but this does not exclude care in explaining and distinguishing apparently adverse precedents, or seeking reasonable interpretations of statutory provisions; and
- Consequences: the decisions mandated by the ruling in question should be more acceptable in evaluative terms than those that would be mandated by the opposite view.[10]

In MacCormick's estimation, it is (especially) with respect to the former two desiderata that legal and moral reasoning diverge. This divergence arises because legal systems contain vast numbers of authoritative texts 'that give their special character to arguments concerning coherence and consistency in law.'[11] These aspects of legal texts and reasoning are not irrelevant to moral reasoning, but that reasoning 'knows no single authoritative rule-book and lacks the deeply institutional character of legal reasoning.'[12]

For me, two further conclusions may be drawn from all this, both of which bear heavily on the narrative theory of law and democracy as I have stated it. First, if moral and legal reasoning are, as MacCormick maintains, related – yet differing – strains of practical reason, then tensions will inevitably arise in difficult cases between the results of general moral reasoning and specialized legal reasoning. This again takes us back to the issues we examined with respect to interpretive communities in the context of jury decisions. There, our focus was on how juries process evidence and construct coherent narratives out of it. But a (non-hung) jury does more than construct a shared factual narrative:[13] it also makes a decision that assesses the legal consequences of that narrative in light of its interpretation of the law it is given (in the form of jury instructions).

These are not separate processes, however. For as Darryl Brown has persuasively argued,

> factual interpretation and statutory interpretation … likely have an interactive or reciprocal relationship: a factual story will make a particular application of a statute seem obvious, appropriate, or most plausible. Conversely, statutory language that seems to compel one result in light of an initial factual understanding may prompt a jury to reconsider its construction of facts if that initial result is discomforting – if it conflicts with a 'considered judgment' about the proper moral assessment of the defendant's action.[14]

In drawing a link between 'considered judgment' and 'proper moral assessment,' Brown is suggesting, I think, that jurors use lay practical reason to harmonize – in the form of a verdict that is a sort of narrative conclusion – the evidence they have heard and the instructions they have been given. There may be, from time to time, a divergence between lay and professional outcomes on any given set of facts and rules, but this is part of the democratic point–counterpoint structure that seeks an equilibrium between overheated group passions and cold systemic formalism. As Brown puts it in the context of criminal law, 'individualized assessments of moral culpability, sensitive to circumstances and background norms, are not only a theoretical goal of criminal law; they are also part of the popular understanding of the criminal law's purpose.'[15]

Turning now to my second point, *Donoghue v. Stevenson* presents a further problem because of the procedural posture in which it was decided. MacCormick notes that Stevenson defended the case by way of a 'plea to the relevancy' of the case – that is, with a purely legal defence akin to a general demurrer or motion to dismiss for failure to state a claim. In other words, he argued that a manufacturer owes no duty to a consumer; as a consequence, there was no duty to breach and, as a further consequence, no possibility of a negligence claim for want of a mandatory element. Stevenson lost the issue in the first instance, so the case went up on appeal (finally to the House of Lords) on a very one-sided narrative, one based on *allegations*, not proven facts. (But as the lawyers over in Fort Worth say, 'No matter how flat a pancake gets, it still has two sides.') When MacCormick revisited the case after thirty years, he emphasized that reasoning takes place in context and that a too-limited context can lead to what may be described as 'narrative prematurity' – that is, a narrative that is too quickly shaped and, therefore, unready to be assessed for its legal consequences. That may very well have been the case in *Donoghue v. Stevenson*, which never ripened into a fully litigated controversy (and it settled after the appeals, so we have no way of reconstructing it now). It is one thing to make a moral judgment on hypothetical or partial facts, but it seems quite another to make a legal judgment that will be institutionalized (with generalized precedential effect) on a one-sided narrative that has not withstood the assault of a countervailing narrative. In sum, to allow anything less than a complete clash of narratives is undemocratic because modern democratic forms presume that laws of general application will be created only after full public debate (albeit on a representative basis). There's an even more important point here, though – namely, that, as MacCormick notes, there is only so much information narrated in a court's opinion and missing information might actually change how we view the correctness of whatever rule is laid down in the case. This point needs further investigation. But first we must stop to consider the more fundamental issue of how lawyers come to be members of their specialized interpretive community, a community that drives them to create narratives of a very special sort.

## Law-as-Discipline

As I've noted before, lawyers belong to a professional interpretive community, one in which its members read, write, and therefore think in ways that they did not prior to crossing the bar. The process of entering this new community begins in law school, which Philip Kissam likens to a Foucaultian discipline, and is completed (some might say exacerbated) in law practice. In *The Discipline of Law Schools: The Making of Modern Lawyers*, Kissam is concerned to test many of the cherished assumptions upon which American legal education has rested for a century or more.[16] His critique is comprehensive (and we must cut it short here), so I want to focus on just a couple of his points – viz., how law schools teach students in ways that are ultimately constraining (and needlessly so):

> The discipline teaches *instrumentalist habits of reading and writing* that both empower and limit future lawyers. These habits consist of quick, productive but often superficial ways of reading legal texts and writing about law, and they are linked to law school's distinctive oral culture, which celebrates oral heroism and tacitly devalues complex reading and writing. The law school's distinctive oral culture in turn rests upon the discipline's case method, its large amphitheater classrooms, its Moot Court exercises and the speech-like forms of effective final examination writing. But this oral culture and the instrumentalist reading and writing habits of law schools tend to subordinate more complicated, more reflective, more critical and more imaginative ways of reading, writing and thinking about the law.[17]

For me, one aspect of this stands out above all others: the reliance on the study of cases (mostly excerpted appellate opinions) and the specialized narrative form upon which they are based. And just as law students and teachers rely on compendiums of cases (in the form of casebooks), American practitioners rely quite heavily on cases as sources of legal authority (either in raw reporter form or in treatises that resemble casebooks in design, if not purpose).

Casebooks (and treatises) are, as Kissam aptly and ironically describes them, 'large heavy books that are bound in serious, somber colors, blue, black or deep red, and carry serious, somber titles such as "Contracts Law: Cases and Materials" or "Federal Income Taxation."'[18] As I just mentioned, these books consist largely of excerpts of appellate court opinions (in some subjects mostly from the United States Supreme Court), together with summaries of related cases, blurbs from scholarly writing, and a few discussion questions and hypotheticals. Some casebooks – especially those prepared by editors with cross-disciplinary leanings (e.g., economics) – may also include materials designed to provide an analytical framework within which to evaluate particular decisions. But, as Michael Hoeflich has observed, even in doctrinally expansive casebooks, 'the editors rarely consider the broader context of the case as published nor do they suggest that reported decisions may not, in fact, give full accounts of "what really happened."'[19] By 'broader context' Hoeflich is thinking principally of things social and historical – that is, the sort of materials that would make it possible for a reader 'to understand and evaluate the origin, historic rationale, or legitimacy of the decision.'[20] As a consequence of all this, Kissam concludes, 'the structure of casebooks makes it difficult to understand opinions as comprehensible narratives, as comprehensible parts of larger coherent doctrinal or social contexts, or as useful subjects for the development of legal arguments, counter-arguments and criticism.'[21]

There are good reasons why law teachers use casebooks and practising lawyers use treatises: they offer a convenient way to teach and recall rules quickly and economically. This economy comes, however, at a significant associated cost. There is a basic polarity in how lawyers think and thereby perform their greater social functions. In one mode, the analytical, 'things and events are detached from the situations of everyday life and represented in more abstract and systematic ways.'[22] This way of thinking promotes stability and consistency. In the other mode, the narrative, 'things and events are given significance through being placed in a story, an ongoing context of meaningful interaction.'[23] Things *human* (e.g., meaning and values) reside here. Both modes are vital and significant, but thinking about law solely in case/rule terms privileges the former over the latter.[24]

With this backcloth stitched into place, we can begin to foreground the central feature of the casebooks and treatises – viz., the edited or summarized appellate opinion – and what that feature implies. An appellate opinion almost always takes a narrative shape, but that narrative is highly concentrated and formalized. The last opinion in any given case stands at the head of a series of narrative regressions, those resulting from opinions below, testimony of parties and witnesses, statements and briefs of counsel, and no doubt others. The opinion we find in a reporter is thus just the last – not the only – narrative in the record of a case, even though over time it may be the only generally available trace of a matter that is left to posterity.[25] But by no means can the opinion be taken as a complete statement of 'what really happened' as a matter of history. For as we've just seen in the discussion of *Donoghue v. Stevenson*, sometimes the 'facts' are no more than naked allegations. In sum, narrative coherence can come at the expense of narrative completeness.

The version of an opinion that we find in a casebook or treatise (because of editing, topical organization, and surrounding commentary) is in some sense a revision and recontextualization of a case's final narrative – extrajudicial, yet of great importance because many bedrock cases are never read in full by lawyers. As such, a casebook/treatise suffers from two inherent deficiencies. First, as Karl Llewellyn once remarked, 'only by happenstance will an opinion accurately report the process of deciding.'[26] So, as with the full version published in a reporter, the casebook/treatise version is not only cut off from the underlying narrative record upon which it is based but as well from the deliberative process that led to the decision. We must thus take it on faith that the judge who wrote a particular opinion did so in good faith and fairly and accurately described the facts (as well as how she analysed them), but this cannot always be the case: 'we must also, in this post-Realist world, accept the possibility that judges edit the facts and analysis which they include in their published opinions.'[27] Consequently, as Llewellyn further suggests, 'vital factors may go unmentioned; pseudo factors may be put forward; emphasis and weighing of factors may be hugely skewed; any statements of policy may be not for revelation but merely for consumption; the very alleged statement of "the facts" may be only a lawyer's argumentative arranged selection, omission, emphasis, distortion, all flavored to make the result tolerable or toothsome.'[28]

The reasons for judicial editing can range from the benign (trying to keep an opinion to a manageable length), to the problematic (tailoring the facts, perhaps subconsciously, to fit a personal or political agenda), to the corrupt (reaching a decision based on bribery). And we must remain largely ignorant of these reasons (or even a judge-author's basic editorial choices) because we have no way to test the final, published narrative against its building blocks in the overall record – all we see is what the judge wants us to see. In short, the decision to conceal or foreground a narrative is a rhetorical decision (one sometimes born of compromise rather than individual belief) that was made long before the printed page passes before our eyes. But we can sometimes catch that decision's shadow in a case in which multiple judges write opinions or in which a dissent, 'for instance, pounds home facts or authorities the majority has found it convenient to ignore.'[29]

Let's take an example. *Ake v. Oklahoma* grew out of an especially horrid multiple homicide that took place outside Oklahoma City in the late 1970s.[30] The crime had a deep public impact, so much so that I recall people still talking about it in private conversations when I practised law in Oklahoma City some fifteen years later. One of the murderers, Glen Burton Ake, was convicted of the crime, but he appealed to the United States Supreme Court, arguing that the State of Oklahoma had violated his due process rights by failing to provide him with a psychiatrist to testify in his defence. Of the crime itself, here's what Justice Marshall, writing for the majority, had to say: 'Late in 1979, Glen Burton Ake was arrested and charged with murdering a couple and wounding their two children.'[31] The remainder of his factual recitation deals with Ake's mental instability, pretrial psychiatric treatment, and competence to stand trial. Justice Rehnquist, in dissent, had a much different story to tell:

> Petitioner Ake and his codefendant Hatch quit their jobs on an oil field rig in October 1979, borrowed a car, and went looking for a location to burglarize. They drove to the rural home of Reverend and Mrs. Richard Douglass, and gained entrance to the home by a ruse. Holding Reverend and Mrs. Douglass and their children, Brooks and Leslie, at gunpoint, they ransacked the home; they then bound and gagged the mother, father, and son, and forced them to lie on the living room floor. Ake and Hatch then took turns attempting to rape 12-year-old Leslie Douglass in a nearby bedroom. Having failed in these efforts, they forced her to lie on the living room floor with the other members of her family.
>
> Ake then shot Reverend Douglass and Leslie each twice, and Mrs Douglass and Brooks once, with a .357 magnum pistol, and fled. Mrs Douglass died almost immediately as a result of the gunshot wound; Reverend Douglass's death was caused by a combination of the gunshots he received and strangulation from the manner in which he was bound. Leslie and Brooks managed to untie themselves and to drive to the home of a nearby doctor. Ake and his accomplice were apprehended in Colorado following a month-long crime spree that took them through Arkansas, Louisiana, Texas, and other states in the western half of the United States.[32]

Why such a contrast between the two opinions? Justice Marshall concluded that Ake's rights had been violated and that his conviction should be reversed. Straying into the facts of the crime itself would only have detracted from the rhetorical inevitability of that holding.[33] Justice Rehnquist, on the other hand, thought that Ake was a faker (he later pointed to evidence in the record in which Ake told a cellmate that he was going to 'play crazy'), so he wanted to paint Ake as acting with conscious deliberation (look back at the verbs he selected) as he went about his heinous acts – that is, he may have been Satanic, but he was sane. We can't go further here (we don't have enough evidence before us), but we can see that Justice Marshall needed to shunt the multiple-murder-attempted-rape-of-a-twelve-year-old story to the side to stake his claim to authority and that Justice Rehnquist needed to do just the opposite.

Getting now to the second of our two points, a casebook editor or treatise author further eliminates content, generally to draw attention to a particular doctrinal aspect of a case. And because an editor or author selects cases because he or she believes that each of them well illustrates a rule, the development of a rule, or the application of a rule, each case is edited (or summarized) and slotted in a casebook or treatise according to the editor or author's overall organizational rubric. If context adds meaning – and I think it indisputably does – then *where* an opinion is placed in a casebook/treatise adds an important dimension to the opinion. Here's an illustration: I have just pulled five antitrust books from my bookshelf, one that I use in the course I teach at Southern Methodist University from time to time,[34] one from a practitioners' seminar I took about ten years ago,[35] a couple of others that publishers have sent me for review,[36] and a hornbook (i.e., a one-volume treatise) that I often consult when I'm just starting to work though an antitrust issue.[37] I have searched through each to see what the editors have done with one of the most-cited cases in all of private antitrust litigation, *Brunswick Corp. v. Pueblo Bowl-O-Mat, Inc.*[38] The case is important because it limits the category of private plaintiffs entitled to sue under the federal antitrust laws to those who can show '*antitrust injury*,' a concept that has proven slippery in subsequent attempts at application.[39] Andersen and Rogers edit the case down to a bit more than five pages (including eight of the opinion's original footnotes) and place it as the first case in a section titled 'Private Enforcement.' That placement makes sense, given – as I already mentioned – that the case is more important in the civil litigation context than in others (such as criminal enforcement). Morgan slims the case down by another page (largely by eliminating all but two footnotes) and lodges it at the end of the first subsection ('The Transition Cases') in a chapter focusing on developments since 1975. Morgan emphasizes history over practical application in his casebook, so he has selected *Brunswick* as one of several examples of the modern Supreme Court's application of economic analysis to antitrust problems, as well as to show how the Court began to change (most often by limiting) the field of operation of the federal antitrust laws, a process that continues to this day.[40] In short, he locates the case within a historical narrative and uses it as an element of his retelling of that narrative. The other two casebooks, Areeda/Kaplow and Goetz/McChesney, do not reprint *Brunswick* at all, though Areeda and Kaplow do include a summary of the case (including a quotation of the sentence for which *Brunswick* is most often cited) in a subsection titled 'Antitrust Injury,' and Goetz and McChesney reprint cases that cite to *Brunswick*. Sullivan and Grimes's hornbook, which has the purpose of more directly stating antitrust standards than would a casebook, cites the case several times and summarizes it, as expected, in a subsection dealing with antitrust injury.

What do these various approaches tell us? At the one extreme, Goetz and McChesney imply that *Brunswick* itself is less important than more recent cases that cite it. In some ways, though, this is like reading the last chapter in Dworkin's chain novel without reading the first chapter. Granted, a casebook or treatise cannot include all – or even many – cases in a series, but it seems to me that foundational cases that have led to splintered or confused subsequent authority are worth direct analysis. One step up the ladder are Areeda and Kaplow's and Sullivan and Grimes's brief summaries of *Brunswick*, which reduce the case to a rule supported by a few sentences of factual recitation and commentary. If there is a teleology to casebook and treatise construction, the Areeda/ Kaplow and Sullivan/Grimes approaches to *Brunswick* neatly illustrate it: important cases can be boiled down to an essence. This may often be true, but it presents a very narrow, rule-focused view of the law.

The other two antitrust casebooks we have been discussing attempt to avoid the rule-based trap by placing *Brunswick* in a larger context. I must admit that the practitioner in me favours the Andersen and Rogers approach because it underscores the foundational importance of the case to civil litigation. But ultimately, this is to locate *Brunswick* and the rule it enunciates within a larger set of rules (the rules – principally Section 4 of the Clayton Act – conferring a private right of action on certain persons injured by reason of a violation of the antitrust laws). Morgan, on the other hand, places the case in a historical context, one that reveals an underlying shift in one of the United States' most central public narratives: the story of Big Business. In our discussion of *The Jungle* we saw how that public narrative had tipped in a decidedly populist direction. The Sherman Antitrust Act was a product of that narrative (and the era that gave it birth) no less than the Meat Inspection Act. And its enforcement for the next several decades reflected those origins: many common business practices were considered *per se* illegal, no matter their actual impact on consumer welfare.

In the post–Second World War period, the populist, anti-business narrative waned, and by the 1970s – as Morgan points out – the United States Supreme Court was increasingly directing lower courts and enforcement agencies to consider the 'reasonableness' of practices that had theretofore been deemed unworthy of analysis beyond proof that the alleged conduct had in fact occurred. The reasons for this are complicated and subject to ongoing dispute, but there is no doubt that the Court changed direction and that that change could be marked over the course of the 1960s and 1970s.[41] For our purposes, it is enough to note that this narrative revision happened and that Morgan identifies it, thus signalling a possible way of reinvigorating the tools we use to study and practise law. What I'm thinking of here are the dimensions that a narrative approach to legal materials might offer. What if – in addition to the public-narrative framework that Morgan employs – we were encouraged to examine the personal narratives that gave rise to particular disputes in the first place? Such an approach, it seems to me, would remind students, judges, and practitioners of how a number of rules are formed and provide a corrective to the greatest shortcoming of appellate opinions: viz., their inherent narrowness of scope, a subject that we must look at more closely.

## The Problem with Appellate Practice and Appellate Opinions

Lawyers become so accustomed to reading appellate opinions for rules that it's easy for them to forget how tightly those opinions are cast – for example, they have a limited purpose, are subject to powerful generic constraints, and are built on a rhetoric of justification, not description. First, and in some ways most important, appeals are based on particularized points of asserted error in the proceedings below. At the level of the United States Supreme Court, then, it is most unusual for the Court to consider more than one or two closely framed issues, and those are selected because of their general importance, not because of their impact on the actual litigants before the Court. These limitations are not a matter of speculation or practitioners' folklore; they are institutionalized in the Court's rules. For example, Rule 10, which sets forth the considerations governing review on a writ of *certiorari*, specifically states that only extraordinary cases are subject to review, typically cases that involve conflicting decisions among United States courts of appeals or between those courts and state courts of last resort on an 'important matter.' This means that 'a petition for a writ of certiorari is rarely granted when the asserted error consists of erroneous factual findings or the misapplication of a properly stated rule of law.'[42]

This rule ensures that only a certain type of case is heard; another rule ensures that the case is narrowly presented in a way that suppresses the matter's narrative aspects. Rule 14, which mandates the content (and thereby the non-content) of a petition for a writ of *certiorari*, reveals a decidedly anti-narrative bias, one focused on carefully compassed legal questions. It essentially directs that all appellants use a one-size-fits-all formula:

- The questions presented for review [must be] expressed concisely in relation to the circumstances of the case, without unnecessary detail. The questions should be short and should not be argumentative or repetitive. The questions shall be set out on the first page following the cover, and no other information may appear on that page.
- A concise statement of the case set[s] out the facts material to consideration of the questions presented.
- A direct and concise argument amplif[ies] the reasons relied on for allowance of the writ.
- A petition for a writ of certiorari should be stated briefly and in plain terms.
- The failure of a petitioner to present with accuracy, brevity, and clarity whatever is essential to ready and adequate understanding of the points requiring consideration is sufficient reason for the Court to deny a petition.[43]

This emphasis on concision, directness, and brevity has certain consequences, the most important being that from the very outset, a Supreme Court appeal will have a tightly circumscribed, rule-focused ambit. It should come as no surprise, then, that most appellate opinions mirror the petitions, of which they are mere culminations.

Robert Ferguson has identified a number of generic characteristics in appellate opinions: a monologic voice, an interrogative mode, a declarative tone, all of which cohere in what he calls a 'rhetoric of inevitability.'[44] As Ferguson correctly notes, the question a court chooses to answer – and the way it chooses to frame that question – is so fundamental as to make that process 'the methodological anchor of judicial rhetoric.'[45] Not surprisingly, therefore, appellate counsel devote much energy to hitting just the right notes in the version of the question presented that they will sponsor because 'they understand what an earlier member of the profession, Francis Bacon, observed four centuries ago: the questions we ask shape our knowledge far more than do the theories we propose.'[46] In practice, this means that every stroke of the oar – from start to finish in the appellate process – is aimed at guiding the court to a 'correct' statement of a question (or a few questions).

By emphasizing the generic importance of questions presented in appellate opinions, I do not mean to deny that those opinions have a narrative dimension. They do. But it is a type of narrative quite different from the complex of narratives that makes up the case prior to its arrival at the appellate court. The appellate narrative is, as Ferguson explains it, driven by a declarative tone, one designed at once to simplify and to convey certitude:

> The courtroom, as forum, takes the complexity of event – the original disruption that provokes legal action in the first place – and transfers aspects of that complexity into a narrative, the written form of which is a literal transcript of what has been said in court. The judicial opinion then appropriates, molds and condenses that transcript in a far more cohesive narrative of judgment, one that gives the possibility of final interpretation by turning original event into a legal incident for judgment. Judgment, in turn, guides a general cultural understanding of the original event for consumption beyond the courtroom … Every step of the process requires an unavoidable series of simplifications. Judgment must reduce event to an incident, and further reduce incident to a narrative about acceptable behavior. This is its mission. Everything about the enterprise, including the listener-reader of the judicial opinion, welcomes the declarative tones that make it possible.[47]

This is, I think, just another aspect of what we have earlier discussed as the process by which particulars can become universals and of how ontological narratives can become strands in a higher-order narrative fabric. We have seen that this process of narrative distillation is effective at *making* rules, but that it impedes the process of *understanding* rules because it necessarily obscures their narrative roots. And the editing of opinions for inclusion in casebooks and treatises thickens the cloak that is always already wrapped about an appellate opinion. Is there a solvent that will help strip away this cloak?

## (Re)Introducing Narratives across the Profession

I think there is: more exposure to the narratives large and small that underlie case opinions. I am not suggesting the displacement of all rule-based teaching, judging, and lawyering in favour of an ad hoc approach to legal questions; rather, I am advocating the greater use of narrative material across the spectrum so that all participants will have another set of tools with which to evaluate and criticize legal propositions. This process must begin in the classroom and can perhaps most easily be deployed as a strategy in the context of scholarship, but in cases of extraordinary moment and complexity – cases that, therefore, warrant a commensurate expenditure of resources – both advocates and judges could find the technique both practical and illuminating.[48] If, as we have previously seen, the original justification for common law rules usually follows the rubric of the normative/narrative syllogism, then in any given case, it would be helpful to know what narrative elements figured (or did not figure) in the formulation of the premises that led to the conclusion. Armed with that information, a reader has an important critical tool with which to evaluate the original legitimacy or the continuing vitality of precedent. As the leading report on legal education puts it, 'awareness of narrative and context bring[s] … principles alive while also giving conceptual nuance to their meaning.'[49]

A couple of examples may help us here. First, there are the relatively easy situations in which certain lines of cases are tainted because of corruption. We earlier looked at the Oklahoma Supreme Court scandal and how opinions authored by Justice Corn are generally viewed as suspect by Oklahoma practitioners. But relatively few readers outside Oklahoma know that, and the opinions still appear right there in the *Pacific Reporter*, waiting for the unwitting to read and rely on them.[50] They bear no evident mark of the bribes that may have influenced any one of them. In fact, most of them seem reasonable, and an impartial, uncorrupted judge may very well have decided them the same way. But they are nonetheless illegitimate, and we can only know that through narratives existing outside the opinions themselves.

More troublesome are opinions that are driven by bias yet manage to mask the fact with an admixture of authoritative tone and high-sounding rhetorical devices.[51] This is to say that not all biased decisions proudly announce themselves as such in the transparent manner of *Plessy*, *Muller*, or *Bowers*. Hoeflich neatly illustrates this in a discussion of a case, *Taft v. Hyatt*,[52] that is often cited for a basic contract principle and sometimes anthologized or summarized in casebooks and treatises.[53] I first offer my own summary of the case, followed by Hoeflich's conclusions based on his reading of it, followed in turn by some of my own observations that will leave us suspended in a state of indeterminacy that is nonetheless instructive. The case was essentially an interpleader action in which members of a group that had offered a reward for apprehension of a criminal pled (i.e., paid) money into a court so that rival claimants could set up their respective claims to the reward. One of the three claimants had prevailed in the trial court, as we will soon see.[54] The background facts are these: on 16 May 1917, residents of a small southeastern Kansas town, Parsons, learned that Agnes Smith – the wife of a local physician, Dr Asa Smith – had been assaulted (she later died). Another physician, Dr Robert Smith, was suspected of the crime; he soon went into hiding. All three of the Smiths were African Americans. At some point before the afternoon of 17 May, a local group that Hoeflich identifies as the Anti-Horse Thief Association (referred to as A.H.T.A. in the opinion) offered and publicized a $750 reward for the arrest or information leading to the arrest of Robert Smith. Dr Asa Smith was a member of this group.

During the afternoon of 17 May, William Hyatt, a Parsons attorney, learned that Robert Smith wanted to meet with him. Hyatt went to Smith's hideout, where 'the two talked together for an hour or more, but were unable to reach an agreement as to the employment of Hyatt to defend Smith.'[55] Before this meeting, Hyatt knew of the reward. In what may be a recurring lawyer fantasy (unacted upon, one would hope), in the face of a potential client unwilling to put up a retainer, Hyatt returned from the meeting and immediately told the county attorney where Smith was hiding. He even accompanied the deputy sheriff on the mission to arrest Smith. But in the meantime, Smith had been spirited away to nearby Oswego, Kansas, by a group of five members of the Lodge of Colored Masons and Thomas Murry, the chief of police of Parsons, all of whom considered Smith's fears of mob violence well founded. Before the party left for Oswego, where Smith was ultimately placed in the custody of the Labette County sheriff, Murry placed Smith under arrest. At the time of that arrest, Murry knew of the reward; the rest of the group did not. Hyatt, Murry, and the five members of the Colored Masons all claimed that the reward was theirs.

At trial, Hyatt prevailed. The other claimants appealed that judgment. The Kansas Supreme Court took each of the rivalling claims in turn and found them all wanting. Hyatt, the Court held, was not eligible to receive the reward because his actions (even setting aside his unconscionable use of prospective client information for his own pecuniary gain) did not lead to the arrest of Smith. It surely could have – had Smith remained at their meeting place – but it did not:

> The court finds that the information Hyatt gave would lead to the arrest of the guilty person if it had been acted upon promptly, and the fact that it did not bring about this result was through no fault of Hyatt's. But this finding does not help Hyatt's case. It may have been that the officers to whom he confided his information were too slow. Whatever the reason, before any action was taken by them which resulted in apprehending the accused, the latter was on his way to the county jail in the custody of another officer, having, with the aid of his friends, surrendered himself. So far as the apprehension of the guilty person was concerned, Hyatt might as well have kept his information to himself.[56]

Murry's actions, on the contrary, actually did lead to Smith's arrest – he in fact arrested him. But the Court acknowledged and relied on well-settled law that a police officer may not 'claim a reward for merely doing his duty':

> Murry cannot recover, because, as chief of police of the city of Parsons, it was his duty to make an arrest of fugitives from justice or persons charged with or suspected of crimes. The fact that he was not armed with a warrant or other process for the arrest of the accused is immaterial, because there was reasonable ground for believing that Smith had committed the particular offense charged against him, and his subsequent conviction established his actual guilt.[57]

That leaves the collective claim of the members of the Colored Masons. It is this claim that led to the establishment of the rule for which the case is most often cited.[58] The critical facts for the Court were that this group of claimants 'had not heard of the offer of the reward until after the accused had been surrendered to the sheriff' and that they acted out of a desire to protect Smith from mob violence, not to bring him to justice.[59] These facts, coupled with the legal holding that the private (as opposed to a statutory) offer of a reward should be analysed under contract principles, stymied the group's attempt to secure the reward:

> A private offer of reward for the apprehension of a fugitive from justice or of a person suspected or charged with an offense stands, as a general rule, upon a different footing from a statutory offer, or one made by virtue of a statute. The offer of a private individual is a mere proposal, which, when accepted, becomes a contract. Until it is accepted by some person who upon the strength of the offer takes some steps to earn the reward, there is no contract. *Van Vlissingen v. Manning*, 105 Ill. App. 255. There must be a meeting of the minds of the parties – on the one side, of the person who makes the offer; on the other, of the person who performs the service. Where a claimant for the reward was not aware that it had been offered until after he had performed his services, there has been no meeting of minds which would constitute a contract. Besides, the undisputed facts with respect to those defendants who called the chief of police to assist them in taking the accused to Oswego are that these claimants were simply assisting the accused in surrendering himself. Their testimony is that what they did was for the purpose of protecting him from mob violence. They had never heard of the reward, and, of course, are not entitled to any part of it.[60]

This holding, as Hoeflich notes, was not compelled in any legal sense.[61] The issue presented was one of first impression in Kansas, as the Court's citation to a single out-of-state opinion reveals. From this, Hoeflich begins to wonder whether there was something else afoot, so he digs deeper. The opinion itself tells us that Hyatt and Smith were 'unable to reach an agreement as to the employment of Hyatt to defend Smith,' and at least part of the reason was because 'they did not agree upon the fee to be paid for the defense.'[62] Hoeflich's investigation of the appellate record shows that at trial only the members of the Colored Masons were asked *why* they wanted the reward. One claimant's response (as abstracted in the record) is particularly telling: 'Witness testified that he was a friend of Dr. Smith; that he was interested in seeing that mob violence was not resorted to; *that he did not obligate himself or pay anything towards the defense of Smith.*'[63] In other words, the group wanted the reward to pay for Smith's defence.

Because these questions have no relevance to the issue of knowledge of the reward, Hoeflich is compelled to ask *why* they were asked. Could it have something to do with the setting and circumstances – that is, a black man accused of murder in small Kansas town that was already on the verge of forming a lynch mob? Did the townsfolk want to prevent Smith from mounting an adequate defence through the use of the reward money? Could this have influenced the outcome at trial and, perhaps, on appeal? It is of course impossible to answer these questions with certainty. I am inclined to think that the appellate court would not have been directly swayed by a desire to withhold the reward money to keep Smith from using it for his defence, for this simple reason: Smith had by that time been convicted and that conviction had already been affirmed.[64] On the other hand, there are good reasons to think that the Supreme Court may have been indirectly influenced, if only because of the institutional tendency to show deference to trial court decisions. And – based on my further investigation of the underlying murder case – there are even better reasons to think that the trial court may have been swept along by the racial undercurrents that Hoeflich senses in *Taft v. Hyatt*.

In *Taft*, the murder of Agnes Smith was reduced to the passing reference that she had been 'assaulted' and then, in a parenthetical aside, to the fact that she had died and that Robert Smith had been charged and convicted of her murder.[65] But this was no ordinary murder. The narrative has plot elements straight out of Greek tragedy and is reminiscent of modern Greek-influenced dramas like Eugene O'Neill's *Desire Under the Elms*. The list of major dramatis personae might read something like this:

Dr. Asa Smith: A black physician; once widowed; now over 60.
Robert Smith: Also a black physician; now 33; employed by Asa Smith since he was 13.
Agnes Smith: Wife of Asa Smith for one year; lived with the first Mrs Smith prior to her death; partially educated by Asa; now 24.[66]

The respective ages of the players suggest a couple of familiar plotlines, one of which is borne out by the facts of the case. At trial, Smith was convicted largely on the strength of Mrs Smith's 'dying statement,' a large portion of which was read to the jury as an exception to the general rule against hearsay:

I know that I am about to die and this is my statement in the fear of death. Bob Smith came in at about 11 o'clock A. M., May 16th and says, 'Why·

don't you treat me better – why have you got it in for me?' I picked up some scissors, off the table, and he started for me and he took them away from me and seized me by the throat and choked me and threw me on the floor. He choked me and poured something in my mouth and face and ran out, and I got up and got to Mrs. Neighbors' and lost consciousness.'[67]

From the testimony of one of the attending physicians, we learn what the 'something' was that led to her particularly gruesome and drawn out death (she survived for about a week):

Agnes Smith was found to be burned with carbolic acid. Dr. Boardman testified that: 'The odor was very strong. The acid was up in her hair, over her face, and down on her upper chest. The acid was upon her cheeks, around the back of her neck, and around her ears. Her eyes were entirely burned. One had turned entirely white. *** She was unconscious.'[68]

On appeal, Smith's most significant claim of error was that Agnes Smith's dying declaration should not have been received into evidence. For reasons that are unimportant to our discussion, the Court concluded that the statement was proper evidence. More telling, perhaps, was the Court's quotation of the portion of the statement that was *not* read to the jury: 'I told him to get out of the house, and *** *I feared he would rape me.*'[69] Since this excised portion of Agnes Smith's statement was not directly at issue in the appeal, it seems to me that it may signal the crux of the matter for the Supreme Court. If we recall that the dominant racial narrative in predominantly white interpretive communities in the *late* twentieth century portrayed young black males as feral and threatening to civil society (think of the King beating case), then so much the more so would this have been true in the *early* twentieth century. In other words, the Supreme Court may well have concluded that Smith was just another out-of-control black man unable to control his appetites, despite overwhelming evidence of his good character and at least something more than a mere suggestion that Agnes Smith was suicidal. In other words, a murder and attempted rape could have seemed the only coherent narrative available to the all-white, all-male Kansas Supreme Court of a hundred years ago. I may be overreading a bit, but I hear an echo of that in the Court's last substantive paragraph: 'The record leads to the inevitable conviction that the cruel and atrocious crime charged was committed, and *whatever influences actuated him, or whatever their source*, the defendant was legally found guilty.'[70]

At a minimum, all of this buttresses Hoeflich's suspicion that race may have played some part in *Taft v. Hyatt*. It does not mean that the Supreme Court strained to deprive the Colored Masons of the reward for racist reasons. Perhaps nothing was amiss at all. But perhaps there was a desire to keep solidarity with the decisions of the trial court below and with the Court's own holdings only a year before in *State v. Smith*. The point is, though, that one cannot even have this type of discussion – cannot engage in critical reading – without going outside the four corners of an appellate opinion. *A fortiori*, one cannot have this type of discussion when salient facts have been bobbed from a casebook/treatise version or, even more to the point, when the facts have been sanitized so as to present an intentionally unparticularized statement of the case, presumably to minimize distraction from the statement of universalized doctrine. Take, for example, the version of *Taft v. Hyatt* that appeared in Lon Fuller and Melvin Eisenberg's contracts casebook:

> Smith, a member of a masonic lodge, was suspected of a murder which had aroused the indignation of the community. Smith conveyed his fears of mob violence to certain of his masonic brothers and asked their protection. They accompanied a police officer to his hiding place and in the company of the officer took Smith to the sheriff, who placed him in the county jail. Just before the party got into the cab to go to the sheriff's office, Smith was told by the officers that he was under arrest. The masons now claim a reward of $750 which had been offered by the husband of the murdered woman 'for the arrest or information which will lead to the arrest' of Smith. Held, they were not entitled because (1) they did not know of the offer until after Smith was arrested, and (2) they merely assisted Smith in surrendering himself and therefore did not arrest him or give information leading to his arrest within the meaning of the offer.[71]

Every hint of race is erased from this summary, making it impossible to ask the questions about the case that we just asked.[72] In fairness, casebook editors and hornbook authors have to make choices, and not every case can be presented in an extensive form. And lawyers need fingertip reference materials to get them started in the analysis of legal problems. By the same token, law students need a handy resource from which to learn the valuable lawyerly skill of extracting legal rules from cases and then manipulating them. I nonetheless think that those who write and speak about law (including in/on general audience forums like newspapers and television) can use narrative background materials to create more nuanced portraits of the cases they discuss, which, in turn, will give their audiences a better sense of how cases are decided and how rules are made. Similarly, law students can sharpen their critical reading skills and, thereby, their analytical writing skills by learning to dig into cases from time to time.[73] Now is a perfect time to add narrative tools to our critical arsenals, because it has never been easier to accomplish. As most courts have migrated to electronic filing, all manner of case materials have become readily available for review and analysis. It has therefore become a much simpler matter to go behind published opinions and find the raw stuff upon which they are based, including pleadings, briefs, documentary evidence, and testimony. The value of the reading-for-narratives approach that I am advocating can be expressed in a number of ways, but none is more important, I think, than the possibility of revealing the narratives that competed for victory, universalization, and institutionalization in any particular case. In that way, all citizens can more fully understand that litigation is often no more than a competition to convince *this* judge, *this* jury, and a majority of *this* appellate panel that one story or another deserves favourable judgment. But it may be that in another time and place, that story is no longer convincing. In short, as Robert Ferguson suggests (following Thoreau), we must carefully attend to what we read:

> 'Books,' writes Henry Thoreau, 'must be read as deliberately and reservedly as they were written.' The judicial opinion deserves the same injunction. Judges use words to secure shared explanations and identifications; they also use them as weapons of control. Deliberation with reservation explores that distinction, and the result is more than understanding. Here and elsewhere, a practiced appreciation or resourcefulness in language is the first safeguard in a republic of laws.[74]

## Democratic Education, Practical Reason, and the Law

What I have been arguing for here is, I suppose, a more thorough melding of black-letter law and theory in legal education, writing and practice.[75] But I don't think that the advantages of this type of approach would be limited to placing yet another argumentative arrow in the litigator's quiver. I think, rather, that Ferguson is exactly right to suggest that a 'readerly' approach to the law can help shore up the democratic values that the easy rhetoric of formalism and the rules that drive it so often obscure. Over twenty years ago, Neil MacCormick suggested that

there are six questions to which any serious approach to higher education ought to allow of some answer, preferably one reached after substantial reflection. In quick and summary form, the questions are: (1) What is
there? (2) What is the structure of the things there are, and how do different kinds of existence interrelate? (3) How do we know what there is, and
how do we have acquaintance with the things that exist[]? (4) By what
method should we explain and expound the various matters open to our
knowledge? What is the place of human beings as rational agents in relation to whatever else there is? and (6) In light of all this, how are we to live
and conduct ourselves?[76]

None of these questions is peculiar to law, but that is MacCormick's
point. For if one is truly to understand law, one must learn more than
the substance of a set of legal rules, rules that are always subject to
defeasance at the whim of a legislature or high court. This 'more than'
is not a single identifiable tactic but rather a range of skills that permit
one to evaluate laws critically in their social context. MacCormick's six
questions mark a path along which to gather these skills and, also, to
build the quality of intellect necessary to maintain the cornerstone role
that law-as-profession holds in a thriving democracy: 'The questions
are ones which ought to remain open and alive for every law teach-
er, law student and indeed legal practitioner of whatever rank and
eminence.'[77]

But this is not all. The structural importance of philosophical questions (by whatever name) is not limited to lawyering and legal education: MacCormick suggests that they are threaded through 'the
tradition of the Democratic Intellect.' How best, then, are we to analyse
and decide legal questions in a way that bolsters this tradition? As I
hope my discussions of *Taft v. Hyatt* and *Mutual Life Insurance v. Hillmon*
show, a contextual, historicist approach can help us 'rejudge' received
authoritative narratives. It seems to me that Llewellyn was correct to
observe that we can learn much 'from our friends across the alley, in the
work called History' because

they have learned, not merely as a matter of individual intuition but as
a moderately transmissible and moderately reliable craft-skill, to mark
off even in a private diary, like that of Pepys, passion or prejudice from
reporting, observation of a facet from observation of a whole, interpretation from accurate record of the event. They read letters or pronuncia-
mentos, speeches, or reports, with moderately effective corrections for the

twisting of facts by the nature and bias of the writer, by his sources of information, by his known or seeming purpose, and the like. They have learned to test and supplement one piece of evidence by another, and each single piece both by its immediate context, by its inherent probability in the circumstances, and by the shape, color, flavor of the great whole.[78]

Yet as we've seen, narrative context is just as important to the process of reasoning itself. And as Detmold suggests, this has deep civil (and I would argue democratic) implications: 'Law is for citizens before judges (judges are for citizens, not citizens for judges) and there is something very wrong in a theory which overlooks this.'[79] Detmold's point is that 'the fullness of law as practical reason is achieved when the law that judges apply is ... in a true sense the citizen's law; when law is common law.'[80] This requires a mutually corresponding relationship between system and citizen; that is, 'the fullness of practical reason *in law*, and its central case, is achieved only in so far as the legal system has (and recognizes that it has) serious citizens (those mature in the matter of law; those who have law as common law).' What, then, can we do to ensure that all citizens (not just lawyers) are 'mature' with respect to law?

Commentators from Dewey to Dworkin have argued that education is key to the development of a truly democratic society.[81] The emphasis of this commentary typically focuses somewhat narrowly on the *content* of secondary education or the general need for *access* to higher education. Dworkin, for instance, believes that many of the most important social issues of the day are so complicated that they are beyond the judgment of many ordinary voters, thus causing them to vote (if at all) for candidates based on religious affiliation or personal attractiveness. As an antidote, he suggests that the secondary curriculum be over-hauled to include 'courses that take up issues that are among the most contentious political controversies of the day.'[82] This aim – though laudable – is one likely difficult to achieve (as Dworkin readily concedes), so I want to set my sights somewhat lower and consider whether the narrative theory of law that we have developed offers opportunities to introduce reforms in education (in the most general and public sense) that could facilitate democratic ends without creating the political difficulties inherent in Dworkin's proposal.

If we think about the word *education*, and consider the fossilized metaphor within it – 'to lead' – we instantly see that the process is something at once broader and deeper than schoolhouse teaching and learning. To say this is not to deny a link between narrative theory and education (in fact, I've elsewhere argued that important reforms in *legal* education could be facilitated through application of narrative theory to law school pedagogy),[83] but I think that all legal actors – not just teachers – can help law do its democratic work by thinking, teaching, and writing about law in ways that foreground it as a key component in an overarching cultural narrative. What would this entail? I have no simple prescription, but I think we can start by reconsidering how we present law to people outside (or just entering) the profession.

It sometimes seems as if there are as many accounts of law as there are theorists to sponsor them: formalistic/scientific, realistic, autopoietic, positivist, pragmatic, feminist, CLS, institutional, post-colonial, and on and on. As I hope I have already sufficiently shown, narrative offers a partial (yet nonetheless significant) account of some aspects of legal systems and related democratic institutions. It is not a comprehensive normative theory of how judges, legislators, and other legal actors should conduct the business of the law. In this respect, I think the narrative theory as I have stated it bears some resemblance to the most current version of law and economic theory. When I say 'current,' I'm thinking foremost of Judge Posner's latest reflections on the subject; his thoughts are of special importance because he was an early and certainly the most visible proponent of economic legal analysis.[84] Plainly, Posner once hoped that economics held the interdisciplinary key that would unlock the secret to a perfectly functioning legal system (and explain the breakdowns in less than perfectly functioning legal systems). Thus, in 1975, he was able to opine that an

> important finding emerging from the recent law and economics research is that the legal system itself – its doctrines, procedures and institutions – has been strongly influenced by a concern (more often implicit than explicit) with promoting economic efficiency … The idea that the logic of the law is really economics is, of course, repulsive to many academic lawyers, who see in it an attempt by practitioners of an alien discipline to wrest their field from them. Yet the positive economic analysis of legal institutions is one of the most promising as well as most controversial branches of the new law and economics. It seeks to define and illuminate the basic character of the legal system, and it has made at least some progress toward that ambitious goal.[85]

More recently, however, Posner has retreated from the notion of an all-embracing theory of law formed by yoking the precepts of a unified normative system (like utilitarianism) to the teachings of economics: 'It has been many years since I flirted with such an approach.'[86]

But that does not mean that economics does not inform legal analysis in deep and significant ways. For good or ill, economic concepts have swamped all others in my primary practice area (antitrust). In most federal courts, an antitrust plaintiff cannot get out of the gate in most types of cases brought under the Sherman Act unless he can plead – in his initial complaint – that competition has been injured in a market defined in precise *economic* terms.[87] And this is so no matter how ruthlessly anticompetitive the conduct at issue is alleged to be. As a consequence, it is impossible to practise, teach, or write about antitrust law without having a solid working knowledge of economic concepts. Antitrust law thus illustrates one doctrinal corner (among many) of the law that has become inherently interdisciplinary as a matter of both practice and pedagogy. As Posner aptly observes, 'one by-product of [law and economics] research that has considerable pedagogical importance has been the assignment of precise economic explanations to a number of fundamental legal concepts that had previously puzzled students and their professors, such as "assumption of risk," "pain and suffering" as a category of tort damages, contract damages for loss of expectation, plea bargaining, and the choice between damages and injunctive relief.'[88]

What is important here is the way that economics has been seamlessly integrated into a wide range of judicial practices, legal commentary, and doctrinal law school courses, rather than being cabined solely in 'Law and Economics' seminars or specialized academic journals, as are so many supposed 'interdisciplinary' enterprises. It is this aspect that is worth exploring at some length in the context of our narrative theory. For instance, can narrative be used to explain – even challenge – legal concepts and rules in the same way that economics can? And, if so, can't this be done not just in law schools, but as well in undergraduate and secondary courses and even in popular media discussions of legal issues?

Robert Ferguson has spoken of the 'continuum of publication' that marks a trial, from things like pleadings (intended for lawyer consumption) to things like fictional projections (intended for public consumption).[89] I thus think it makes sense to compare the various narrative approaches deployed across such a continuum. As an example, let's take the case of *Silkwood v. Kerr-McGee*.[90] The case is important for a number of reasons (e.g., it continues to affect nuclear and environmental policy, as well as whistle-blower protection laws),[91] but I want to focus on just one: punitive damages. *Silkwood* was on the leading edge of what became the modern wave of huge punitive-damages awards, a subject that the United States Supreme Court has revisited with some regularity over the last twenty-five years. The issue is especially germane to our larger discussion because the reasoning process that a jury undertakes in deciding whether to award punitive damages is acknowledged – *in law* – as a 'discretionary *moral judgment*.'[92] It thus stands as a particularly robust example of something close to pure lay practical reasoning in a legal context. (Other reasoning by jurors, though lay, is coloured by the need to assess evidence in light of the rules of law embodied in jury instructions.)

In the Supreme Court opinion, Karen Silkwood plays a minor role. We learn only that she

> was a laboratory analyst for Kerr-McGee at its Cimarron plant near Crescent, Okla. The plant fabricated plutonium fuel pins for use as reactor fuel in nuclear powerplants ... During a 3-day period of November, 1974, Silkwood was contaminated by plutonium from the Cimarron plant. On November 5, Silkwood was grinding and polishing plutonium samples, utilizing glove boxes designed for that purpose. In accordance with established procedures, she checked her hands for contamination when she withdrew them from the glove box. When some contamination was detected, a more extensive check was performed ... She was immediately decontaminated, and at the end of her shift, the monitors detected no contamination ... The next day, Silkwood arrived at the plant and began doing paperwork in the laboratory. Upon leaving the laboratory, Silkwood monitored herself and again discovered surface contamination. Once again, she was decontaminated. On the third day, November 7, Silkwood was monitored upon her arrival at the plant. High levels of contamination were detected ... Suspecting that the contamination had spread to areas outside the plant, the company directed a decontamination squad to accompany Silkwood to her apartment ... The squad ... monitored the apartment, finding contamination in several rooms, with especially high levels in the bathroom, the kitchen, and Silkwood's bedroom. Silkwood ... was sent to the Los Alamos Scientific Laboratory to determine the extent of contamination in her vital body organs. She returned to work on November 13. That night, she was killed in an unrelated automobile accident.[93]

Silkwood's personal narrative is thus reduced to these few lines and then silted over with page upon page of the history of and intent behind the Atomic Energy Act of 1954 and its subsequent amendments, all to show whether or to what extent federal law pre-empted the basis of the punitive damages awarded to Silkwood's estate.

So why did an Oklahoma City jury whack Kerr-McGee with the then astonishing sum of $10,000,000 in punitive damages (on top of $500,000 in personal injury damages)? After all, Silkwood could not have suffered for long, given that she died – in an 'unrelated' automobile accident – within a month of her exposure to plutonium.[94] It's impossible to say exactly what actuated the trial judge and jury in the case, but we know that Silkwood's story is much more complicated than the Supreme Court makes it out to be.[95] From the trial court's post-trial opinion we learn a few more details about Silkwood, including that the evidence presented

> a Kafka-like picture of a young woman who was contaminated by an originally unknown amount of plutonium that was inexplicably found in her apartment. She was fearful of a slow death from cancer, became hysterical at times, and approached a nervous breakdown as she became the focus of federal agency and industry investigation into the incident. Because of the uniqueness of her injury, she was compelled to place herself for medical care in the custody of those whom she distrusted.[96]

We also learn that Kerr-McGee defended the case principally on legal grounds, which included federal pre-emption and the exclusive remedies of Oklahoma's workers' compensation scheme. But, alternatively, Kerr-McGee put forth arguments and evidence designed to show that Silkwood had contaminated herself, though Silkwood's motives for such an act remain mostly unexplained in the opinion. One of the Tenth Circuit's opinions states, however, that there was 'evidence that Silkwood was unhappy with a reprimand she had received shortly before her November 5 contamination and that she wanted to embarrass Kerr-McGee.'[97] For more on this point, we need to look outside the judicial opinions, though we don't need to go outside the case record, which has been amply dissected by many others, including investigative journalist Richard Rashke.[98]

Flamboyant trial lawyer Gerry Spence – best known these days as a basso-voiced television legal pundit and for his fringed leather jacket and huge, decorated cowboy hat (both of which were part of his get-up for the *Silkwood* trial) – led the Silkwood estate's trial team. William 'Bill' Paul, a courtly Oklahoma City trial attorney and later president of the American Bar Association, led Kerr-McGee's defence. The trial lasted ten weeks, longer than any trial in Oklahoma history. By all accounts, the trial was hard (even bitterly) fought, with each side by turns attempting to direct and then redirect the in-court reconstruction of Karen Silkwood's personal narrative through introduction of evidence not directly relevant to the ultimate issue of the trial (i.e., whether Kerr-McGee was negligent in its handling of plutonium). For its part, the company sought to impugn Silkwood's character through introduction of 'evidence on numerous matters regarding Silkwood's sexual involvements, use of drugs, and purported suicide attempts.'[99] The trial court largely stymied this effort, though, by excluding the evidence. The Silkwood lawyers took a tack that proved more successful. They introduced evidence that Silkwood was an effective union agitator and worker safety whistle-blower, thus sowing the seed that the company had reason to dislike her (though it requires a significant leap to conclude that this dislike then translated into the affirmative acts of contaminating her with plutonium and planting it in her apartment).

But perhaps the most damaging aspect of the case may have been the circumstances surrounding Silkwood's death. In its instructions to the jury, the court specifically admonished its members: 'You are not to consider her death in awarding damages in this action.'[100] Why was that necessary? Part of the answer may be that Spence had effectively introduced testimony suggesting that Silkwood had obtained documents showing that Kerr-McGee had falsified records and that she was on her way to turn over documentary proof of that fact to a union official and a reporter from the *New York Times* at the time of her fatal car crash.[101] From this testimony, could the jury have inferred that Kerr-McGee had some hand in Silkwood's death and punished it accordingly? We can't say with certainty, but we *can* say that the Supreme Court's categorical statement that the car crash was 'unrelated' is an assertion, not a fact that was proven to an appropriate evidentiary standard. It may well have been (and probably was), but the matter is not as unequivocal – especially from the jury's perspective – as the Supreme Court would have us think. We know this because we know that in deciding 'what happened' in a case, jurors go beyond testimony from the witness stand – they also develop narratives about what '*could* have happened.'[102]

Here, the jury was left with essentially two options: to build the facts surrounding Silkwood's death into its narrative of corporate malfeasance, or to disregard them as a mere coincidence. One reason that it might have been difficult simply to disregard these facts was that 'there was evidence that Kerr-McGee's supervisory employees knew Silkwood was attempting to gather evidence of Kerr-McGee's negligent and improper practices in the operation of the plant and that some disapproved of her and these activities.'[103] But more important, writing Silkwood's death off as an extraneous 'coincidence' runs counter to our human impulse to create all-encompassing narratives.[104] Once the trial judge allowed the jury to hear testimony that Silkwood was on her way to meet a *New York Times* reporter to turn over damning evidence of wrongdoing, he made it possible for (and in some sense compelled) the jury to fold those facts into a narrative that would support its 'moral judgment' as to whether Kerr-McGee should be punished.

We can take at least two things away from this. First, I think a case like *Silkwood* offers an 'educational' opportunity to explore the intersection of legal and moral reasoning in a way that doesn't carry with it the sorts of political ramifications inherent in Dworkin's proposal to open the secondary school system to vigorous debate on religiously loaded topics like abortion, intelligent design, or school prayer. Second, *Silkwood* reminds us of Ferguson's observation that some legal narratives escape their bottles and take different shapes as novels, plays, or films. In taking a more popular form, the legal narrative becomes democratized. *Silkwood* presents just such a case, having inspired much journalism, a motion picture, and a host of conspiracy theories. To help us understand what the *Silkwood* opinions have obscured and what might have concerned the jury members when they constructed a narrative of Karen Silkwood's life and death, it's useful to look at the closing lines of the film's screenplay, which takes the form of an interview of Silkwood's boyfriend, Drew Stephens, by two reporters:

DREW:  She had a union meeting that afternoon, and she'd bamboozled me into going out to the airport and meeting that reporter from the New York Times and the union guy, Paul Nathan. I took them over to the Holiday Inn, which was where the interview was supposed to be, and we waited for a while, and I started to notice Karen's late. Paul Nathan, he got the call. She'd hit the culvert on 74. A trucker found her. I talked to the towing people later, they said her arm was sticking out like a limb on a tree ...

What we did was to drive out to where they said the accident was. Paul and the reporter, they were all concerned with looking for her documents because they heard the cop had seen papers blowing around. But if there were any papers they were gone ... We went into town looking for the car, but they had it all locked up, we couldn't get into the garage, and I don't know who it was found out the police were saying she fell asleep at the wheel ...

She didn't fall asleep at any wheel. Her tire marks were absolutely straight on the shoulder on the wrong side of the road for almost 200 yards. Somebody tried to push her off the road, probably didn't even mean to kill her, but being Karen she had to try to stay on the road so she hit the culvert.

WOMAN REPORTER: Do you have a theory as to who killed her?

DREW: I don't know who killed her.

MAN REPORTER: Do you think we'll ever know who killed her?

DREW: No.[105]

We don't either, and we probably never will. But our curiosity is not satisfied. That's a good thing, though. For our curiosity drives us, in cases like *Silkwood*, to interrogate and look behind law's narratives and, in the process, to make them more complete and accessible. In this way, we make law's narratives democracy's narratives.

I'm not sure whether *Silkwood* was properly decided anywhere along the way or, if it was, which decision is correct. I do know, though, that Judge Doyle, dissenting from the majority's opinion in the last decision in the case, accurately describes the enduring cultural power that legal narratives can achieve:

Our brothers, Judges McKay and Logan, refuse to face the general nature of this case. They fail to recognize its total magnitude of the condition created by Kerr-McGee. There has not been a previous situation which brought into focus the tremendous power of the material. It is understandable that Kerr-McGee's reaction is one which clings to its effort to treat the condition as an ordinary result and which also turns away from the reality of this tragedy. The truth though is that the treatment of Silkwood shook the entire nation. Her suffering and death will not be soon forgotten.

The punitive damages are the sole reminders of her life and death. The evidence and the verdict serve to call attention to the danger from the misuse of the material and its tragic result. How can a new trial and a different verdict improve the present result? How can a different result serve to remind those who remain of the true symbol of the material and what it stands for?[106]

Where he's wrong, though, is in his belief that the cultural significance of Karen Silkwood's personal narrative turns on the affirmance or reversal of the jury verdict in her case. For by the time it reached him, Silkwood's story had already slipped its legal bonds to become a cultural artefact. And that artefact has crept back into the law in myriad ways[107] – and thereby rehumanized it.

In the end, the programmatic and structural issues I have sketched throughout this chapter with respect to legal reasoning, education, and practice are a specific application of a larger cultural critique. When Edward Said called for a 'democratic criticism' rooted in humanism, he was urging us to find ways of overcoming the burden of too much (yet too facilely packaged) information, on the one hand, and too much Balkanized (and jargon-laden) expertise, on the other:

> We are bombarded by prepackaged and reified representations of the world that usurp consciousness and preempt democratic critique, and it is to the overturning and dismantling of these alien objects that, as C. Wright Mills put so correctly, the intellectual humanist's work ought to be devoted ... Expertise as a distancing device has gotten out of control, especially in some academic forms of expression, to the extent that they have become antidemocratic and even anti-intellectual.[108]

The remedy lies, Said suggests, in forms of discourse that mandate reflection and that are built on what he calls 'detail,' a word he uses in much the same sense that I have used 'narrative' throughout this work. For lawyers, this means that each of us must work to read legal texts in ways that allow us to penetrate the omnipresent fog of rules and see the stories for which those rules are often more or less accurate shorthand and to write our own legal texts in ways that are both revealing and intelligible to non-specialists. All this is to say that we should teach, practise, and write about law democratically.

# A Conclusion of Sorts

The narrative dimensions of law are manifold. Disputes or crimes that are tried in court take the form of a story (or many stories). The ultimate disposition of a case quite often results in a written opinion that takes a narrative shape. And as we've seen, stories told to legal actors (be they legislators or judges) can actually become laws. That's not all, though, because the law exists and changes across time, which means that its history can be narrated, as in fact it is every time someone sets out to state what the law *is* on a particular subject. It's these recurring (and most often prosaic) narrative reconstructions – each executed in an ever-moving present and amidst a swirl of ephemeral public and personal narratives – that allow us a glimpse of the law's narrative genetic structure and, thereby, insight into how the law develops across cultures and over time.

In 'Tradition and the Individual Talent,' T.S. Eliot describes a relationship between the poet and the past that is a useful analogue to the relationships I have just noted.[1] He begins this essay by lamenting that 'in English we seldom speak of *tradition*,' a word that – when used at all – tends to appear only in a 'phrase of censure.'[2] The crux of his argument is that we all too readily embrace novelty (i.e., difference from predecessors, especially immediate predecessors) and are thereby blinded by prejudice. But 'if we approach a poet without this prejudice we shall often find that not only the best, but the most individual parts of his work may be those in which the dead poets, his ancestors, assert their immortality.'[3]

Eliot immediately cautions, though, that 'tradition' is much more than 'timid adherence' to the immediately preceding generation and its most obvious successes, which are often 'currents soon lost in the sand.' He has something else in mind:

> Tradition is a matter of much wider significance. It cannot be inherited, and if you want it you must obtain it by great labor. It involves, in the first place, the historical sense ...; and the historical sense involves a perception, not only of the pastness of the past, but of its presence ... This historical sense, which is a sense of the timeless as well as the temporal and of the timeless and the temporal together, is what makes a writer traditional. And it is at the same time what makes a writer most acutely conscious of his place in time, of his own contemporaneity.[4]

Thus conceived, Eliot's ideal writer is suspended in a ceaseless temporal oscillation between 'now' and 'then.' As a consequence, 'no poet, no artist of any art, has his complete meaning alone.' He becomes part of a fabric that he at once alters and is altered by: 'The necessity that he shall conform, that he shall cohere, is not one-sided; what happens when a new work of art is created is something that happens simultaneously to all the works of art which preceded it.' The properly attuned writer 'will not find it preposterous that the past should be altered by the present as much as the present is directed by the past' and, moreover, 'will be aware of great difficulties and responsibilities.'[5]

What Eliot ultimately develops here is a general theory of the relationship between past and present narratives, one suggesting that the narrative cosmos is neither an undifferentiated lump ('an indiscriminate bolus'), nor 'one or two private admirations,' nor 'one preferred period.' Instead, it is all these things, and more: viz., a main road that may change course from time to time but that does not superannuate the principal milestones along the route.[6] Pitched at this level, Eliot's critical theory may be seen as a general humanistic statement of what we have observed more particularly in aspects of Dworkin's concept of 'integrity' or MacCormick's suggestion of an ultimate convergence of narrative and normative coherence. For example, Dworkin argues that integrity 'insists that the law – the rights and duties that flow from past collective decisions and for that reason license or require coercion – contains not only the narrow explicit content of these decisions [read: the specific narratives embodied in those decisions] but also, more broadly, the scheme of principles necessary to justify them.' And 'scheme of principles' is but another name for a high-order narrative, one that Dworkin calls 'an overall story worth telling now.'[7]

Deciding what story to tell now is as much an act of judgment as of creation, and this fact holds as much for the literary writer as for the lawyer/judge. In considering the position of the poet, Eliot posits simultaneous cross-judgments between the past and present:

In a peculiar sense [the poet] will be aware … that he must inevitably be judged by the standards of the past. I say judged, not amputated, by them; not judged to be as good as, or worse or better than, the dead; and certainly not judged by the canons of dead critics. It is a judgment, a comparison, in which two things are measured by each other. To conform merely would be for the new work not really to conform at all; it would not be new, and would therefore not be a work of art. And we do not quite say that the new is more valuable because it fits in; but its fitting in is a test of its value – a test, it is true, which can only be slowly and cautiously applied, for we are none of us infallible judges of conformity.[8]

In urging this bilateral judgment based on 'fit,' Eliot sets forth a critical theory that subsumes quite well the theory of narrative and normative coherence that I have described and elaborated on throughout this work.[9] Indeed, the interpretive work of the poet and of Dworkin's common law judge largely coincide:

Law as integrity asks a judge deciding a common-law case … to think of himself as an author in the chain of common law. He knows that other judges have decided cases that, although not exactly like his case, deal with related problems; he must think of their decisions as part of a long story he must interpret and then continue, according to his own judgment of how to make the developing story as good as it can be … The judge's decision – his postinterpretive conclusions – must be drawn from an interpretation that both fits and justifies what has gone before, so far as that is possible. But in law as in literature the interplay between fit and justification is complex.[10]

Both Dworkin and Eliot understand that any narrative – be it legal or literary – exists on more than one plane: as part of a horizontal patchwork of all present narratives (some more generically related than others) and as part of a vertical column of generically related narratives stretching back through time. The trick for the present author, then, is to craft a narrative that fits in both dimensions. For example, a judge faced with an abortion case must craft a justificatory narrative that fits with *Roe*, *Casey*, and *Carhart and* with the current state of 'privacy' and other relevant laws. This process preserves continuity with the past while allowing for development in light of changing circumstances. The law is thus enslaved neither by its own past nor by fads of the day. As Eliot explains, 'the difference between the present and the past is that the conscious present is an awareness of the past in a way and to an extent which the past's awareness of itself cannot show.'[11] In sum, though the past cannot be relived, its history can be (and indeed must be continually) reworked.

Taking all this into account, we can say that a proper narrative theory of the law is one that balances past and present. This entails acceptance of authoritative standards of practice articulated and adhered to in the past, but 'that initial acceptance ... does not preclude subsequent critique of the practice.'[12] As a mode of argument, then, narrative 'suggests that the way law changes is through the advancement of stories or accounts of the practice that have an internal unity that captures the significant elements of the practice while pointing in a direction different from the current understanding of the enterprise.'[13] In this way, law – like literature – 'develops' (Eliot is careful to observe that change may be a 'refinement, perhaps, complication certainly' but not necessarily an 'improvement'). At the end of the day, development is, I suppose, an inevitable adjunct of the accumulation of institutional knowledge. But as Eliot posits, our newest knowledge merely teeters at the always already displaced mouth of a narrative stream stretching back to the time when humans first began to 'know' at all:

> Someone said: 'The dead writers are remote from us because we know so much more than they did.' Precisely, and they are that which we know.[14]

The same may be said of lawyers.

# Notes

## Introduction

1 Neil MacCormick, *Institutions of Law: An Essay in Legal Theory* (Oxford: Oxford University Press, 2007), 1.

## 1. Law and Narrative: Re-examining the Relationship

1 It seems to me that Richard Rorty is exactly right when he says that 'the rhetoric of scientific objectivity, pressed too hard and taken too seriously, has led us to people like B.F. Skinner on the one hand and like Althusser on the other – two equally pointless fantasies, both produced by the attempt to be "scientific" about our moral and political lives.' Richard Rorty, 'Solidarity or Objectivity?' in *From Modernism to Postmodernism*, ed. Lawrence Cahoone (Malden: Blackwell, 1996), 573 at 585. The human calculus is, I think, more complicated than a deterministic behaviourist's rat-in-a-box experiments or a structuralist Marxist's hypotheticals would suggest.

2 Charles Fried, 'Jurisprudential Responses to Legal Realism,' *Cornell Law Review* 73 (1987–8): 331 at 333–4.

3 See, for example, Richard Posner, 'Law and Literature: A Relation Reargued,' *Virginia Law Review* 72 (1986): 1351 at 1392.

4 *Id.*

5 Cf. David Howarth, 'Is Law a Humanity (or Is It More Like Engineering)?' *Arts and Humanities in Higher Education* 3 (2004): 9. Howarth argues that 'law is connected with the humanities, but it is no more connected by those means than any other creative or practical activity. Otherwise, law stands in relation to the Humanities and the Social Sciences as engineering does

to the Sciences … Law is a user of the Humanities and the Social Sciences, albeit sometimes a reluctant and covert user.' *Id.*, 23.

6  James Boyd White, 'The Judicial Opinion and the Poem,' reprinted in *Law and Literature*, ed. Lenora Ledwon (New York: Garland, 1996), 5 at 21.

7  *Id.*, 331.

8  Richard A. Posner, 'The Decline of Law as an Autonomous Discipline: 1962–1987,' *Harvard Law Review* 100 (1987): 761; see also Richard A. Posner, 'Conventionalism: The Key to Law as an Autonomous Discipline?' *Toronto Law Journal* 38 (1988): 333 (describing efforts to refurbish the idea that law is best left in the hands of those trained in law and only law as 'conventionalism,' and concluding that this conventionalism does not effectively compete with or refute contending interdisciplinary theories of law's nature and operation).

9  *Id.*, 762.

10  Brian H. Bix, 'Law as an Autonomous Discipline,' in *The Oxford Handbook of Legal Studies*, ed. Peter Cane and Mark Tushnet (New York: Oxford University Press, 2003), http://ssrn.com/abstract _id=315719 at 1.

11  Neil MacCormick, *Rhetoric and the Rule of Law: A Theory of Legal Reasoning* (Oxford: Oxford University Press, 2005), 14.

12  Percy Shelley, *A Declaration of Rights* (1812), http://terpconnect.umd.edu/~djb/shelley/declaration1880.html.

13  Paul H. Fry, *The Reach of Criticism: Method and Perception in Literary Theory* (New Haven: Yale University Press, 1983), 145.

14  *Id.*

15  White, 'The Judicial Opinion,' 21.

16  I should probably state what I have in mind when I apply the label 'humanities.' For present purposes, I propose that we think of the humanities as imaginative representations (I would include the descriptive and analytical under this umbrella) of the human condition. This roughly coincides with Nietzsche's definition of truth – that is, 'a mobile army of metaphors, metonyms, and anthromorphisms – in short a sum of human relations, which have been enhanced, transposed, and embellished poetically and rhetorically and which after long use seem firm, canonical, and obligatory to a people.' Rorty, 'Solidarity or Objectivity?' 584 (quoting Nietzsche). So conceived, the humanities are a storehouse of morals, values, and standards of right conduct across cultures and over time.

17  I offer autopoiesis as *an* example. Other theories of law's relative autonomy would serve to illustrate the point just as well. For instance, Kelsen's 'pure theory' and neoformalism are often cited for the proposition. See Bix, 'Law as an Autonomous Discipline,' 9.

18  Gunther Teubner, 'Introduction to Autopoietic Law,' in *Autopoietic Law: A New Approach to Law and Society*, ed. Gunther Teubner (New York: de Gruyter, 1988), 3; see also Niklas Luhmann, *Social Systems*, trans. John Bednarz, Jr, and Dirk Baecker (Stanford: Stanford University Press, 1995).

19  Zenon Bankowski, 'How Does It Feel to Be on Your Own? The Person in the Sight of Autopoiesis,' *Ratio Juris* 7 (1994): 254 at 256. See also Howarth, 'Is Law a Humanity?' 23 ('Law's central activity of making structures and devices out of legal rules has its own internal logic and standards, an activity that cannot be taught by reference to any other discipline, just as one cannot become an engineer merely by knowing mathematics and the relevant sciences').

20  Hugh Baxter, 'Autopoiesis and the "Relative Autonomy" of Law,' *Cardozo Law Review* 19 (1997–8): 1987 at 1992.

21  Though the humanities are not a system of the same order as, say, ecology or the economy, they exhibit a degree of self-reflexivity, structure, and generic constraint sufficient to qualify as a system for purposes of this discussion. Indeed, it is the systemic nature of literature that postmodernist writers like John Barth (who crafts a short story from a Möbius strip that endlessly loops, 'ONCE UPON A TIME THERE WAS A STORY THAT BEGAN ONCE UPON A TIME THERE WAS A STORY THAT BEGAN …') have parodied and pilloried. John Barth, 'Frame-Tale,' in *Lost in the Funhouse* (Garden City: Doubleday, 1968), 1–2.

22  William Witteveen advances this notion another step when he suggests that the language of law can be a tool for mediating between systems. William Witteveen, 'The Hidden Truth of Autopoiesis,' in *Law and Literature*, ed. Michael Freeman and Andrew D.E. Lewis (Oxford: Oxford University Press, 1999), 645 at 665.

23  Gunther Teubner makes this point, I think, in arguing that 'the law autonomously processes information, creates worlds of meaning, sets goals and purposes, produces reality constructions, and defines normative expectations – and all this quite apart from the world constructions in lawyers' minds.' Gunther Teubner, 'How the Law Thinks: Toward a Constructivist Epistemology of Law,' *Law and Society Review* 23 (1989): 727 at 739.

24  I intend the metaphor to capture not only the notion of changing one thing into another but also the fact that there is often a gap between the aims and ends of such a process.

25  See Michael H. Graham, *Evidence: Text, Rules, Illustrations, and Problems*, rev. 2nd ed. (Notre Dame: National Institute for Trial Advocacy, 1989), 567–8. Graham notes that certain questions (e.g., 'Tell us everything that was said that night?' or 'How did the accident happen?') are objectionable because

they call for a 'narrative' answer that may include irrelevant or hearsay matters. *Id.*, 567. Nonetheless, 'there is … some scientific indication that a spontaneous narration is more accurate, while interrogation by specific questions is said to present a more complete picture of the facts.' Ibid.; see also *Goings v. United States*, 377 F.2d 753, 762–3 (8th Cir. 1967) ('Ritualistic formality in presenting evidence should not deter untrained witnesses from telling their story in their own words. We hold here, it is only when evidence which is traditionally considered unworthy or unreliable, assumes the stature of undue significance that we must recognize error').

26 Albert Camus, *The Stranger*, trans. Matthew Ward (1942; New York: Vintage, 1989).

27 *Id.*, 3.

28 *Id.*, 8.

29 *Id.*, 10.

30 *Id.*, 38.

31 *Id.*, 55–6.

32 *Id.*, 58–9.

33 *Id.*, 64.

34 *Id.*, 65. This would appear to be a problem invariant across legal systems. What practising lawyer has not had a client seemingly determined to say exactly the wrong thing – or to say something in exactly the wrong tone – in his defence? I admit to my share.

35 *Id.*, 68–9.

36 To those reading with eyes trained under an 'adversarial' system, this type of testimony seems strange, erroneous even. But under a French-influenced system, a deep exploration of a defendant's individual background is both relevant and necessary: 'The first phase of a trial in the *Cour d'assises* reflects the French interest in the psychology and personal circumstances of the defendant and is called the "personality" (*personnalité*). The defendant's life history and personality are explored over the course of a day or two … The French do not share American concerns about character evidence and poisoning the well, reflected in the United States' elaborate rules of evidence.' Renée Lettow Lerner, 'The Intersection of Two Systems: An American on Trial for an American Murder in the French *Cour D'Assises*,' *University of Illinois Law Review* (2001): 791 at 822.

37 Camus, *The Stranger*, 94.

38 *Id.*, 99.

39 *Id.*, 107.

40 Ian Ward makes the more generalized, historicist point that 'if the most immediate context for literature is the writer's context, then there is much

to be gained from ascertaining precisely the cultural context that Camus perceived.' Ian Ward, *Law and Literature: Possibilities and Perspectives* (Cambridge: Cambridge University Press, 1995), 144.

41  See, for example, Posner, 'Law and Literature,' 1392ff.

42  Ben Jonson, 'Discoveries,' in *The Works of Ben Johnson*, ed. Francis Cunningham, vol. 3 (Chatto and Windus, 1903), 403 (emphasis added).

43  Upton Sinclair, *The Jungle* (1906; New York: Penguin, 1985).

44  *Id.*, 44.

45  *Id.*, 44–5.

46  *Id.*, 118–19.

47  *Id.*, 149–50.

48  *Id.*, 51.

49  *Id.*, 51–2.

50  *Id.*, 133.

51  *Id.*, 115.

52  *Id.*, 77–8.

53  *Id.*, 115–16.

54  *Id.*, 46.

55  *Id.*, 117–18.

56  *Id.*, 163.

57  Quoted in James Harvey Young, *Pure Food* (Princeton: Princeton University Press, 1989), 229.

58  With respect to the novel, see, for example, Ian Watt, *The Rise of the Novel: Studies in Defoe, Richardson, and Fielding* (Berkeley: University of California Press, 1957); with respect to the regulatory state, see, for example, Lisa Heinzerling and Mark V. Tushnet, *The Regulatory and Administrative State* (New York: Oxford University Press, 2006).

59  James Harvey Young, 'The Long Struggle for the 1906 Law,' *FDA Consumer* 1, June 1981, http://www.fda.gov/AboutFDA/WhatWeDo/History/CentennialofFDA/TheLongStrugglefortheLaw/default.htm.

60  Quoted in *id*.

61  *Id.*

62  Young, *Pure Food*, 229.

63  *Id.*

64  *Id.*

65  One of the most contentious items taken up in the House hearings involved the now infamous 'pig that fell into a privy': 'As an extreme example of the entire disregard on the part of employees of any notion of cleanliness in handling dressed meat, we saw a hog that had just been killed, cleaned and washed, and started on its way to the cooling room fall

from the sliding rail to a dirty wooden door and slide part way into a filthy men's privy. It was picked up by two employees, placed upon a truck, carried into the cooling room and hung up with other carcasses, no effort being made to clean it.' *Id.*, 242 (quoting *Conditions in the Stockyards*, 59th Cong. 1 sess., House Doc. 873).

66 *Id.*

67 *Id.*, 251 (quoting Senator Lodge's reference to 'a man who wrote a book').

68 *Id.*, 233 (quoting from Roosevelt's papers).

69 *Id.*, 235.

70 *Id.*, 235–46 (discussing, among other things, the Neill-Reynolds Report and the testimony of its two authors).

71 Interestingly, Roosevelt almost immediately sought to distance himself from Sinclair once his legislative agenda was achieved. The correspondence between Roosevelt and Sinclair shows that Roosevelt always saw Sinclair as a mixed blessing – a useful tool yet a constant irritant. Once the usefulness was past, only the irritant (mostly Sinclair's strident socialism, with which Roosevelt had little sympathy) remained. This explains the position that Roosevelt took in a letter to Kansas newspaper editor William Allen White: 'Thus in the beef packing business I found that Sinclair was of real use. I have an utter contempt for him. He is hysterical, unbalanced, and untruthful. Three-fourths of the things he said were absolute falsehoods. For some of the remainder there was only a basis of truth. Nevertheless, in this particular crisis he was of service to us, and yet I had to explain again and again to well-meaning people that I could not afford to disregard ugly things that had been found out simply because I did not like the man who had helped in finding them out.' *Id.*, 251 (quoting Theodore Roosevelt, *Theodore Roosevelt: An Autobiography* [New York: Scribner's, 1920], 443).

72 According to Wiley, *The Jungle* 'brought public opinion to the pitch of indignant excitement' at a time when 'President Roosevelt was eagerly in quest of a law supervising the packing of our animal food products.' Harvey W. Wiley, *The History of a Crime against the Food Law*, ch. 7 (Washington: Wiley, 1929), www.soilandhealth.org/03sov/ 0303critic/030305wylie/03 0305toc.html. Though Sinclair was initially disappointed that he had not ameliorated the overall plight of the workers, he later conceded with some pride that he had 'helped to clean up the yards and improve the country's meat supply.' Quoted in Young, *Pure Food*, 252.

73 See, for example, Young, 'The Long Struggle,' 1 (Sinclair's 'few pages describing filthy conditions in Chicago's packing plants, widely reported and confirmed by government inquiry, cut meat sales in half, angered President Roosevelt, and pushed a meat inspection bill aimed at protect-

ing the domestic market through the Congress'); C.C. Regier, 'The Struggle for Federal Food and Drugs Legislation,' *Law and Contemporary Problems* 1, no. 1 (1933–4): 3 at 13 (Roosevelt 'had received the Neill-Reynolds report on June 2, and two days later he sent … the first part of the much feared report [to the House], which was immediately broadcast by the press. This compelled favorable action on the part of the committee'); Thomas A. Bailey, 'Congressional Opposition to Pure Food Legislation, 1879–1906,' *American Journal of Sociology* 36 (1930): 52 at 62 ('Roosevelt sent … the first part of the Neill-Reynolds report [to the House]. Startled by the revelations given forth in this manner, an indignant public, which flooded the House with telegrams, would not thereafter permit further dilatory action on the part of Congress').

74 See, for example, *Baur v. Veneman*, 352 F.3d 625, 645 n.1 (2d Cir. 2003) (dissenting op.) ('It bears noting … that the federal government's initial efforts to regulate American meat quality were motivated in no small part by public reaction to *The Jungle*, Upton Sinclair's 1906 novel about Chicago's meat packing plants'); *IBP, Inc. v. Alvarez*, 339 F.3d 894, 897–8 (9th Cir. 2003) ('[P]ublication of Upton Sinclair's novel *The Jungle* provoked President Theodore Roosevelt to secure passage of the Meat Inspection Act of 1906 …'); *U.S. v. Espy*, 145 F.3d 1369, 1371 (D.C. Cir. 1998) ('The [Meat Inspection] Act was passed in response to Upton Sinclair's famous book *The Jungle*').

75 Gary D. Libecap and Mark T. Law, 'Corruption and Reform? The Emergence of the 1906 Food and Drug Act and the 1906 Meat Inspection Act,' International Center for Economic Research, Working Paper No. 20, 2003, http://www.icer.it/docs/wp2003/Libecap20-03.pdf at 31. With respect to the narrower issue of the impact of *The Jungle* on the Meat Inspection Act, Law and Libecap state that 'the direct result of Upton Sinclair's muckraking was the 1906 Meat Inspection Act, which significantly expanded the USDA's inspection of the slaughtering, packing, and canning of meats.' *Id.*, 20.

76 Leo Tolstoy, *War and Peace*, trans. Aylmer Maude, vol. 2 (1865–9; Oxford University Press, 1933), 257–9, excerpted in *The Modern Tradition*, ed. Richard Ellman and Charles Feidelson, Jr. (New York: Oxford University Press, 1965), 265–7.

77 Rachel Carson, *Silent Spring* (1962; Wilmington: Mariner, 2002), 1–3.

78 *Id.*, 7–8.

79 *Id.*, 15–16.

80 *Id.*, 67–8.

81 *Id.*, 72.

82 Quoted in Paul Brooks, *The House of Life: Rachel Carson at Work* (Boston: Houghton Mifflin, 1972), 13.

83 Quoted in *id.*, 305.

84 President's Science Advisory Committee, *Use of Pesticides* (1963); see also Christopher J. Bosso, *Pesticides and Politics* (Pittsburgh: University of Pittsburgh Press, 1987), 122. (The PSAC panel 'clearly vindicated Carson.')

85 Quoted in Linda Lear, *Rachel Carson: Witness for Nature* (New York: Holt, 1997), 452.

86 Terence Kehoe and Charles Jacobson, 'Environmental Decisionmaking and DDT Production at Montrose Chemical Corporation of California,' *Enterprise and Society* 4 (2003): 640 at 662.

87 See Bosso, *Pesticides and Politics*, 125–32.

88 See Kehoe and Jacobson, 'Environmental Decisionmaking,' 661–2.

89 *Hearings on S. 1250 and S. 1251 Before the S. Comm. on Commerce*, 88th Congress 1 sess. (1963) (Statement of Rachel Carson). In the hearings, Senators Ribicoff and Gruening both compared Carson to Harriett Beecher Stowe. Ribicoff's opening remarks even echoed Lincoln's (legendary) remark to Stowe that she was 'the little woman who wrote the book that started this Great War!' 'Miss Carson,' Ribicoff told her, 'we welcome you here. You are the lady who started all this. Will you please proceed … There can be no doubt that you are the person most responsible for the current public concern over pesticide hazards.' Senator Gruening (D-Alaska) also compared her to Stowe (at the close of testimony). In addition, Carson testified before another Senate subcommittee. See *Interagency Coordination in Environmental Hazards (Pesticides): Hearings Before the U.S. Senate Subcommittee on Reorganization and International Organizations of the Committee on Government Operations*, June 4, 1963, 88th Congress 1 sess. (1963) (testimony of Rachel Carson); see also, Lear, *Rachel Carson*, 454–5.

90 See, for example, *Environmental Defense Fund v. Environmental Protection Agency*, 598 F.2d 62, 72 n.32 (D.C. Cir. 1978) ('One of the most influential publications in the eventual enactment of the 1972 [Federal Water Pollution Control] Act [Amendments] was R. Carson, Silent Spring (1962), which devoted considerable attention to the carcinogenic nature of some heavy metals and some chlorinated hydrocarbon pesticides'); Mary Jane Angelo, 'Embracing Uncertainty, Complexity, and Change: An Eco-pragmatic Reinvention of a First-Generation Environmental Law,' *Ecology Law Quarterly* 33 (2006): 105 at 155 ('Rachel Carson's 1962 book Silent Spring first brought to the public's attention the downside of the seemingly miracle pesticide [DDT] … Carson's book led to a public outcry against the threats of DDT and other persistent pesticides').

91 See Caula A. Beyl, 'Rachel Carson, *Silent Spring*, and the Environmental Movement,' *HortTechology* 2 (1992): 272 at 275; Brooks, *The House of Life*, 311–12.

92 Roland Barthes, *Image Music Text*, trans. Stephen Heath (1977; New York: Noonday, 1988), 79.

93 Hayden White, 'The Value of Narrativity in the Representation of Reality,' *Critical Inquiry* 7 (1980): 5 at 5.

94 See, for example, Peter Brooks, 'Narrativity of the Law,' *Law and Literature* 14 (2002): 1 at 1.

95 Jan M. van Dunne, 'Narrative Coherence and Its Function in Judicial Decision Making and Legislation,' *American Journal of Comparative Law* 44 (1996): 463 at 466. Van Dunne goes on to recount a modern equivalent: 'In Dutch literature there is the intriguing story told by Ter Haar, the specialist on the "Adat law" of then the Netherlands East Indies, now Indonesia. On one of his field trips in Java, he interviewed the local village chief and judge, and wanted to know the rule of law according to the indigenous law, say, for example on inheritance. The chief looked blank and told him he could not tell him. Ter Haar persisted, and repeated his question. Finally, the village chief said: "Give me a case, then I will tell you what the law is." There was no *Adat* law tradition based on abstract, general rules. Incidentally, in my experience, legal practitioners in Europe will have the same response when asked what the substantive law in a certain field is (e.g., the rule on *force majeure* in contract law).'

96 See, for example, Daniel A. Farber and Suzanna Sherry, 'Telling Stories out of School: An Essay on Legal Narratives,' *Stanford Law Review* 45 (1993): 807 (discussing claims of various 'storytelling' schools of scholarship).

97 See Richard A. Posner, *Law and Literature*, rev. ed. (Cambridge, MA: Harvard University Press, 1998).

98 Ward, *Law and Literature*, 3.

99 Kieran Dolin, *A Critical Introduction to Law and Literature* (Cambridge: Cambridge University Press, 2007), 10–11.

100 For an overview of law and literature's successes and failures, see Judith Resnik, 'Singular and Aggregate Voices: Audiences and Authority in Law & Literature and in Law & Feminism,' in *Law and Literature*, ed. Michael Freeman and Andrew D.E. Lewis (Oxford: Oxford University Press, 1999), 687; and Richard H. Weisberg, 'Literature's Twenty-Year Crossing into the Domain of Law: Continuing Trespass or Right by Adverse Possession?' in *Law and Literature*, ed. Michael Freeman and Andrew D.E. Lewis (Oxford: Oxford University Press, 1999), 47.

101 For a good compendium of literary citations in court opinions, see John M. DeStephano, 'On Literature as Legal Authority,' *Arizona Law Review* 49 (2007): 522.

102 *United States v. City of Chicago*, 870 F.2d 1256, 1259 (7th Cir. 1989) ('Decrees that vest federal district judges with supervisory powers over organs of state or local government are extraordinary, and the goal should be to wind them up as fast as possible rather than to perpetuate them indefinitely through liberal grants of petitions to intervene. The parallel to the interminable equity proceedings mocked in Dicken's novel *Bleak House* will not be missed by those of a literary bent').

103 For a critical overview of work in this area, see Guyora Binder and Robert Weisberg, *Literary Criticisms of Law* (Princeton: Princeton University Press, 2000), 292–377. For Binder and Weisberg, 'while the claim that law is really a kind of literature has an air of paradox, identifying law with rhetoric – the art of persuasion – seems almost obvious. Yet the venerable history of "rhetoric" gives the Law as Rhetoric trope connotations that are more esoteric than self-evident.' *Id.*, 292.

104 *Plaut v. Spendthrift Farm, Inc.*, 514 U.S. 211 (1995).

105 *Id.*, 239.

106 *Id.*

107 Dolin, *Critical Introduction*, 2.

108 *Plaut*, 514 U.S. at 245.

109 Robert Frost, *Mending Wall* (1915).

110 Dolin, *Critical Introduction*, 4.

111 Ibid. (quoting Robert M. Cover, 'Forward: *Nomos* and Narrative,' *Harvard Law Review* 97 [1983]: 4 at 4).

112 David Ray Papke and Kathleen H. McManus, 'Narrative and the Appellate Opinion,' *Legal Studies Forum* 23 (1999): 449 at 449.

113 Lawrence Stone, 'The Revival of Narrative: Reflections on a New Old History,' *Past and Present* 85 (1979): 3 at 3.

114 Mark A. Clawson, 'Telling Stories: Romance and Dissonance in Progressive Legal Narratives,' *Legal Studies Forum* 22 (1998): 353 at 364 (citing and partially quoting Patricia Ewick and Susan S. Silbey, 'Subversive Stories and Hegemonic Tales: Towards a Sociology of Narrative,' *Law and Society Review* 29 [1995]: 197 at 200).

115 Brooks, 'Narrativity of the Law,' 1.

116 Van Dunne, 'Narrative Coherence,' 463.

117 White, 'Value of Narrativity,' 6.

118 Binder and Weisberg, *Literary Criticisms*, 201.

119 Ibid., 209. One of those claims – the one that Judge Posner seizes on – is

the asserted 'relation between storytelling and truthtelling.' Posner, *Law and Literature*, 355. As an example, he dissects a personal anecdote told by Patricia Williams in her 1991 book on race and rights. In her telling, she was shopping one day and saw a sweater in a store window that she wanted to buy for her mother. She 'pressed [her] brown round face to the window' and finger to the admittance buzzer on the door. A 'narrow-eyed, white teenager … glared out' at her and 'after about five seconds … mouthed "We're closed" and blew pink rubber [from bubble gum] at [her]. It was two Saturdays before Christmas, at one o'clock in the afternoon; there were several white people in the store who appeared to be shopping for things for *their* mother.' Posner recognizes the power of this story, which he locates in its compression, vivid contrasts, and use of metaphor. But he also recognizes these as the techniques of fiction. So he asks, 'Did Williams, who is not a child, who is a mature woman, *really* press her face to the window …? Or is she embroidering the facts for dramatic effect – making the insult to her seem graver because it shattered a childlike eagerness and innocence?' We have no way to answer these questions (and the others he asks), but there are good reasons to believe that Posner is on to something (one of Williams' admirers, Robin West, has stated that the stories in Williams's book 'may not have been factually accurate'). *Id.*, 357n.32 (quoting Robin West, 'Constitutional Fictions and Meritocratic Success Stories,' *Washington and Lee Law Review* 53 [1996]: 995 at 998). So even if Posner is wrong to suspect the veracity of Williams's story, he's right that we can't simply assume that narratives have a truth value independent of their form and content.

120 Richard Weisberg, *Poethics and Other Strategies of Law and Literature* (New York: Columbia University Press, 1992), 35.

121 Binder and Weisberg, *Literary Criticisms*, 291.

122 Dolin, *A Critical Introduction*, 29–40 (noting, among other things, Robin West's suggestion that the law of self-defence would look much different had it developed around a narrative of domestic violence rather than one based on fights between men in bars and alleys).

123 Jonathan Hearn, 'Narrative, Agency, and Mood: On the Social Construction of National History in Scotland,' *Comparative Studies in Sociology and History* 44 (2002): 745; Margaret R. Somers, 'The Narrative Constitution of Identity: A Relational and Network Approach,' *Theory and Society* 23 (1994): 605.

124 Somers, 'The Narrative Constitution,' 617.

125 *Id.*

126 Barthes, *Image Music Text*, 79.

127  Hearn, 'Narrative, Agency, and Mood,' 748.
128  *Id.*
129  *Id.*, 748–9.
130  *Id.*, 749.
131  *Id.*
132  *Id.*
133  *Id.*, 749–50.
134  410 U.S. 113, 117 (1973).
135  *Id.*, 165.
136  505 U.S. 833 (1992).
137  127 S. Ct. 1610 (2007).
138  *Id.*, 1622–3.
139  Hearn, 'Narrative, Agency, and Mood,' 750.
140  Somers, 'The Narrative Constitution,' 618.
141  Regier, 'The Struggle,' 4–5 ('There were those who objected on constitutional grounds. They did not wish to have the federal government extend its police power into the states').
142  Bailey, 'Congressional Opposition,' 64 ('There were those who were personally interested in the perpetuation of frauds that would be illegal under a pure food statute … This group was the most dangerous, for it fought most persistently and most insidiously').
143  Young, *Pure Food*, 40–1.
144  Quoted in Regier, 'The Struggle,' 6.
145  Quoted in Young, *Pure Food*, 174.
146  Young, *Pure Food*, 201.
147  *Id.*, 289.
148  *Id.*, 290.
149  *Id.*, 135 (quoting Exhibit 18, *Food Furnished by Subsistence Department to Troops in the Field*, 56 Cong. 1 sess., Senate Doc. 270 (1898)).
150  *Id.*, 136.
151  *Id.*, 138 (quoting Carl Sandburg, *Always the Young Strangers* [New York: Harcourt, 1952], 417).
152  *Id.*, (quoting *Food Furnished by Subsistence*, 1100–7).
153  *Id.*
154  *Id.*, 138–9.
155  Brook Thomas, 'Reflections on the Law and Literature Revival,' *Critical Inquiry* 17 (1991): 510 at 535.
156  Hippolyte Taine, *History of English Literature*, trans. Henry von Laun, rev. ed. (1864; New York: Colonial, 1900), excerpted in *The Modern Tradition*, ed. Richard Ellman and Charles Feidelson, Jr (New York: Oxford University Press, 1965), 254.

157 *Id.*, 258.

158 *Id.*, 259.

159 *Id.*, 260–1.

160 *Id.*, 254.

161 *Id.*

162 *Id.*, 264.

163 *Id.*, 255.

164 See, for example, Stephen Greenblatt, *Renaissance Self-Fashioning: From More to Shakespeare* (Chicago: University of Chicago Press, 1980); Louis Adrian Montrose, 'The Purpose of Playing: Reflections on a Shakespearean Anthropology,' *Helios* 32 (1980): 28.

165 H. Aram Veeser, 'The New Historicism,' in *The New Historicism Reader*, ed. H. Aram Veeser (New York: Routledge, 1994), 1.

166 Ross Murfin and Supryia M. Ray, *The Bedford Glossary of Critical and Literary Terms*, 2nd ed. (Boston: Bedford/St Martin's, 2003), 299.

167 Catherine Gallagher and Stephen Greenblatt, *Practicing New Historicism* (Chicago: University of Chicago Press, 2000), 13.

168 Brook Thomas, *The New Historicism and Other Old-Fashioned Topics* (Princeton: Princeton University Press, 1991), 39.

169 See, for example, Stephen Orgel, 'The Role of King,' in *The New Historicism Reader*, ed. H. Aram Veeser (New York: Routledge, 1994), 35 at 44 (arguing that the full force of Caroline idealism is found in the masques of Inigo Jones, 'not in the promulgation of edicts, erratically obeyed, nor in military power, inadequately furnished').

170 Binder and Weisberg, *Literary Criticisms*, 479.

171 Gregg D. Crane, 'The Path of Law and Literature,' *American Literary History* 9 (1997): 758 at 772.

172 145 U.S. 909 (1892).

173 Marianne Wesson, '"Remarkable Stratagems and Conspiracies": How Unscrupulous Lawyers and Credulous Judges Created an Exception to the Hearsay Rule,' *Fordham Law Review* 76 (2007): 1675; 'Particular Intentions: The Hillmon Case and the Supreme Court,' *Law and Literature* 18 (2006): 343. Wearing her novelist hat, Professor Wesson is working on a fictionalized account of the case. The factual account that I'm reciting is based on the Supreme Court opinion cited above, fleshed out here and there by Wesson's investigatory findings.

174 There was also an exhumation of the corpse from Medicine Lodge, followed by a third inquest in Lawrence. James W. Green, the then County Attorney and later Dean of the University of Kansas Law School, conducted that inquest and later appeared as counsel for the defence (itself an interesting issue of professional ethics). Today his statue adorns a leafy

stretch of Jayhawk Boulevard in the middle of the KU campus. I've probably walked past it hundreds of times, with no idea until recently that he played a central part in the famous *Hillmon* case.

175 *Hillmon*, 145 U.S. at 287.

176 *Id.*, 288–9.

177 Wesson, 'Particular Intentions,' 349–50.

178 *Hillmon*, 145 U.S. at 294.

179 *Id.*, 295.

180 Wesson, 'Particular Intentions,' 350. For a very good application of structuralist principles to legal fact finding via narrative, see Bernard S. Jackson, *Law, Fact and Narrative Coherence* (Roby: Deborah Charles, 1988), 61–88 (discussing Bennett and Feldman's theory of fact finding at trial: 'People carry around with them a stock of socially-constructed narratives, acquired through the whole range of their social experience (including their education). A significant factor affecting the plausibility of a newly-communicated story is the degree to which it fits a narrative which already exists within this stock of social knowledge').

181 Frederick Jackson Turner, *The Frontier in American History* (1893; New York: Holt, 1920), 32–3n.49. Turner's positions have been qualified and debunked over the years, so I don't offer them for the truth of the matter – maybe as a 'state of the American mind' exception to hearsay.

182 The image of places like Dodge City and Tombstone as pits of teeming lawlessness was exaggerated (as were the legends that grew up around Bat Masterson, the Earps, Bill Cody, and others) and fuelled by an endless supply of dime-novel Westerns and ludicrous newspaper reports. Daryl Jones, *The Dime Novel Western* (Bowling Green: Popular Press of Bowling Green University, 1978). One need only look at the covers of dime novels to get the drift. *Richard J. 'Diamond Dick' Tanner Dime Novels,* Nebraska State Historical Society, http://www.nebraskahistory.org/lib-arch/research/treasures/diamond_dick_tanner.htm. These types of images persist to some degree today, even though the academic literature (and the literature-literature) has moved off this flat-footed position since Turner's time. See, for example, John Phillip Reid, *Law for the Elephant: Property and Social Behavior on the Overland Trail* (San Marino: Huntington Library Press, 1996); Sam Shepard, *True West* (New York: Samuel French, 1981).

183 Wesson's conclusion is based on several factors. At one point, she was convinced that the letter was a simple forgery, but she came around to the view that Walters probably did write the letter – just not when and where stated. She found persuasive evidence that Walters was alive well after he

was supposedly killed, that the insurance companies had fabricated other evidence, and – based on modern forensic tests – that Hillmon probably was the person killed at Crooked Creek.

184 This quotation is usually ascribed to Horace Greeley, though the evidence shows little more than that he said things sort of like that. I was crestfallen to learn that he had not actually penned those words, which were carved into my memory in childhood. For you see, in the small town in which I grew up, we maintained a diorama of a stagecoach stop (Station 15) featuring Greeley and a few other notables who had passed through on the way west. History, like memory, is a slippery thing ...

185 In the next chapter I will discuss the central importance of coherence to the plausibility of narratives. For now, we can simply register Neil Mac-Cormick's observation that 'narrative coherence ... is a necessary but not a sufficient condition of real-world credibility.' MacCormick, *Rhetoric and the Rule of Law*, 227; cf. Jackson, *Law, Fact*, 71–6 (critiquing Bennett and Feldman's account of fact construction at trial). For MacCormick, the difference between a fictional and a non-fictional narrative is that the non-fictional narrative must be 'anchored' in reality. But he also notes the warning of others against 'too ready reliance on a good story as solidifying belief in "facts" established by it.' And that is exactly the situation in the next example that we will take up: a good story that is anchored, but the anchor is false evidence.

186 Jonathan H. Adler, 'Fables of the Cuyahoga: Reconstructing a History of Environmental Protection,' *Fordham Environmental Law Journal* 14 (2002): 89.

187 *Solid Waste Agency of Northern Cook County v. U.S. Army Corps of Engineers*, 351 U.S. 159, 174–5 (2001) (Stevens, J., dissenting) ('In 1969, the Cuyahoga River in Cleveland, Ohio, coated with a slick of industrial waste, caught fire. Congress responded to that dramatic event, and to others like it, by enacting the Federal Water Pollution Control Act of (FWPCA) Amendments of 1972').

188 http://www.cnn.com/NATURE/9906/22/saving.cuyahoga.

189 Quoted in Ohio Historical Society, 'Cuyahoga River Fire,' *Ohio History Central: An Online Encyclopedia of Ohio History*. http://www.ohiohistoryc-entral.org.

190 *Id.* ('Fires occurred on the Cuyahoga River in 1868, 1883, 1887, 1912, 1922, 1936, 1941, 1948, and in 1952.').

191 Adler, 'Fables of the Cuyahoga,' 96.

192 *Id.*, 98; Ohio Historical Society, 'Cuyahoga River Fire,' 190.

193 Jonathan H. Adler, 'Smoking Out the Cuyahoga Fire Fable: Smoke and

Mirrors Surrounding Cleveland,' *National Review Online*, 22 June 2004. http://www.nationalreview.com/adler/adler200406220845.asp; see also Adler, 'Fables of the Cuyahoga,' 139–40.

194 As Hearn has already reminded us, narratives usually have protagonists. The Cuyahoga had some help in achieving this status, at least in part, through Randy Newman's song about the fire. Randy Newman, 'Burn On,' on *Sail Away* (Warner Bros. Records, 1972).

195 See John Wargo, *Our Children's Toxic Legacy: How Science and Law Fail to Protect Us from Pesticides*, 2d ed. (New Haven: Yale University Press, 1998), 80.

196 Quoted in *id.,* 81.

197 Ibid. (quoting Secretary Freeman).

198 The feminine public narrative was radically revised over the course of the twentieth century. It is difficult to overestimate the impact these revisions had on law. More on that will follow.

199 Lear, *Rachel Carson*, 429.

200 *Id.*

201 *Id.*, 430.

202 Robert Penn Warren, *All the King's Men* (1946; New York: Bantam, 1971), 188–9.

## 2. Institutionalizing Narratives

\* This chapter profited from comments on an earlier version presented to seminars at the Institute for Advanced Studies in the Humanities and the Legal Theory Reading Group at the University of Edinburgh. Thanks to Susan Manning and Maks Del Mar, respectively, for organizing the events.

1 See, for example, Neil MacCormick, 'Notes on Narrativity and the Normative Syllogism,' *International Journal for the Semiotics of Law* 4 (1991): 163 at 168–9.

2 *See* Bernard S. Jackson, *Law, Fact, and Narrative Coherence* (Roby: Deborah Charles, 1988), 37–60.

3 *Id.*, 41, 195.

4 *Id.*, 37.

5 Jackson's concern here is with one of the eight requirements of the Rule of Law as enunciated by Lon Fuller. See Lon L. Fuller, *The Morality of Law*, rev. ed. (New Haven: Yale University Press, 1969), 39 ('Certainly there can be no rational ground for asserting that a man can have a moral obligation to obey a legal rule … that came into existence only after he had acted').

6  Neil MacCormick, *Rhetoric and the Rule of Law: A Theory of Legal Reasoning* (Oxford: Oxford University Press, 2005), 57–9.
7  For a thorough discussion of classification/categorization, see Anthony G. Amsterdam and Jerome Bruner, *Minding the Law* (Cambridge, MA: Harvard University Press, 2000), 17–109.
8  Jackson, *Narrative Coherence*, 97–8. Amsterdam and Bruner make a similar point in arguing that each category of common law writ is essentially a plot précis: 'the very writs that defined causes of action at common law (quare clausum fregit and so forth) were rather like plot summaries of the founding narratives of various myth-like genres.' Amsterdam and Bruner, *Minding the Law*, 112; see also Guyora Binder and Robert Weisberg, *Literary Criticisms of Law* (Princeton: Princeton University Press, 2000), 499–500 (observing, in a discussion of William Ian Miller's study of Icelandic law, that 'Icelandic law looks as if it were "abstracted from specific cases rather than deduced from disembodied principle"').
9  Oliver Wendell Holmes, Jr., *The Common Law* (Boston: Little, Brown, 1881), excerpted in Stephen B. Presser and Jamil S. Zainaldin, *Law and Jurisprudence in American History*, 2nd ed. (St Paul: West, 1989), 731.
10  *Hynes v. New York Cent. R. Co.*, 176 N.Y.S. 795, 795 (N.Y. App. Div. 1919).
11  *Id.*, 796.
12  *Id.*, 796–7.
13  Jackson, *Narrative Coherence*, 116.
14  This case is a staple on the 'law' side of law and literature scholarship. But its importance is hotly disputed. Weisberg praises the opinion as a perfect melding of style and justice; Binder and Weisberg condemn it as little more than 'Hallmark card cliché.' Cf. Richard Weisberg, *Poethics and Other Strategies of Law and Literature* (New York: Columbia University Press, 1992), 17–20, with Binder and Weisberg, *Literary Criticisms of Law*, 237. I won't attempt to resolve the aesthetic dispute other than to note that I think everyone could agree that Cardozo's opinion is more rhetorically convincing and narrativistically rounded than Putnam's opinion. The facts *do* matter, even if you believe that Cardozo could have done better or, more generally, that narrative can be used to distort facts (and thereby mislead).
15  *Hynes v. New York Cent. R. Co.*, 231 N.Y. 229, 230-32 (N.Y. 1921).
16  *Id.*, 232–3.
17  *Id.*, 234–5.
18  Of course, Cardozo's decision remains something of a 'gut' (rather than tightly reasoned) reaction to the facts of the case. Judge Posner has criticized Cardozo on this count. Richard Posner, *Cardozo: A Study in Reputa-*

*tion* (Chicago: University of Chicago Press, 1990), 53 (stating that Cardozo gives 'no reason' for the *Hynes* decision).

19  See MacCormick, *Rhetoric and the Rule of Law,* 49–52.

20  *Id.,* 235–6.

21  Zenon Bankowski, *Living Lawfully: Love in Law and Law in Love* (Boston: Kluwer, 2001), 28–43; Martha Nussbaum, *The Fragility of Goodness: Luck and Ethics in Greek Tragedy and Philosophy* (New York: Cambridge University Press, 1986), 51–82.

22  Bankowski, *Living Lawfully,* 29.

23  Sophocles, *Antigone,* in *The Three Theban Plays,* trans. Robert Fagles (New York: Penguin, 1984), ll. 203–35.

24  I'll turn more directly in the next chapter to the question of how members of particular groups interpret what they see, hear, or read.

25  *Id.,* ll. 499–525.

26  Zenon Bankowski, 'Legal Reasoning from the Inside Out,' in *Stressing Legal Decisions,* ed. Tadeusz Biernat et al. (Krakow: Polonia, 2003), 27–46. In this piece Bankowski discusses, among other things, Nussbaum's recent work on narrative in legal proceedings. Nussbaum has argued that current death penalty cases insufficiently account for defendants' overall life narratives. See Martha Nussbaum, 'Equity and Mercy,' in *Sex and Social Justice* (New York: Oxford University Press, 1999). Interestingly, Robin West has made the (somewhat) opposite (but not inconsistent) point – namely, that too much narrative appears in death penalty cases at the U.S. Supreme Court level because they often recite grisly, yet legally irrelevant, details of crimes tacitly to justify affirmance of death penalty convictions. See Robin West, *Narrative, Authority, and Law* (Ann Arbor: University of Michigan Press, 1993), 428–39. In any event, the Supreme Court acknowledges that both logic and narrative are essential threads in the adjudicative fabric: 'In sum, the accepted rule that the prosecution is entitled to prove its case free from any defendant's option to stipulate the evidence away rests on good sense. A syllogism is not a story, and a naked proposition in a courtroom may be no match for the robust evidence that would be used to prove it. People who hear a story interrupted by gaps of abstraction may be puzzled at the missing chapters, and jurors asked to rest a momentous decision on the story's truth can feel put upon at being asked to take responsibility knowing that more could be said than they have heard. A convincing tale can be told with economy, but when economy becomes a break in the natural sequence of narrative evidence, an assurance that the missing link is really there is never more than second best.' *Old Chief v. United States,* 519 U.S. 172, 189 (1997).

27  Nussbaum, *The Fragility of Goodness,* 55.

28  25 S. Ct. 539 (1905).

29  *Id.*, 546.

30  *Muller v. Oregon*, 208 U.S. 412 (1908).

31  *Id.*, 421–3.

32  For a useful compendium of various approaches to law and narrative, see Peter Brooks and Paul Gewirtz, eds., *Law's Stories: Narrative and Rhetoric in the Law* (New Haven: Yale University Press, 1996).

33  693 P.2d 475 (Kan. 1985).

34  *Id.*, 475.

35  *Id.*, 476.

36  *State v. Scott*, 21 P.3d 516 (Kan. 2001). In Kansas, a syllabus point is a statement of law prepared by the justice delivering the opinion and is often cited as such.

37  Judges typically decline to elaborate on the law once the jury is charged. The privileged status of instructions is underscored when a trial judge declines to answer inquiries from a jury other than with a directive to review the instructions. See *State v. Lawrence*, 135 P.3d 1211 (Kan. 2006).

38  Susie Cho, 'Capital Confusion: The Effect of Jury Instructions on the Decision to Impose Death,' *Journal of Criminal Law and Criminology* 85 (1994): 532 at 549 (also noting that 'drafters of standard instructions do not rely on a specific set of facts, and courts use those instructions in all cases involving the issue which they cover'); see also Lawrence J. Severance et al., 'Toward Criminal Jury Instructions That Jurors Can Understand,' *Journal of Criminal Law and Criminology* 75 (1984): 198 at 201.

39  See, for example, Zenon Bankowski and James MacLean, eds., *The Universal and the Particular in Legal Reasoning* (Burlington: Ashgate, 2006); MacCormick, *Rhetoric and the Rule of Law*, 78–100.

40  Jeremy Waldron, 'The Concept and the Rule of Law,' New York University Law School Colloquium in Legal, Political, and Social Philosophy, Paper No. 2, 2006, http://www.law.nyu.edu/clppt/program2006/readings/Concept%20and%20Rule%20of%20Law%20WALDRON.pdf at 12–13.

41  Cf. Joseph Raz, 'The Rule of Law and Its Virtue,' *Law Quarterly Review* 93 (1977): 195 ('There cannot be institutions of any kind unless there are general rules setting them up. A particular norm can authorize adjudication in a particular dispute, but no number of particular norms can set up an institution').

42  MacCormick, *Rhetoric and the Rule of Law*, 99.

43  The trick is to hold the particular and the universal in our gaze at the same time. It will not do to focus solely on the universal and evaluate justice only at that level. Justice cannot be assured if 'micro counterexamples do

not tell.' Robert Nozick, *Anarchy, State, and Utopia* (New York: Basic, 1974), 205.

44 The real problem with jury instructions is not that jurors do not try to apply them but that they often don't understand them. For this reason, judges, practitioners, and scholars have devoted considerable effort over the past few decades to developing comprehensible jury instructions. See Cho, 'Capital Confusion,' 551–2 ('Researchers who have conducted experiments to test juror comprehension have found that psycholinguistic principles can be applied to jury instructions to eliminate confusing language, simplify meaning, and present instructions clearly and logically'); Severance, 'Toward Criminal Jury Instructions,' 233 ('Our findings demonstrate that simplified language and organized presentations of legal concepts can effectively help jurors, particularly when coupled with the opportunity to discuss and deliberate. Proper attention to devising jury instructions that are meaningful to lay people, as well as legally accurate, can accomplish the important task of informing jurors of the relevant legal concepts').

45 693 P.2d at 477. The statutory source of the instruction was Kan. Stat. Ann. § 21-3211, which stated: 'A person is justified in the use of force against an aggressor when and to the extent it appears to him and he reasonably believes that such conduct is necessary to defend himself or another against such aggressor's imminent use of unlawful force.'

46 *Id.*

47 'The PIK committee explained "immediate" was inserted in the self-defense instruction for "imminent" because it is a "better understood term." PIK Crim.2d 54.17, Comment.' 693 P.2d at 478. This makes good sense. It is implausible that the jury made the fine distinction that the majority opinion posits. This was not, after all, a case in which the defendant was not allowed to put on evidence in support of a self-defence claim. Indeed, the jury seems to have largely credited her story in declining to convict her of the charged offence (second-degree murder) and choosing instead to convict her of a lesser included offence (involuntary manslaughter).

48 *Id.*, 478. In dissent, Justice McFarland, the only woman on the Court, conceded that there is a 'fine' distinction between 'imminent' and 'immediate' and that there are situations in which that distinction might control. But she did not believe that Betty Hundley's story constituted such a case, because Betty was in neither imminent nor immediate danger. Justice McFarland sought to demonstrate this by juxtaposing two hypotheticals, one an alternative version of how Betty's story could have played out:

Probably it would be better to utilize the statutory term 'imminent' rather than 'immediate' in a self-defense instruction. In a factual situation involving matters of seconds the distinction could be significant and the use of 'immediate' could constitute reversible error. An example of such situation would be two men arguing in the middle of a parking lot. One man sees the other reach for the door of his automobile while stating he is going to kill him and he knows the man has a gun or a knife therein. The danger in such circumstances may be imminent but not immediate. But the facts before us do not show imminent or immediate danger of harm.

There were only two persons in the motel room. One admits killing the other. The only version of what transpired is that of the defendant herein. Taking this as true, the deceased told the defendant to leave the premises, giving her money to buy cigarettes. The deceased then sat on the bed in his shorts, not even looking in defendant's direction. The defendant reached for her purse by the door, took a gun therefrom and fired five shots at the deceased. The parties were in a motel room in a busy part of the city of Topeka in the early evening hours. They were not in some remote area where help would be difficult to obtain. At the very least, defendant would have had a five minute head start on the defendant [sic, 'deceased'] had she failed to return with the cigarettes. I fail to see how, in this factual situation, it could be reversible error to use 'immediate' rather than 'imminent' in the self-defense instruction as it would not have altered the outcome. (Ibid., 470)

49 The Court specifically located the underlying problem as one rooted in historical prejudice: 'Wife beating is steeped in the concept of marital privacy, and the belief wives are the personal property of the husband. In Blackstone's Commentaries the theory of coverture was advanced, making punishment for mistreatment of a wife impossible since husband and wife were considered one. 1 Blackstone, *Commentaries on the Laws of England*, 3rd ed. (1884): 432 at 442–4.' Ibid., 479.

50 *Id.*

51 *Id.*

52 *Id.*

53 Though the State may not appeal an acquittal, Kansas law permits the State to reserve questions for appeal, but only if those questions are of state-wide interest and essential to the administration of criminal justice. *State v. Martin*, 658 P.2d 1024, 1024 (1983).

54 763 P.2d 572 (1988).

55 *Id.*, 579. 'This addition was apparently encouraged by the following language in *State v. Hodges*, 716 P.2d 563 (1986): "Where the battered woman syndrome is an issue in the case, the standard for reasonableness concern-

ing an accused's belief in asserting self-defense is not an objective, but a subjective standard. The jury must determine, from the viewpoint of defendant's mental state, whether defendant's belief in the need to defend herself was reasonable."' Ibid.

56  *Id.*, 577; see also *id.*, Syl. § 4.

57  *Id.*, 579.

58  763 P. 2d at 582 (Herd, J., dissenting) (citations omitted): 'The majority implies its decision is necessary to keep the battered woman syndrome from operating as a defense in and of itself. It has always been clear the syndrome is not a defense itself. Evidence of the syndrome is admissible only because of its relevance to the issue of self-defense. The majority of jurisdictions have held it beyond the ordinary jury's understanding why a battered woman may feel she cannot escape, and have held evidence of the battered woman syndrome proper to explain it. The expert testimony explains how people react to circumstances in which the average juror has not been involved. It assists the jury in evaluating the sincerity of the defendant's belief she was in imminent danger requiring self-defense and whether she was in fact in imminent danger.'

59  It's possible to chart the shift in legal discourse within the justice–gender nexus by looking at temporally spaced cases. See, for example, Kieran Dolin, *A Critical Introduction to Law and Literature* (Cambridge: Cambridge University Press, 2007), 33–40. For a law-and-literature approach to the issue, see Melanie Williams, '*Tess of the D'Urbervilles* and the Law of Provocation,' in *Law and Literature*, ed. Michael Freeman and Andrew D.E. Lewis (Oxford: Oxford University Press, 1999).

60  Pattern Instructions in Kansas, 3d.

61  This process is not unique to jury instructions. Indeed, that's how the common law has always worked. It's just that we forget that, for example, 'The Rule in *Shelley's Case*' or 'The Rule in *Spencer's Case*' grew out of stories.

62  In recent years it has become easier to identify laws with individual narratives because legislators have actually started to name particular acts after individuals (usually victims of injustice, crimes, or gross negligence). I'm thinking of things like Texas's Tim Cole Act (wrongful conviction), New York's Libby Zion Act (medical negligence), and widespread Megan's and Amber's Laws (child abductions and sex crimes).

63  Amy Devitt, 'Integrating Rhetorical and Literary Theories of Genre,' *College English* 62 (2000): 696 at 710 (quoting Catherine F. Schryer with respect to genre stability).

64  I have found it useful to think of coherence in two ways. The first, and more familiar, is that of a chain. The problem with that metaphor is that a

story may be said to fail if any link breaks or doesn't fit. I think a logician must have first coined the trope, for as we all know, storytellers spin yarns, not chains. Anyway, yarn does not depend on the integrity of any single strand. Mosaics and tapestries are also appropriately analogous, I think, in that they can lose pieces or threads and still convey a message.

65 MacCormick, *Rhetoric and the Rule of Law,* 233.

66 Ronald Dworkin, *Law's Empire* (Cambridge, MA: Belknap, 1986), 228–38.

67 As a native Kansan, I would have offered the World's Largest Ball of Twine (to which farmers have been adding segments for over fifty years) as more apt: http://skyways.lib.ks.us/towns/Cawker/twine.html. But alas, I was not the first author to enter on the scene.

68 Post-structuralists would deny that the novel is a closed form because it remains open to interpretation. See, for example, Terry Eagleton, *Literary Theory: An Introduction* (Minneapolis: University of Minnesota Press, 1983), 138 (arguing that the shift from structuralism to post-structuralism is a movement from seeing 'the poem or novel as a closed entity, equipped with definite meanings which it is the critic's task to decipher, to seeing it as irreducibly plural, an endless play of signifiers which can never be finally nailed down to a single centre, essence or meaning'). For our purposes, I mean only that a novel has left its author's hands.

69 See, for example, Stefanie A. Linquist and Frank B. Cross, 'Empirically Testing Dworkin's Chain Novel Theory: Studying the Path of Precedent,' *New York University Law Review* 80 (2005): 1156–7 (finding only limited support for chain-novel theory and concluding that Dworkin's 'thesis does not describe fully the operation of U.S. law').

70 For a good summary of the Dworkin–Fish matchup, as well as of third-party commentary on the matchup, see Binder and Weisberg, *Literary Criticisms,* 169–81.

71 *Id.,* 1158.

72 *Black's Law Dictionary,* 8th ed. (2004), 1443 (definition of *stare decisis*).

73 See, for example, Robert Nozick, *Invariances: The Structure of the Objective World* (Cambridge, MA: Belknap, 2001), 75–114; Gerald Postema, 'Objectivity Fit for Law,' in *Objectivity in Law and Morals,* ed. Brian Leiter (New York: Cambridge University Press, 2001), 99 at 108.

74 See, for example, *Lawrence v. Texas,* 539 U.S. 558 (2003) (Scalia, J., dissenting) ('I do not myself believe in rigid adherence to *stare decisis* in constitutional cases; but I do believe that we should be consistent rather than manipulative in invoking the doctrine. Today's opinions in support of reversal do not bother to distinguish – or indeed, even bother to mention – the paean to *stare decisis* coauthored by three Members of today's majority in *Planned*

*Parenthood v. Casey.'*).

75  Zenon Bankowski et al., 'Rationales for Precedent,' in *Interpreting Precedents*, ed. D. Neil MacCormick and Robert S. Summers (Aldershot: Ashgate/Dartmouth, 1997), 481 at 487; see also *Planned Parenthood of Southeastern Pa. v. Casey*, 505 U.S. 833, 844 (1992) ('Liberty finds no refuge in a jurisprudence of doubt').

76  *Id.*, 488; see also *id.*, 487 (linking predictability to the Rule of Law by suggesting that it is 'definitive for the idea of a rational legal discourse').

77  Linquist and Cross, 'Empirically Testing,' 1167.

78  Stanley Fish, 'Working on the Chain Gang: Interpretation in the Law and in Literary Criticism,' *Critical Inquiry* 9 (1982): 201 at 202 (quoting Ronald Dworkin, 'Law as Interpretation,' *Critical Inquiry* 9 [1982]: 179 at 192–3); see also Dworkin, *Law's Empire*, 229 ('[A] group of novelists writes a novel, *seriatim*; each novelist in the chain interprets the chapters he has been given in order to write a new chapter, which is then added to what the next novelist receives, and so on').

79  *Id.*, 205–6 (quoting Dworkin).

80  *Id.*, 203.

81  *Id.* What Fish has in mind here, I think, is the notion that different literary modes carry with them different sets of conventions. For example, in Ian Watt's famous study of the early development of the realistic novel, he catalogues the shared expectations of both readers and writers of realistic novels: 'The narrative method whereby the novel embodies [a] circumstantial view of life may be called its formal realism; formal, because the term realism does not here refer to any special literary doctrine or purpose, but only to a set of narrative procedures which are so commonly found together in the novel, and so rarely in other literary genres, that they may be regarded as typical of the form itself. Formal realism, in fact, is the narrative embodiment of a premise that Defoe and Richardson accepted very literally, but which is implicit in the novel form in general: the premise, or primary convention, that the novel is a full and authentic report of human experience, and is therefore under an obligation to satisfy its reader with such details of the story as the individuality of the actors concerned, the particulars of the times and places of their actions, details which are presented through a more largely referential use of language than is common in other literary forms.' Ian Watt, 'Realism and the Novel Form,' excerpted in *Law and Literature*, ed. Lenora Ledwon (New York: Garland, 1996), 463 at 464.

82  Fish, 'Chain Gang,' 204.

83  *Id.*

84  This seems wrong to me, or at least an overstatement. Though I agree that information comes in interpreted form, interpretation also comes in light of other interpretations. Absent misreading of what has come before, this additional context should indeed guide (or constrain) future interpretations, if they are to be coherent.

85  *Id.*, 204.

86  Derrida's notion of 'supplement' – which carries the sense of both 'addition to' and 'substitution for' – helps explain this relationship. See Jacques Derrida, *Of Grammatology*, trans. Gayatri Chakravorty Spivak (Baltimore: Johns Hopkins University Press, 1976), 144–52. If, for example, I pull a volume of the Federal Digest off the shelf, I have in my hand a 'complete' statement of the law on a particular subject. But every so often, the publisher puts out a new edition (and every year puts out a new pocket part) that updates the cases previously digested and adds new ones. Each new edition thus 'adds to' and 'substitutes for' its predecessor in a never-to-be-completed cycle. See Jack M. Balkin, 'Deconstructive Practice and Legal Theory,' *Yale Law Journal* 96 (1987): 743 at 758–9.

87  Novelists occasionally revise their work after publication. The New York edition of Henry James's novels is an example. Those novels are in most respects the same as their predecessors – they are still recognizable as the same works – but they are different (and by most accounts hardly improved). The same is true of black-letter law: judges no longer need to add substantive chapters; at most, they edit a bit, add a footnote here and there, or – occasionally – slap on an afterward. There is not, of course, a bright line between actual novelizing and mere editing, but we know that the legal novel is essentially finished once courts begin to quote settled precedent, with no further pretence of pronouncement. But when times change, there's always room for a sequel.

88  I actually think Fish overstates the power of genre constraints, in one important respect. He uses as an example a judge who deems a defendant guilty of a crime for no reason other than that the defendant has red hair. This is not 'striking out in a new direction,' according to Fish. Rather, this person 'would simply not be acting as a judge because he could give no reasons for his decision that would be seen as reasons by competent members of the legal community.' Fish, 'Chain Gang,' 206. The problem here is that there is no line to be drawn between 'bad' decisions made within the legal genre and 'extrajudicial' decisions made without it. To return to the analogy to fiction, literary history is replete with examples – from A. Conan Doyle's Sherlock Holmes detective series to Aaron Spelling's *Dallas* television series – in which characters have been killed off in one episode

only to reappear later in the series. And this happens within subgenres that are ostensibly in a 'realistic' vein. Are the implausible contrivances that bring the dead back to the page or screen generic breaches or merely bad realism? I don't think one could construct a test that would satisfy all members of the interpretive community any more than one could devise a rubric for separating 'bad' or 'stupid' or 'wrong' judicial decisions from those that Fish would identify as extrajudicial.

89 See Kan. Stat. Ann. § 60-518; 12 Okla. Stat. tit. 12, § 100; see, generally, *Lepak v. McClain*, 844 P.2d 852 (1992) (Opala, J., concurring) (discussing issues relating to Oklahoma statutes adopted from Kansas).

90 The current versions of the statutes read as follows:

If any action be commenced within due time, and the plaintiff fail in such action otherwise than upon the merits, and the time limited for the same shall have expired, the plaintiff, or, if the plaintiff die, and the cause of action survive, his or her representatives may commence a new action within six (6) months after such failure. Kan. Stat. Ann. § 60-518.

If any action is commenced within due time, and a judgment thereon for the plaintiff is reversed, or if the plaintiff fail in such action otherwise than upon the merits, the plaintiff, or, if he should die, and the cause of action survive, his representatives may commence a new action within one (1) year after the reversal or failure although the time limit for commencing the action shall have expired before the new action is filed. 12 Okla. Stat., tit. 12, § 100.

91 220 P. 59 (Okla. 1923).

92 222 P. 1114 (Kan. 1924).

93 *Prince v. Leesona Corp., Inc.*, 720 F.2d 1166, 1168 (10th Cir. 1983).

94 *Allen v. Greyhound Lines, Inc.*, 656 F.2d 418, 422 (9th Cir. 1981).

95 *Id.*, 422–3.

96 *Morris v. Wise*, 293 P.2d 547, 550 (Okla. 1955).

97 *Grider v. USX Corp.*, 847 P.2d 779, 788 n.7 (Okla. 1993) (Opala, J., concurring) ('Morris holds § 100 uninvocable to save an action which was originally brought in federal district court in Texas and was later recommenced in an Oklahoma state court').

98 917 P.2d 810 (Kan. 1996) (discussing with apparent approval the position that the trend against applying savings statutes to cases first filed in other jurisdictions had 'reversed').

99 *Prince v. Leesona Corp.*, 720 F.2d 1166 (10th Cir. 1983).

100  *Harnett v. Parris*, 1995 WL 55036 at *6 (D. Kan.) ('This court is bound to
     follow the Tenth Circuit's decision' in *Prince*). By way of full disclosure,
     I was one of counsel in *Harnett*, a case with its own interesting narrative
     twists. The case involved a number of racing greyhounds allegedly stolen
     from Harnett, an Irish citizen, by a once prominent (but by then impris-
     oned) former Oklahoma legislator, Parris, and others through the use
     of forged registration documents. For details of the alleged scheme, see
     *Harnett v. Parris*, 925 F. Supp. 1496 (D. Kan. 1996). But I digress …

101  See, e.g., *Bockweg v. Anderson*, 402 S.E.2d 627, 633 (1991).

102  *Grider v. USX Corp.*, 847 P.2d 779, 788n.7 (Okla. 1993) (Opala, J., concur-
     ring) ('The teaching of Morris came under severe criticism … for afford-
     ing out-of-state dismissals dehors the merits a different treatment from
     that which is accorded in-state federal-court dismissals').

103  See http://www.time.com/time/magazine/article/0,9171,841846.00.
     html.

104  This is an example of an interpretive community having a subcom-
     munity – one whose members are aware of important context not even
     inferable by someone outside that subcommunity. This is to say that a
     lawyer sitting in a library in New York would be unlikely to discover
     that Oklahoma authority from the late 1950s is tainted, absent resort to
     non-legal materials. Plainly, the normal resources used for evaluating the
     subsequent history of a case (e.g., Shepard's or KeyCite) would raise no
     cautionary flags.

105  Amy Devitt, *Standardizing Written English: Diffusion in the Case of Scotland*,
     1520–1659 (Cambridge: Cambridge University Press, 1989).

106  Idem, *Writing Genres* (Carbondale: Southern Illinois University Press,
     2004), 31.

107  Devitt evaluated five different English forms in five different genres in
     twenty-year tranches over the period in question. Specifically, she looked
     at how quickly certain Anglo-English forms replaced Scots-English forms:

     '-ing' replacing '-and' as the inflection marking the present participle;
     'no/not' replacing 'na/nocht' as the negative particle;
     indefinite article 'a' before consonants and 'an' before vowels replacing
        'ane' in all environments;
     '-ed' replacing '-it' as the inflection marking the past tense; *and*
     'wh-' replacing 'quh-' in the spelling of relative pronouns.

     As genres, she examined

religious treatises;
official correspondence;
private records (mostly diaries);
private correspondence; *and*
national public records (e.g., records of the Scots Privy Council).

108  Devitt, *Standardizing Written English*, 65.
109  The specific records that Devitt examined were:

Ancient criminal trials;
Records of the Convention of the Royal Burghs;
Register of the Privy Council;
Trials for witchcraft; and
Selected justiciary cases.
*Id.*, 78 (Appendix II).

110  *Id.*, 65–6.
111  Jonathan Hearn, 'Narrative, Agency, and Mood: On the Social Construction of National History in Scotland,' *Comparative Studies in Sociology and History* 44 (2002): 745 at 745.
112  Caroline McCracken-Flesher, 'Thinking Nationally/Writing Colonially? Scott, Stevenson, and England,' *Novel* 24 (1991): 296 at 296–7 (quoting N.T. Phillipson, 'Nationalism and Ideology,' in *Government and Nationalism in Scotland*, ed. J.N. Wolfe [Edinburgh: Edinburgh University Press, 1969], 177).
113  Hearn, 'Narrative, Agency, and Mood,' 753; see also Michael Fry, 'The Whig Interpretation of Scottish History,' in *The Manufacture of Scottish History*, ed. Ian Donnachie and Christopher Whatley (Edinburgh: Polygon, 1992), 72–89.
114  McCracken-Flesher, 'Thinking Nationally,' 298.
115  *Id.*
116  *Id.*, 298–9 (quoting J.G. Lockhart, *Memoirs of the Life of Sir Walter Scott, Bart.* [Boston: Houghton Mifflin, 1901], 223–4).
117  Lindsay Farmer, '"The Genius of our Law …": Criminal Law and the Scottish Legal Tradition,' *Modern Law Review* (1992): 25 at 25.
118  *Id.*, 32 (quoting Baron Hume, 1 *Commentaries on the Law of Scotland Respecting Crimes*, 4th ed., ed. B. Bell [Edinburgh: Bell and Bradfute, 1844], 12–13).
119  *Id.*
120  *Id.*, 26.

121  *Id.*, 42.

122  *Id.*, 33–4.

123  In particular, Farmer points to the work of Lord Cooper and Professor T.B. Smith, which he capsules as follows: 'The story of development since 1800 is that the effect of the Union has been felt as the smaller Scottish system has come under the assimilating influence of the English. Criminal law alone has resisted this intrusion, largely due to the institutional separation from the House of Lords, but also because the "native genius" of the Scots gave rise to a system of sufficient flexibility to make legislative intervention unnecessary in the face of social change. It thereby avoided the harshness and confusion that was the hallmark of the English criminal law in the early nineteenth century. As the High Court has developed and renewed its own precedents, the English system has come to benefit through the statutory adoption of concepts developed in Scotland … The implications of this nationalism start to become clear when we set this thesis beside the familiar concern, shared by Cooper and Smith, that the profusion of statute law threatens to undermine the principles of the common law. Here the threat is not only statute law but United Kingdom statute law. What is being threatened is an idea of Scotland and Scottish identity – the native genius of our law' (*Id.*, 34).

124  Peter Railton, 'Marx and the Objectivity of Science,' in *The Philosophy of Science*, ed. Richard Boyd et al. (Cambridge, MA: MIT, 1991), 763.

125  See *Berry v. Chaplin*, 169 P.2d 442 (Cal. App. 1946).

126  *Id.*, 445–6.

127  On appeal, the Court agreed with the decision of the lower court not to enforce the stipulation. In a nutshell, the Court found that the parties had no power to enter into the stipulation and that the judge had no power to approve it, absent evidence that the stipulation was fair and reasonable and in the best interests of the child. The Court also found that the parties were improperly attempting to manipulate the judicial system by agreeing as to the force that particular evidence was to carry. *Id.*, 446–8.

128  *Id.*, 449.

129  *Id.*, 450–1 (emphasis supplied). Though no scientific evidence was offered to rebut the blood-group evidence, the trial court did allow a cruder form of hereditary testing: it made Chaplin stand in front of the jury next to Joan Berry with the baby cradled in her arms so that the jury could compare features. Chaplin unsuccessfully advanced this as a point of error on appeal, the Court holding that the salacious testimony presented at trial would have disabused the jury of any inclination to envision a Madonna and Child. Ibid., 452. This begs the real question presented – that

is, whether lay phenotyping is a proper rebuttal to professional genotyping.

130 *Id.*, 451.

131 *Id.*, 453. Interestingly, one of the leading evidentiary authorities of the time had already moved to the position that negative blood-type evidence (or at least unchallenged negative blood-type evidence) should inferentially resolve the issue of paternity. See John Henry Wigmore, 1 *Evidence in Trials at Common Law*, 3d ed. (Boston: Little, Brown, 1940), § 165b ('But at this point comes into play the great discovery of science (emerging after many years of patient research by numerous scientists, but now accepted as correct by all) viz. that no particular gene A, B, or O, will appear in the progeny unless it was present in one of the parents. This universal negative truth of heredity is the basis of the inferences to be examined later').

132 For a thorough and engaging discussion of the history of scientific expert testimony, see Tal Golan, *Laws of Men and Laws of Nature* (Cambridge, MA: Harvard University Press, 2004). Golan's thesis – which seems right to me – is that science and law began to intersect in the late eighteenth century and that each influenced the other in deep and interesting ways. Golan shows, for example, how the attempt to delineate science from non-science has shaped our modern rules of evidence.

133 As it turned out, *Berry v. Chaplin* was on the tipping point: the California legislature acted fairly quickly to give conclusive weight to undisputed blood-test evidence of non-paternity. See *Dodd v. Henkel*, 84 Cal. App.3d 604, 609 (Cal.App. 1978) ('[T]he California statutes authorizing a determination of nonpaternity based upon undisputed findings of the "experts" were enacted in the wake of considerable criticism of the holding ... followed in the celebrated case of Berry v. Chaplin.').

134 Three constitutional provisions recognize – and therefore arguably legitimize – slavery. U.S. Const. art. 1, § 2, cl. 3, directs that the apportionment of legislators and direct taxes among the several states be 'determined by adding to the whole Number of free Persons, ... three fifths of all other Persons.' Art. 1, § 9, prohibits Congress from outlawing the slave trade (the 'Migration or Importation of ... Persons') before 1808. Art. 4, § 2, cl. 3 – the fugitive-slave clause – holds that a slave ('a Person held to Service or Labour') escaping from one state to another 'shall be delivered up' on claim of his or her owner.

135 Geoffrey R. Stone et al., *Constitutional Law* (Boston: Little, Brown, 1986), 436–7 (quoting Robinson, *Slavery in the Structure of American Politics 1765–1820* [New York: Harcourt, 1971], 209, 210, and 244–6).

136 *Id.*, 440 (quoting D. Fehrenbacher, *The* Dred Scott *Case: Its Significance in American Law and Politics* [New York: Oxford University Press, 1978], 192–4, 206–8).

137 *Id.*

138 The United States Constitution enumerates the categories of cases over which federal courts have jurisdiction. One of those categories is 'Controversies … between Citizens of different States.' U.S. Const. art. 3, § 2.

139 Act of March 6, 1820, 3 Stat. 545.

140 60 U.S. 393, 407 (1857).

141 *Id.*, 534–5.

142 According to some commentators, the problem with this type of originalism is that it equates the constitutional text of the United States to the text of the Constitution (i.e., other documents such as the Declaration of Independence should be considered 'constitutional'). See Binder and Weisberg, *Literary Criticisms*, 353–9.

143 *Id.*, 405.

144 See, for example, U.S. Const. amends. XIII (abolishing slavery), XIV (conferring citizenship on all persons born or naturalized in the United States), and XV (conferring the right to vote on all citizens, without regard to race, colour, or previous condition of servitude).

145 163 U.S. 537 (1896).

146 See *Id.*, 549–50: '[I]t is also suggested by the learned counsel for the plaintiff in error that the same argument that will justify the state legislature in requiring railways to provide separate accommodations for the two races will also authorize them to require separate cars to be provided for people whose hair is of a certain color, or who are aliens, or who belong to certain nationalities, or to enact laws requiring colored people to walk upon one side of the street, and white people upon the other, or requiring white men's houses to be painted white, and colored men's black, or their vehicles or business signs to be of different colors, upon the theory that one side of the street is as good as the other, or that a house or vehicle of one color is as good as one of another color.'

147 *Id.*, 551–2.

148 *Id.*, 557, 559.

149 *Id.*, 560.

150 *Id.*, 560–1.

151 347 U.S. 483 (1954).

152 Kieran Dolin neatly argues that a perfect explanation for the 'why' is that – by the middle of the last century – lawyers, writers, and critics had

begun to talk across the disciplinary wall between law and literature.
Dolin, *Critical Introduction*, 182–206.

153 *Id.*, 489–94.

154 *Id.*, 494n.11. The Court also cited a similarly generalized finding by one
of the Kansas courts below: 'Segregation of white and colored children
in public schools has a detrimental effect upon the colored children. The
impact is greater when it has the sanction of the law; for the policy of
separating the races is usually interpreted as denoting the inferiority of
the negro group. A sense of inferiority affects the motivation of a child to
learn. Segregation with the sanction of law, therefore, has a tendency to
[retard] the educational and mental development of negro children and
to deprive them of some of the benefits they would receive in a racial[ly]
integrated school system.'

155 None of this means that *Brown* put matters of race to rest in the United
States. Even today, race bedevils the courts and many social institutions.
Most recently, the debate has moved into the arena of affirmative action
and on to topics such as, for instance, whether educational institutions
can grant preferences to members of minority groups that have been
historically underrepresented in those institutions. See, for example, *Grut-*
*ter v. Bollinger*, 539 U.S. 306, 343 (2003), where, in approving a preferential
admission system at the University of Michigan Law School, the Court
(somewhat wistfully) opined that race-based preferences would not be
necessary in another generation: 'We expect that 25 years from now, the
use of racial preferences will no longer be necessary to further the interest
approved today.'

156 To put this in the terminology of legal theory, the ideal of racial equality
had hardened into what Dworkin calls an 'interpretive' fact. See Dworkin's discussion of Edmund Cahn's position in Ronald Dworkin, 'Social
Sciences and Constitutional Rights – The Consequences of Uncertainty,'
*Journal of Law and Education* 6 (1977): 3 at 5: 'We don't need evidence for
the proposition that segregation is an insult to the Black community –
we know it; we know it the way that a cold causes snuffles. It is not that
we don't need to know it nor that there isn't something there to know.
There is a fact of the matter, namely that segregation is an insult, but
we need no evidence for that fact – we just know it. It's an interpretive
fact.'

157 Watt, 'Realism,' 463–4.

158 *Id.*, 464.

159 Paul Veyne, *Writing History*, trans. Mina Moore-Rinvolucri (Middletown:
Wesleyan University Press, 1984), 4–5.

160  *Id.*

161  Robert Browning, *The Ring and the Book*, ed. Richard D. Altick and Thomas J. Collins (1868–9; Peterborough: Broadview, 2001).

162  *Id.*, bk. XII, ll. 866–7. Preceding summaries based on ibid., vii–xi.

163  Marie Hockenhull Smith, 'The Lawyer, the Novelist, and the Discourse of Authority,' in *Law and Literature*, ed. Michael Freeman and Andrew D.E. Lewis (Oxford: Oxford University Press, 1999), 239 at 242.

164  *Id.*

165  Browning, *The Ring and the Book*, bk I, ll. 1330–5.

166  *Id.*, bk I, ll. 86, 117.

167  *Id.*, bk I, ll. 18–30.

168  *Id.*, bk I, ll. 141–8. To similar effect, Browning writes: 'This is the bookful; thus far take the truth, / The untempered gold, the fact untampered with, / The mere ring-metal ere the ring be made!' *Id.*, bk I, ll. 364–6.

169  *Id.*, bk I, ll. 451–68.

170  *Id.*, bk I, ll. 713, 717–19.

171  *Id.*, bk I, ll. 827–9.

172  *Id.*, bk I, ll. 1105–14.

173  See ibid., bk XII, ll. 576–78 (noting 'The inadequacy and inaptitude / Of that self-same machine, that very law / Man vaunts, devised to dissipate the gloom').

174  For Browning, it is error to accept any single piece of testimonial evidence at face value because it is always already infected with bias, blindness, or confusion: 'who trusts / To human testimony for a fact / Gets this sole fact – himself is proved a fool.' Ibid., bk XII, ll. 601–3. This explains, at least partially, his faith in narrative interplay.

175  See *id.*, Appendix A, General Note 5 at 771–2.

176  *Id.*, bk II, ll. 1075–81.

177  *Id.*, bk II, ll. 1130–60; see also Albert Borowitz, 'The Ring and the Book and the Murder,' *Legal Studies Forum* 29 (2005): 849 (comparing commentaries on evidence of Half-Rome and Other Half-Rome).

178  *Id.*, bk II, ll. 1500–3.

179  *Id.*, bk III, ll. 907–11.

180  *Id.*, bk III, ll. 923–5.

181  *Id.*, bk III, ll. 1308–17.

182  *Id.*, bk IX, ll. 443–8; 457–8; 473–81; 509–11; 525–8.

183  *Id.*, bk V, ll. 1867–77.

184  *Id.*, bk VI, ll. 528–38; 725–38; 1650–93.

185  *Id.*, bk VII, ll. 688–710; 1093–186.

186  *Id.*, bk X, ll. 212–17; 229–32.

187  *Id.*, bk X, ll. 647–56. The 'other Arentine' to which the Pope refers is Pietro Arentino, a lewd sonneteer of the sixteenth century.

188  See, e.g., *id.*, bk. VIII, l. 425.

189  *Id.*, bk X, ll. 543–4.

190  *Id.*, bk X, ll. 598–602.

191  *Id.*, bk X, ll. 1242–4.

192  Robert Langbaum, 'The Ring and the Book: A Relativist Poem,' 71 *PMLA* (1956): 131 at 141.

193  *Id.*, 140–1.

## 3. Law, Narrative, and Democracy

1  See, for example, Jose Maria Maravall, 'The Rule of Law as a Political Weapon,' in *Democracy and the Rule of Law*, ed. Jose Maria Maravall and Adam Przeworski (New York: Cambridge University Press, 2003), 261–6 (demonstrating how 'the rule of law and democracy can undermine each other through politics').

2  See, for example, Richard Posner, *Law, Pragmatism, and Democracy* (Cambridge, MA: Harvard University Press, 2004), 15, 280 (discussing various meanings of both terms).

3  See Neil MacCormick, 'Jurisprudence, Democracy, and the Death of the Weimar Republic,' *Texas Law Review* 77 (1999): 1095 at 1096. MacCormick notes the difficulties inherent in any attempt to define what we popularly think of as a constitutional democracy. He helpfully precedes this observation with a catalogue of what a representative democracy is not: a 'people's democracy' of the Chinese sort, fascism, or military dictatorship. The common thread in the 'nots' is that each of these other forms has tended to result in personal (or at best oligarchical) dictatorships.

4  Ronald Dworkin, *Is Democracy Possible Here? Principles for a New Political Debate* (Princeton: Princeton University Press, 2006), 131–47 (broadly contrasting features of 'majoritarian' and 'partnership' views of democracy); see also Ronald Dworkin, 'Moral Reading,' in *Law and Democracy*, ed. Tom Campbell and Adrienne Stone (Burlington: Ashgate, 2003), 113 (distinguishing 'majoritarian' from 'constitutional' conceptions of democracy).

5  Neil MacCormick, *Rhetoric and the Rule of Law: A Theory of Legal Reasoning* (Oxford: Oxford University Press, 2005), 2 ('Respecting the Rule of Law is of profound political value in states or confederations of states … To have properly published and prospective laws, equality of citizens before them, and limitation of official power with respect to them, are foundations for democratic liberty and essentials for a stable economy').

6 Guillermo O'Donnell, 'The Quality of Democracy: Why the Rule of Law Matters,' *Journal of Democracy* 15 (2004): 32 at 33.

7 The German and French expressions emphasize the link between the 'law' and 'state.' See, for example, Jürgen Habermas, *Between Facts and Norms*, trans. William Rehg (1992; Cambridge, MA: MIT, 1996), xxxv ('When contrasted with the English equivalent, "rule of law," *Rechtsstaat* – which literally means "law-state" – reveals the greater emphasis that the German legal tradition places on the state. Depending on the context, I translate *Rechtsstaat* either as "rule of law" or "constitutional state." I also use "government by law," as a way to split the difference'); Marise Cremona, 'The European Neighborhood Policy: Legal and Institutional Issues,' CDDRL, Working Paper No. 25, 2004, http://cddrl.stanford.edu at 10.

8 See O'Donnell, 'The Quality of Democracy,' 33.

9 Cremona, 'European Neighborhood,' 10 (citing A.V. Dicey, *Lectures Introductory to the Study of the Law of the Constitution* [London: MacMillan, 1885]). According to Cremona, Dicey's approach is reflected in current EU policy. See ibid., 10 (quoting Council Common Position 98/350/CFSP on human rights, democratic principles, the rule of law, and good governance in Africa OJ 1998 L 158/1: 'the rule of law … permits citizens to defend their rights and … implies a legislative and judicial power giving full effect to human rights and fundamental freedoms and a fair, accessible and independent judicial system').

10 Robert Bolt, *A Man for All Seasons* (New York: Vintage, 1990), 65–7 (stage directions and other characters' interjections omitted).

11 Herman Melville, *Billy Budd and Other Stories* (1924; New York: Penguin Classics, 1986).

12 *Id.*, 295.

13 *Id.*, 303.

14 This ambiguity has spawned schools of variant readings in the law-and-literature scholarship. For a good back-and-forth, I would suggest readings of the novella by Judge Posner and Richard Weisberg. Cf. Richard A. Posner, *Law and Literature*, rev. ed. (Cambridge, MA: Harvard University Press, 1998), 165–73 with Richard Weisberg, *Poethics and Other Strategies of Law and Literature* (New York: Columbia University Press, 1992), 104–16.

15 For the conspiracy theorists out there, his name might suggest Edward de Vere, 17th Earl of Oxford, the putative author of Shakespeare's plays.

16 *Billy Budd*, 350.

17 *Id.*, 297.

18 *Id.*, 352.

19 *Id.*, 355.

20 *Id.*, 354.
21 *Id.*, 357.
22 *Id.*, 358.
23 *Id.*, 361.
24 *Id.*, 363.
25 This is of course only possible in the short run because legal narratives often escape that container and assume a non-legal shape. One way of thinking about this phenomenon is by recalling Robert Ferguson's concept of a publication continuum – that is, that though a criminal case may begin with an indictment, it may end with any manner of publication, things like newspaper reports, historical accounts, or even fictionalizations. See Robert A. Ferguson, 'Untold Stories in the Law,' in *Law's Stories*, ed. Peter Brooks and Paul Gewirtz (New Haven: Yale University Press, 1996), 84 at 84. These subsequent publications are manifestations of how different groups have interpreted legal narratives (to make sense to them). For example, *Billy Budd* doesn't end with Billy's death. There is a report in 'a naval chronicle of the time' that shoehorns Billy's story into the British maritime narrative and thereby applauds Claggart as a hero and condemns Billy as a villain. Melville, *Billy Budd*, 382–3. The sailor class, on the contrary, 'instinctively felt that Billy was a sort of man as incapable of mutiny as of willful murder.' They thus carry slivers of the spar from which he was hung as if they were from the True Cross, and they celebrate his end in a ballad, 'Billy in the Darbies.' Ibid., 383–4. For an interesting discussion of the multiple endings (a natural result of what Melville called the 'ragged edges' of truth) of *Billy Budd*, see Barbara Johnson, 'The Execution of Billy Budd,' in *The Critical Difference* (Baltimore: Johns Hopkins University Press, 1980), 79.
26 Melville, *Billy Budd*, 362.
27 See Zenon Bankowski, 'In the Judgment Space,' in *The Universal and the Particular in Legal Reasoning*, ed. Zenon Bankowski and James MacLean (Burlington: Ashgate, 2006), 25 at 33–5.
28 Vere's strict application of the law in Billy's case is not a one-off; rather, it is consistent with his larger world view, which is itself founded on an absolute faith in the power of rules: 'With mankind, he would say, forms, measured forms, are everything; and this is the import couched in the story of Orpheus with his lyre spellbinding the wild denizens of the wood. And this he once applied to the disruption of forms going on across the Channel and the consequences thereof' (Melville, *Billy Budd*, 380). On this count, Vere veers close to the quasi-Hobbesian position of Shakespeare's Angelo in *Measure for Measure*: 'We must not make a scarecrow of the law / Setting it up to fear the birds of prey, / And let it keep one shape, till

custom make it / Their perch and not their terror' (Act II, scene i, ll. 1–4, 3rd ed., ed. David Bevington [Dallas: Scott, 1980]).

29 Cf. MacCormick, *Rhetoric and the Rule of Law*, 31 (emphasizing the 'dynamic aspect' of the Rule of Law, which is 'illustrated by the rights of the defence, and the importance of letting everything that is arguable be argued').

30 O'Donnell, 'Quality of Democracy,' 34.

31 But as Colleen Murphy skilfully illustrates, totalitarian governments aren't really living up to even modest standards. For instance, the use of terror in repressive regimes is effective because it is so arbitrary. And that violates the fundamental prohibition against arbitrary authority over citizens. See Colleen Murphy, 'Lon Fuller and the Moral Value of the Rule of Law,' *Law and Philosophy* 24 (2005): 239 at 252–4.

32 Lon Fuller, *The Morality of Law*, rev. ed. (New Haven: Yale University Press, 1969). For a particularly good discussion of the parable, the case on which it is based, and the practical and theoretical issues at stake, see David Dyzenhaus, 'The Grudge Informer Case Revisited,' *New York University Law Review* 83 (2008): 1000.

33 See Dyzenhaus, 'Grudge Informer,' 1017–18 (demonstrating how Fuller's analytical framework is useful with respect to the issues that arise both before and after the overthrow of a rogue regime like that of the Nazis).

34 Fuller, *Morality of Law*, 39.

35 Joseph Raz, 'The Rule of Law and Its Virtue,' *Law Quarterly Review* 93 (1977): 195 at 196.

36 O'Donnell conceives the rule of law as 'the legally based rule of a democratic state.' He goes on to propose: 'This entails that there exists a legal system that is itself democratic, in three senses: 1) It upholds the political rights, freedoms, and guarantees of a democratic regime; 2) it upholds the civil rights of the whole population; and 3) it establishes networks of responsibility and accountability which entail that all public and private agents, including the highest state officials, are subject to appropriate, legally established controls on the lawfulness of their acts.' O'Donnell, 'Quality of Democracy,' 36. I do not at all disagree with this assessment, but I am more interested in the process by which these ends come to be realized than in how they are framed. Hence, the swerve into Habermas.

37 MacCormick, *Rhetoric and the Rule of Law*, 25–6.

38 William Rehg, 'Habermas' Discourse Theory of Law and Democracy: An Overview of the Argument,' in *The Handbook of Critical Theory*, ed. David M. Rasmussen (Malden: Blackwell, 1996), 166 at 181.

39 *Id.*; see also Michel Rosenfeld, 'Review: Law as Discourse: Bridging the Gap between Democracy and Rights,' *Harvard Law Review* 108 (1995): 1163

at 1175 ('The proceduralist paradigm of law animated by the discourse principle, is, above all, elegantly simple. Starting from a picture of equal "consociates" under law as autonomous and as reciprocally recognizant of each other's dignity, Habermas postulates that these consociates would have to regard as legitimate any laws of which they were both the authors and the addressees'). ·

40  *Id*.

41  Though Habermas is principally concerned with legislation, he 'does acknowledge the need for interpretation in the course of the "discourse of application," as he terms the basic function of the judiciary, and he accepts the propriety of the pressure to achieve internal legal coherence in the process of applying norms.' Tom Campbell, 'Legal Positivism and Deliberative Democracy,' in *Law and Democracy*, ed. Tom Campbell and Adrienne Stone (Burlington: Ashgate, 2003), 342.

42  Habermas, *Between Facts and Norms*, 388–9.

43  Franz Kafka, 'Before the Law,' in *The Penal Colony: Stories and Short Pieces*, trans. Willa and Edwin Muir (1919; New York: Schocken, 1961), 148 at 148–50. Though Kafka separately published the story, it also appears in a slightly different form near the end of his unfinished novel *The Trial*. For an interesting take on the democratic aspects of the story, see Rachel Potter, 'Waiting at the Entrance to the Law: Modernism, Gender, and Democracy,' *Textual Practice* 14 (2000): 253.

44  See, for example, Richard Posner, *Law, Pragmatism, and Democracy* (Cambridge, MA: Harvard University Press, 2004), 109 ('People's interests, preferences, and opinions influence governments, certainly, through the electoral process and otherwise').

45  Rosenfeld, 'Law as Discourse,' 1172.

46  Posner, *Law, Pragmatism and Democracy*, 109. To leave no doubt as to what 'other attributes' might entail, Posner later specifically mentions wealth: 'Successful candidates are not random draws from the public at large. They are smarter, better educated, more ambitious, and wealthier than the average person.' *Id*., 154.

47  *Id*., 16.

48  O'Donnell, 'Quality of Democracy,' 37.

49  See *The Federalist No. 78* (Alexander Hamilton): 'If, then, the courts of justice are to be considered as the bulwarks of a limited Constitution against legislative encroachments, this consideration will afford a strong argument for the permanent tenure of judicial offices, since nothing will contribute so much as this to that independent spirit in the judges as which must be essential to the faithful performance of so arduous a duty.'

50 *Id.* 'The independence of the judges is equally requisite to guard the Constitution and the rights of individuals from the effects of those ill humors
which the arts of designing men, or the influence of particular conjunc-
tures, sometimes disseminate among the people themselves, and which,
though they speedily give place to better information, and more deliberate
reflection, have a tendency, in the meantime, to occasion dangerous inno-
vations in the government, and serious oppressions of the minor party in
the community.'

51 Michael Parenti, *Democracy for the Few* (New York: St Martin's, 1974), 53.

52 See, for example, U.S. Const. amend. I (setting out rights to free speech,
free press, and petition).

53 See U.S. Const. art. 3, § 2, cl. 3 (providing for trial by jury in criminal
cases); U.S. Const. amend. VII (preserving trial by jury in suits at common
law).

54 See U.S. Const. amends. V (no double jeopardy) and VII (no re-examination of facts tried by jury).

55 John Ferejohn and Pasquale Pasquino, 'Rule of Democracy and Rule of Law,'
in *Democracy and the Rule of Law*, ed. J.M. Maravall and A. Przeworski (New
York: Cambridge University Press, 2003), 242 at 243 (noting that jury trials are
one of the few places 'where law and democracy come into close contact').

56 *The Federalist No. 83* (Alexander Hamilton).

57 Alexis de Tocqueville, *Democracy in America*, ed. J. Mayer, trans. George
Lawrence (1835 and 1840; New York: Harper, 1988), 273.

58 *Id.*, 273.

59 *Id.*, 274.

60 *Id.*, 274–5.

61 *Id.*, 275. In light of Tocqueville's position, query whether current methods
of alternative dispute resolution (e.g., private arbitration) are antidemocratic because they take place outside the public's gaze, are effected without public participation, and (usually) result in no public decision.

62 *Id.*, 276.

63 Though New Criticism was given its name by John Crowe Ransom and is
associated with him and a group of Southern intellectuals including Allen
Tate and Cleanth Brooks, it sweeps in a much wider cast of characters,
including T.S. Eliot and I.A. Richards. It held sway from the 1930s to the
1950s and – in my view – continues to colour the way literature is taught in
the United States.

64 Cf. Terry Eagleton, *Literary Theory: An Introduction* (Minneapolis: University of Minnesota Press, 1983), 43 (making the same point with respect to
the work of F.R. Leavis).

65 Perhaps the most influential articulation of the principle of authorial irrelevance may be found in W.K. Wimsatt and Monroe C. Beardsley, 'The Intentional Fallacy,' in *The Verbal Icon: Studies in the Meaning of Poetry* (Lexington: University Press of Kentucky, 1954), 3 ('The design or intention of the author is neither available nor desirable as a standard for judging the success of a work of literary art').

66 *Planned Parenthood of Southeastern Pa. v. Casey*, 505 U.S. 833, 1000-01 (1992) (Scalia, J., dissenting) (bolded emphasis supplied). For a fuller theoretical description of his position, see Antonin Scalia, 'The Rule of Law as a Law of Rules,' *University of Chicago Law Review* 56 (1989): 1175.

67 See Raman Selden, *A Reader's Guide to Contemporary Literary Theory* (Lexington: University Press of Kentucky, 1985), 106–16.

68 *Id.*, 115 (quoting Jauss).

69 For instance, Robert Southey was a well-regarded contemporary of the great Romantic poets, so much so that he was awarded the laureateship in 1813. But by the time I was an undergraduate, he warranted only a single poem of two dozen lines in the fourth edition of the *Norton Anthology of English Literature*.

70 Patrick Harwell with Robert Bentley, *Open to Language* (New York: Oxford University Press, 1982), 352. Answers: (1) deer – a small mammal; (2) meat – edible part of something as opposed to its shell; (3) lets – hinders or prevents; (4) tonight – during last night; (5) bride – bridegroom; (5) road – anchorage (6) unvalued – invaluable (7) occupy – fornicate.

71 Selden, *Reader's Guide*, 112.

72 Umberto Eco, *On Literature*, trans. Martin McLaughlin (2002; Orlando: Harcourt, 2004), 222–3.

73 Ludwig Wittgenstein, *Philosophical Investigations*, 3rd ed., trans. G.E.M. Anscombe (1953; Malden: Blackwell, 2001), 166.

74 According to the notes to the poem, 'Burns's brother said that this poem was composed on the occasion it describes.' *The Norton Anthology of English Literature*, gen. ed. M.H. Abrams, vol. 2 (New York: Norton, 1979), 92.

75 It is equally difficult to trace influences from the writer's side of the equation. In a couple of fascinating essays on the subject of influences, Umberto Eco describes the difficulties inherent in trying to determine whether, how, and to what extent other texts and personal experiences have impacted his own work. See Umberto Eco, 'Borges and My Anxiety of Influence' and 'Intertextual Irony and Levels of Reading,' in Eco, *On Literature*, 118–35, 212–35.

76 *Atkins v. Virginia*, 536 U.S. 304 (2002) (retarded defendant); *Roper v. Simmons*, 125 S. Ct. 1183 (2005) (minor defendant).

77 *Roper*, 125 S. Ct. at 1190.

78  *Stanford v. Kentucky*, 492 U.S. 361 (1989).
79  There are of course ways to cast this discussion other than in the terms of
    reception theory. One could, for instance, think in terms of the interaction
    between 'legal subject' and 'legal object.' For a fascinating and wide-
    ranging analysis that takes this approach, see J.M. Balkin, 'Understanding
    Legal Understanding: The Legal Subject and the Problem of Legal Coher-
    ence,' *Yale Law Journal* 103 (1993): 105.
80  Stanley Fish, *Is There a Text in this Class?* (Cambridge, MA: Harvard Uni-
    versity Press, 1980), 14.
81  Susan Glaspell, 'Trifles,' in *Law and Literature: Text and Theory*, ed. Lenora
    Ledwon (New York: Garland, 1996), 151–64. Glaspell based the play on
    a notorious farmland murder that she covered as a reporter in 1900. For
    further background on that murder, see Patricia Bryan, 'Stories in Fiction
    and in Fact: Susan Glaspell's *A Jury of Her Peers* and the 1901 Murder Trial
    of Margaret Hossack,' *Stanford Law Review* 49 (1997): 1293.
82  *Id.*, 154.
83  This image of masculine cruelty is not unique in female-authored literature
    of the time. An incident in Willa Cather's *A Lost Lady*, in which a boy slits
    the eyes of a woodpecker, comes to mind as a parallel.
84  *Id.*, 157–63.
85  *Id.*, 163.
86  *Id.*, 164.
87  Philip C. Kissam, *The Discipline of Law Schools: The Making of Modern Law-
    yers* (Durham: Carolina Academic Press, 2003), 7.
88  Jeffrey Abramson, *We the Jury: The Jury System and the Ideal of Democracy*
    (New York: Basic, 1994 and 2000), 99.
89  *Id.* (quoting 28 U.S.C. §§ 1861-69).
90  *Taylor v. Louisiana*, 419 U.S. 522, 528 (1975).
91  The cross-sectional ideal has never been fully realized, in part because jury
    pools tend to be based on public records (like voting rolls) that under-
    represent certain groups and because peremptory challenges still have a
    palpable influence on the composition of seated juries, even though they
    can no longer be used to strike prospective jurors solely for racial or gen-
    der reasons. See Abramson, *We the Jury*, 11–12; *Batson v. Kentucky*, 476 U.S.
    79 (1986) (banning race-based peremptory challenges).
92  Abramson persuasively argues that this is a recent phenomenon: 'To look
    at the history of juries in the United States is to see that insistence on dis-
    qualifying prospective jurors for knowing or caring too much about a case
    was not always typical of jury selection.' *Id.*, 21.
93  *Id.*, 22.

94 However true this may be, it runs counter to the historical roots of the jury system, in which the original British juries were comprised of 'men drawn from the neighborhood who were taken to have knowledge of all the relevant facts (anyone who was ignorant was rejected).' Patrick Devlin, *Trial by Jury* (London: Stevens, 1966), 8.

95 Mark Twain, *Roughing It*, ch. 48 (Hartford: American, 1873), http://www.mtwain.com/Roughing_It/49.html.

96 Abramson, *We the Jury*, 53. Abramson goes on to identify the trial of Oliver North on charges stemming from the Iran-Contra Scandal as the 'high-water mark' of the ignorance-as-impartiality theory of jury selection. There, 'the only persons whose impartiality was intact were those rarities who could say that they "saw North on television but it was like watching the Three Stooges or something" or that all they remembered was "that it was about something overseas."' *Id.*, 21.

97 Jewelle Taylor Gibbs, *Race and Justice: Rodney King and O.J. Simpson in a House Divided* (San Francisco: Jossey-Bass, 1996), 28.

98 *Id.*, 29. Unless otherwise noted, the following factual recitations are drawn from Gibbs's account; I have tried, however, to strip them of at least some of Gibbs's pro-King diction.

99 *Id.*, 38.

100 *Id.*, 49.

101 Shortly before the beating, one of the four officers had been called to investigate a domestic-violence incident involving a black family. That officer sent a computer message to officers in another car stating that he had been dealing with 'gorillas in the mist.' *Id.*, 42. The prosecution in the King beating case and subsequent commentators picked up on the phrase as evidence of rampant racism in the LAPD.

102 For an interesting discussion of the 'story' told by a videotape, compare the majority and dissenting opinions of Justice Scalia and Justice Stevens in *Scott v. Harris*, 127 S. Ct. 1769 (2007).

103 *Id.*, 46 (quoting Kimberle Crenshaw and Gary Peller, 'Reel Time/Reel Justice,' in *Reading Rodney King*, ed. Robert Gooding-Williams [New York: Routledge, 1993], 56–70). The presence (some would say omnipresence) of experts in trials adds a layer of interpretive complexity to a jury's task. That is, a typical jury these days must not only interpret and evaluate 'ordinary' trial narratives but also the supposedly disinterested metanarratives of expert authority figures. For a fascinating evaluation of this issue (with a particular focus on the King case), see Curtis E. Renoe, 'Seeing Is Believing?: Expert Testimony and the Construction of Interpretive Authority in an American Trial,' *International Journal of Semiotics* 9 (1996): 115.

104 Crenshaw, 'Reel Time,' 51.

105 *Id.*

106 *Id.*, 51–2.

107 *Id.*, 54 (quoting interview with John W. Mack, 29 October 1993).

108 Langston Hughes, *Harlem* (1951) (italics original).

109 Gibbs, *Race and Justice*, 164–79. For example, Mark Fuhrman, the detective who was responsible for much of the incriminating evidence found on Simpson's estate, was exposed at trial as an extreme racist and a perjurer. And other detectives could not adequately explain the chain of custody for much of the damning blood evidence, which credible defence experts further undermined with testimony of contamination.

110 These numbers reflect the final jury that rendered the decision (i.e., after certain jurors were excused and replaced with alternates). Ibid., 218–19. In another reversal of the King beating case, the district attorney chose to try Simpson 'downtown' rather than in relatively affluent Santa Monica, which was the courthouse closest to where the crimes took place. As a consequence of that decision, the jury pool automatically diversified. Nonetheless, the number of blacks selected as jurors and alternates (fifteen of twenty-four) surprised many. See Abramson, *We the Jury*, xiii.

111 *Id.*

112 *Id.*, xi.

113 Compare, for instance, the contemporaneous reactions of author Shirlee Haizlip and political/social commentator George Will:

The verdict stunningly affirmed the recognition that, along with the non-blacks, the black people on the jury practiced the law-abiding behavior that they had been socialized by and conditioned to: they believed they were obligated to follow both the judge's instructions and the letter of the law. For them, the 'mountain of evidence' was, at best, a sand castle of possibilities.

Incited by Johnnie Cochran to turn the trial into a political caucus, the jurors did that instead of doing their duty of rendering a just verdict concerning two extremely violent deaths. The jurors abused their position in order to send a message about racism or political corruption.

Gibbs, *Race and Justice*, 218, 219–20.

114 *Id.*, xii.

115 With respect to the wrongful death judgment against Simpson, see *Brown v. Simpson*, Case No. SC036876 (LA Sup. Ct.); *Goldman v. Simpson*, Case

No. SC036340 (LA Sup. Ct.). With respect to the Rampart Scandal, see http://www.pbs.org/wgbh/pages/frontline/shows/lapd/scandal.

116 This is another example of the public reinterpretation of legal narratives that we discussed in connection with the multiple endings of *Billy Budd*.

117 Abramson, *We the Jury*, xii.

118 Patrick Colm Hogan, *Cognitive Science, Literature, and the Arts: A Guide for Humanists* (New York: Routledge, 2003).

119 *Id.*, 116.

120 *Id.*, 117.

121 *Id.*; see also William Sullivan et al., *Educating Lawyers: Preparation for the Profession of Law* (San Franciso: Jossey-Bass, 2007), 25 (discussing mastery of 'schemas' as a hallmark of expertise). (This work is popularly known as *The Carnegie Report*.)

122 *Id.*, 117.

123 Gibbs, *Race and Justice*, 227. The idea that different geographic communities may constitute separate interpretive communities would seem to be one that courts and legislatures tacitly accept. For example, certain types of cases (obscenity and medical malpractice come quickly to mind) must be decided according to 'community standards.' See, for example, *Miller v. California*, 413 U.S. 15, 37 (1973) ('obscenity is to be determined by applying "contemporary community standards"'); Tresa Baldas, 'Movement Building to Abolish 'Locality Rules' in Med-Mal Litigation,' *National Law Journal*, 23 July 2007, http://www.law.com/jsp/article. jsp?id=1184956607754 (finding that '21 states still retain laws dictating that a doctor's performance be measured against standards existing in that physician's community').

124 Fish, *Is There a Text*, 338.

125 *Id.*

126 Eagleton, *Literary Theory*, 86.

127 Fish, *Is There a Text*, 199. Put in the form of an aphorism, I think Fish's theory boils down to this: 'We don't see things as *they* are, we see them as *we* are.' Anais Nin, *Seduction of the Minotaur* (Denver: Swallow, 1961), 124.

128 Cf. MacCormick, *Rhetoric and the Rule of Law*, 222 (explaining principles of 'universal causation' and 'rational motivation' as tools for understanding and reconstructing past events).

129 William Butler Yeats, *Easter 1916* (1920), ll. 6, 8.

130 See Paul Butler, 'Racially Based Jury Nullification: Black Power in the Criminal Justice System,' *Yale Law Journal* 105 (1995): 677 at 700: 'Jury nullification occurs when a jury acquits a defendant who it believes is guilty of the crime with which he is charged. In finding the defendant not guilty,

the jury refuses to be bound by the facts of the case or the judge's instructions regarding the law. Instead, the jury votes its conscience.'

131  It is, of course, difficult to tell with any degree of certainty exactly what
motivates any given jury to acquit. Given the sacrosanct 'black box' of the
jury as it deliberates, the most we can typically learn comes after the fact
and is thereby subject to the taint of faulty recollections, rationalizations,
and lies. See, generally, Note, 'Second Circuit Holds That Juror's Intent to
Nullify Is Just Cause for Dismissal,' *Harvard Law Review* 111 (1998): 1347
at 1352.

132  *U.S. v. Barry*, No. 90-0068, 1990 WL 174907 (D. D.C. Oct. 26, 1990), *aff'd*,
938 F.2d 1327 (D.C. Cir. 1991).

133  The following account is drawn from Butler, 'Racially Based Jury Nullification,' 681–2, which is itself based on several accounts in the popular
press.

134  Abramson, *We the Jury*, 65–6. As an interesting and potentially revealing
side note, this judge, Thomas Penfield Jackson, is the jurist criticized by
the Court of Appeals for making improper public statements in the noto-
rious *Microsoft* case. *U.S. v. Microsoft*, 253 F.3d 34, 107-117 (D.C. Cir. 2001).

135  *Id*. Others would no doubt disagree. Devlin, for example, explicitly states
the opposite: 'Each jury is a little parliament.' Devlin, *Trial by Jury*, 164.

136  Regarding *Barry*, some have suggested that the jury was in fact making a
political statement about race relations in the District of Columbia: 'Col-
umnist William Raspberry wrote in the *Washington Post* that "it would
surprise me not at all to learn that all 12 jurors secretly believed the
mayor guilty on virtually all counts" … Raspberry speculated [that] the
jury behaved as if Washington were a "federal colony" with a black population and a white power structure. The jury, Raspberry thought, bridled
at the years-long vendetta of the U.S. Attorney's Office and the FBI to
bring down a popular black mayor. They refused to convict, beyond the
one charge, out of a sense that "occupying forces" had pulled out all the
stops to topple a powerful black man for merely personal sins. There may
have been no legal basis for some juror's refusal to convict on the most
serious charges, but Raspberry congratulated them for using their nullify-
ing powers to send a powerful message to federal authorities about the
nature of life in Washington, D.C.' Abramson, *We the Jury*, 66.

137  See, for example, *Ball v. U.S.*, 163 U.S. 662, 672 (1896) ('A verdict of acquittal, although not followed by any judgment, is a bar to a subsequent
prosecution for the same offense').

138  124 Eng. Rep. 1006 (C.P. 1670). The case arose when Bushell, a juror in the
trial of William Penn for unlawfully (and admittedly) assembling a crowd

on London streets, refused to pay a fine levied on the jury for rendering a verdict contrary to the evidence and against the court's instructions.

139　See Abramson, *We the Jury*, 76 (noting the Georgia Constitution of 1777 and the Pennsylvania Constitution of 1790).

140　*Id.*, 62.

141　For instance, I think Paul Butler's proposal that African-American jurors should harbour a 'presumption in favor of nullification' whenever faced with an African-American defendant charged with a 'victimless' crime is counterproductive and ultimately self-defeating. Butler, 'Racially Based Jury Nullification,' 715. What Butler fails to consider is the inevitable backlash that would occur if black jurors were to begin to acquit black defendants wholesale. This could take a number forms, ranging from more juror dismissals for cause to an overall weakening of the jury system.

142　Abramson, *We the Jury*, xxi–xxii.

143　Devlin suggests that jury nullification provides a vital check on legislation and (especially) executive overreaching. See Devlin, *Trial by Jury*, 160–2 ('The … greater purpose that is served by trial by jury is that it gives protection against laws which the ordinary man may regard as harsh or oppressive. I do not mean by that no more than that it is a protection against tyranny. It is that: but it is also an insurance that the criminal law will conform to the ordinary man's idea of what is fair and just. If it does not, the jury will not be a party to its enforcement').

144　William Shakespeare, *The Merchant of Venice*, act IV, scene i, ll. 182–95, 3rd ed., ed. David Bevington (Dallas: Scott, 1980).

145　Bolt, *Man for All Seasons*, 152.

146　Holmes saw this as the way that law naturally develops. See Oliver Wendell Holmes, 'The Path of the Law,' *Harvard Law Review* 10 (1897): 457 at 466 ('We do not realize how large a part of our law is open to reconsideration upon a slight change in the habit of the public mind').

147　Judge Posner makes a similar point in discussing whether a judge can (or should) dodge precedent or clear legislative intent: 'My answer is that only in the extreme case would the judge be justified in disregarding the legislative judgment. For judges to conduct guerrilla warfare against legislatures and higher courts is destabilizing, and in general a bad thing, but it is not *always* worse than the alternative.' Posner, *Law, Pragmatism, and Democracy*, 71.

148　*See* Karl Llewellyn, *The Common Law Tradition: Deciding Appeals* (Boston: Little, Brown, 1960), 19–20.

149　The 'reasoning' aspect of all this is a subject to which I will return in the next chapter.

150 Stanley Fish, 'Almost Pragmatism: Richard Posner's Jurisprudence,' *University of Chicago Law Review* 57 (1990): 1447 at 1462.

151 Posner, *Law, Pragmatism, and Democracy,* 61–2.

152 Ronald Dworkin, 'Objectivity and Truth: You'd Better Believe It,' *Philosophy and Public Affairs* 25 (1996): 87 at 87.

153 Peter Railton, 'Marx and the Objectivity of Science,' in *The Philosophy of Science,* ed. Richard Boyd et al. (Cambridge, MA: MIT, 1991), 763 at 764.

154 There is no way to carve objectivity and subjectivity at the joint. Nor would this be desirable. For as Neil MacCormick has observed, a 'subjective' inquiry at a level of particularity can aid in the search for 'objective' meaning at a level of generality. See MacCormick, *Rhetoric and the Rule of Law,* 136 (arguing that divining the subjective intention of individual legislators can facilitate the process of ascribing an objective intention to a legislative body).

155 Robert Nozick, *Invariances: The Structure of the Objective World* (Cambridge, MA: Belknap, 2001), 75.

156 Railton, 'Marx,' 764. This sorting process also helps identify the dimensions along which issues concerning a legal system's objectivity might arise. Brian Leiter neatly summarizes four of these dimensions:

- We expect the content of our laws to be objective in the sense of treating people the same unless they are 'relevantly' different;
- We expect judges to be objective in the sense of not being biased against one party or the other;
- We expect legal decisions to be objective in the sense of reaching the result that the law *really* requires without letting bias or prejudice intervene;
- In some areas of the law, we expect the law to employ 'objective' standards of conduct (like 'reasonable person' standards) that do not permit actors to excuse their conduct based on their subjective perceptions at the time.

Brian Leiter, Introduction to *Objectivity in Law and Morals,* ed. Brian Leiter (New York: Cambridge University Press, 2001), 1 at 2–3.

157 Nozick, *Invariances,* 76. In the realm of ethics, Nozick proposes that 'the ethical status of an action or policy is invariant under transformations that substitute one person for another. An ethical statement is (held to be) objective when it exhibits this kind of generality.' Ibid., 289. Within the framework of the law, I think the question of what kind of rule- or reasoning-based invariance should be required is the most interesting. But in practice, the key

component of objectivity is often deemed to be 'invariance across judging subjects.' Gerald Postema, 'Objectivity Fit for Law,' in *Objectivity in Law and Morals*, ed. Brian Leiter (New York: Cambridge University Press, 2001), 108.

158  Fish, 'Almost Pragmatism,' 1448.

159  Posner, *Law, Pragmatism, and Democracy*, 62.

160  For an interesting article that shows, among other things, that 'plain meaning' has no plain meaning, see Clark D. Cunningham et al., 'Plain Meaning and Hard Cases,' *Yale Law Journal* 103 (1994): 1561.

161  Harry Jones, 'The Plain Meaning Rule and Extrinsic Aids in Interpretation of Federal Statutes,' *Washington Law Quarterly* 25 (1939): 2, reprinted in Norman Singer, *Sutherland Statutes and Statutory Construction* 2A, 6th ed. (2002): 785 at 788.

162  In many cases, 'plain meaning' issues become entangled with issues of 'originalism,' 'textualism,' 'organicism,' and other interpretive approaches to legal (especially constitutional) texts. Scholarly materials in this area are legion and well beyond the scope of my argument. A good place to enter this literature is, I think, with the historical perspectives presented in H. Jefferson Powell, 'The Original Understanding of Original Intent,' *Harvard Law Review* 98 (1985): 885; and Mark Tushnet, 'Constitutional Interpretation and Judicial Selection: A View from The Federalist Papers,' *Southern California Law Review* 61 (1988): 1669.

163  MacCormick, *Rhetoric and the Rule of Law*, 204.

164  242 U.S. 470 (1917).

165  Jones, 'Plain Meaning Rule,' 791.

166  478 U.S. 186 (1986).

167  *Id.*, 188.

168  *Id.*, 190.

169  *Id.*, 186, 194.

170  Drucilla Cornell, 'The Violence of the Masquerade: Law Dressed Up as Justice,' *Cardozo Law Review* 11 (1990): 1047 at 1056 (partially quoting Holmes, 'Path of the Law,' 469).

171  *Id.*, 1060.

172  *Id.* (partially quoting Jacques Derrida, 'Force of Law: 'The Mystical Foundation of Authority,' *Cardozo Law Review* 11 [1990]: 919 at 961).

173  *Id.*

174  *Lawrence v. Texas*, 539 U.S. 558 (2003).

175  William Shakespeare, *The First Part of King Henry the Fourth*, Act III, scene i, ll. 51–3, 3rd ed., ed. David Bevington (Dallas: Scott, 1980).

176  Jacques Derrida, *Acts of Literature*, ed. Derek Attridge (New York: Routledge, 1992), 213.

## 4. Narrative as Democratic Reasoning

\* This chapter benefited from comments received at two conferences, the International Conference on the Future of Legal Education (Georgia State) and Law, Culture, and the Humanities (Suffolk). Thanks to Clark Cunningham and Jay Mootz, respectively, for inviting me to participate.

1 Neil MacCormick, *Practical Reason in Law and Morality* (Oxford: Oxford University Press, 2009), 1–2.

2 M.J. Detmold, 'Law as Practical Reason,' *Cambridge Law Journal* 48 (1989): 436 at 436.

3 MacCormick, *Practical Reason*, 13.

4 See Darryl K. Brown, 'Plain Meaning, Practical Reason, and Culpability: Toward a Theory of Jury Interpretation of Criminal Statutes,' *Michigan Law Review* 96 (1998): 1199 at 1215–19.

5 Neil MacCormick, *Legal Reasoning and Legal Theory*, 2nd ed. (Oxford: Clarendon, 1994), 42, 69–70, 80–5, 108–28, 148–9, 157–60, 224–5, 251–4.

6 *Id.*, 183.

7 Throughout the book, MacCormick employs Adam Smith's notion of an impartial spectator to assess the moral implications of various courses of action.

8 *Id.*, 183.

9 *Id.*, 184.

10 *Id.*, 189.

11 *Id.*

12 *Id.*

13 On the subject of co-produced jury narratives, see Robin H. Conley and John M. Conley, 'Stories from the Jury Room: How Jurors Use Narrative to Process Evidence,' *Studies in Law, Politics, and Society* 49 (2009), http://ssrn.com/abstract=1510290 25 at 37.

14 Brown, 'Plain Meaning, Practical Reason, and Culpability: Towards a Theory of Jury Interpretation of Criminal Statutes,' at 1221.

15 *Id.*, 1227.

16 Philip Kissam, *The Discipline of Law Schools: The Making of Modern Lawyers* (Durham: Carolina Academic Press, 2003).

17 *Id.*, 7.

18 *Id.*, 31.

19 M.H. Hoeflich, 'On Reading Cases: The Law Student in Wonderland,' *Syracuse Law Review* 42 (1991): 1163 at 1180.

20 *Id.*; see also Alan Watson, 'Legal Education Reform: Modest Suggestions,' *Journal of Legal Education* 51 (2001): 91 at 93 ('What is going on in the case is very largely incomprehensible').

21 Kissam, *Discipline*, 32.

22 William M. Sullivan et al., *Educating Lawyers: Preparation for the Profession of Law* (San Francisco: Jossey-Bass, 2007), 83. (This work is popularly known as *The Carnegie Report*.)

23 *Id*.

24 *Id*., 84.

25 In a masterful examination of law's untold stories, Robert Ferguson shows how particular narrative pieces of a proceeding can be repressed and contained outside an official trial record. See Robert A. Ferguson, 'Untold Stories in the Law,' in *Law's Stories: Narrative and Rhetoric in the Law*, ed. Peter Brooks and Paul Gewirtz (New Haven: Yale University Press, 1996), 84.

26 Karl N. Llewellyn, *The Common Law Tradition: Deciding Appeals* (Boston: Little, Brown, 1960), 56.

27 Hoeflich, 'On Reading Cases,' 1165.

28 Llewellyn, *The Common Law Tradition*, 56.

29 *Id*.

30 470 U.S. 68 (1985).

31 *Id*., 70.

32 *Id*., 88.

33 For a thorough rhetorical analysis of *Ake*, see Shulamit Almog, 'As I Read, I Weep – In Praise of Judicial Narrative,' *Oklahoma City University Law Review* 26 (2001): 471 at 479–84.

34 William R. Andersen and C. Paul Rogers, *Antitrust Law: Policy and Practice*, 3rd ed. (New York: Mathew Bender, 1999).

35 Phillip Areeda and Louis Kaplow, *Antitrust Analysis: Problems, Text, Cases*, 4th ed. (Boston: Little, Brown, 1988).

36 Thomas D. Morgan, *Cases and Materials on Modern Antitrust Law and Its Origins*, 3rd ed. (St Paul: West, 2005); Charles J. Goetz and Fred S. McChesney, *Antitrust Law: Interpretation and Implementation*, 3rd ed. (New York: Foundation, 2006).

37 Lawrence A. Sullivan and Warren S. Grimes, *The Law of Antitrust: An Integrated Handbook*, 2nd ed. (St Paul: Thomson/West, 2006).

38 429 U.S. 477 (1977).

39 *Id*., 489 ('Plaintiffs must prove *antitrust* injury, which is to say injury of the type that the antitrust laws were intended to prevent and flow from that which makes the defendants' acts unlawful').

40 For instance, the United States Supreme Court recently held that vertical price fixing (resale price maintenance) should no longer be considered

*per se* illegal and should be viewed under the rule of reason. In taking
this step, the Court overruled one of its most venerable precedents, *Dr.
Miles Medical Co. v. John D. Park & Sons*, 220 U.S. 373 (1911). *Leegin Creative
Leather Products v. PSKS Inc.*, 127 S. Ct. 2705 (2007).

41  What Morgan correctly suggests is that change was inevitable by the early
1970s. The economy had become so complex that *per se* rules could no
longer be trusted to produce desired results, and many older decisions
either made little sense in the revised context or could not be logically
extended to new situations or technologies. At the same time, influential
critics like Robert Bork and Richard Posner made powerful thrusts against
the received wisdom; these critics found sympathetic ears among the
judiciary, including the Supreme Court, the composition of which radically
changed with the turnover of four seats between 1970 and 1975.  Morgan,
*Cases and Materials*, 467. But we should also note that *Brunswick*'s oft-
quoted statement that the antitrust laws are designed to protect 'competition, not competitors' is not so inevitable. One could well imagine a society
that would value – and legally protect – a plethora of small businesses for
reasons that post-*Brunswick* cases overlook, reject, or ignore.

42  Sup. Ct. R. 10 (2005).

43  Sup. Ct. R. 14 (2005).

44  Robert A. Ferguson, 'The Judicial Opinion as Literary Genre,' *Yale Journal of
Law and the Humanities* 2 (1990): 201.

45  *Id.*, 208.

46  *Id.*

47  *Id.*, 211. Sanford Levinson has noted how the tone of confidence present in
most appellate opinions often obscures an underlying ambivalence. 'How
often,' he asks, 'does one find a judicial opinion that frankly says that the
question is an exceedingly close one …?' Not often. The reason, he suggests, is that a turn to judicial modesty in the face of a close call might be
taken as a sign of the 'terrifying arbitrariness that underlies much of the
legal system' and as proof that any decision results from something other
than the operation of the Rule of Law. Sanford Levinson, 'The Rhetoric of
the Judicial Opinion,' in Brooks and Gewirtz, *Law's Stories*, 189.

48  With respect to law teaching, it may be that certain types of narrative
materials (I'm thinking especially of literature) may be better suited to
some subjects than to others. Simon Stern proposes, for instance, that novels may contribute to our understanding of evidence law (and vice versa)
because 'the legal question of evidence and the literary question of closure
converge as aspects of legal aesthetics.' Simon Stern, 'Literary Evidence

and Legal Aesthetics,' forthcoming in Austin Sarat, Matthew Anderson, and Catherine Frank, eds., *Teaching Literature and Law* (2010), http://ssrn.com/abstract=1378337, at 10 and 13.

49 Sullivan, *Educating Lawyers*, 124 (discussing interaction of narratives and legal principles in the context of clinical education).

50 A similar – and more widely known – example is that of Judge Martin Manton, a former Chief Judge of the United States Court of Appeals for the Second Circuit. Judge Manton was widely admired for his skill in handling bankruptcy cases. But, alas, Judge Manton fell upon hard times himself (he had built a considerable real estate empire in New York that suffered after the Crash of 1929), and he began to entertain bribes. Thereafter, 'he continued to write model decisions in bankruptcy cases complete with factual and analytic narratives appropriate to the results. What he did not include in these published decisions was the fact that really decided the cases: who paid him the highest bribe.' Hoeflich, 'Reading Cases,' 1167.

51 I am not offering these observations as a sponsorship of a Realist or CLS claim that all legal decisions are arbitrary, political, or elitist. That argument is for another day. Here, I intend for us to test the notion that, for instance, there are prosaic cases that may have been covertly influenced by the type of racial animus that is overtly stated in *Dred Scott* or *Plessy*. We can do this, I think, without deciding how far one should push Llewellyn's famous fillip that 'our government is not a government of laws, but one of laws through men.' Karl N. Llewellyn, 'Some Realism about Realism – Responding to Dean Pound,' *Harvard Law Review* 44 (1931): 1222 at 1243. For a summary of CLS positions on judicial discretion and indeterminacy, see Stephen B. Presser's mimetically titled 'Some Realism about Orphism or The Critical Legal Studies Movement and the New Great Chain of Being,' *Northwestern Law Review* 79 (1984–5): 869.

52 180 P. 213 (Kan. 1919).

53 Hoeflich, 'Reading Cases,' 1168–79.

54 180 P. at 213-14.

55 *Id.*, 214.

56 *Id.*, 215.

57 *Id.*

58 See, for example, *Alexander v. Russo*, 571 P.2d 350 (Kan. App. 1977). As stated in *Taft v. Hyatt*, 105 Kans. 35, 180 P. 213: 'A private offer of reward for the apprehension of an accused person stands, as a general rule, upon a different footing from an offer made by virtue of a statute. When accepted, the offer becomes a contract; until it is accepted by some person, who upon the strength of the offer takes some steps to earn the reward, there is no

contract; and where a claimant of the reward was not aware that it had been offered until after he had acted, he is not entitled to claim the reward' (Syl. 3.)

59  180 P. at 215.
60  *Id.*
61  Cf. Richard Posner, 'Jurisprudential Responses to Legal Realism,' *Cornell Law Review* 73 (1987–8): 326 at 327. In a discussion of how formalists sometimes 'smuggl[e] policy choices into the premises for logical reasoning without analysis or even acknowledgement,' Judge Posner suggests that there may or may not be good reason to recognize a claim for a reward only if the claimant knows of the reward: 'Consider this question of perennial fascination to students of contract law: should a person be allowed to claim, as a matter of contractual entitlement, a reward for returning a lost article, if he did not actually know that a reward had been offered? Langdell said no. And he said it on logical grounds: a contract requires – is defined to require – conscious acceptance; if the person who returned the lost property did not know about the reward he could not have accepted that unilateral offer, and therefore there is no duty to reward this person. Langdell's mistake was to impose a definition on the word "contract" without considering why one might want to make some promises and not others enforceable and what the effect of making this promise enforceable would be. Would it lead to more returns or fewer? Actually this is a difficult question but it is one that Langdell thought he did not even have to consider.'
62  *Id.*, 214–15.
63  Hoeflich, 'Reading Cases,' 1174 (quoting Abstract of Appellants at 14).
64  *State v. Smith*, 174 P. 551 (Kan. 1918).
65  180 P. at 214.
66  174 P. 551 (Kan. 1918).
67  *Id.*, 552.
68  *Id.*, 552.
69  *Id.*, 555 (emphasis supplied).
70  *Id.*, 556 (emphasis supplied).
71  Hoeflich, 'Reading Cases,' 1178 (quoting Lon Fuller and Melvin Eisenberg, *Basic Contract Law*, 3rd ed. [St Paul: West, 1972], 414–15).
72  I don't mean to suggest that the technique I am sponsoring is simply a way to reveal bias in a Realist sort of way. For example, I think one could take a case like *Brunswick* and show how it represents the waning of a public narrative that had romanticized (and legally protected) mom-and-pop businesses and vilified big business from at least the time of Teddy Roosevelt.

73  Philip C. Kissam, 'Lurching Towards the Millennium: The Law School, the Research University, and the Professional Reforms of Legal Education,' *Ohio State Law Journal* 60 (1999): 1965 at 2006–9 (discussing, among other things, the link between reading critically and writing well). The *Carnegie Report* (Sullivan, *Educating Lawyers*, 53) puts it this way: 'It is important … that instructors also give students experience with fuller accounts of cases in which students can grasp the different meaning of "facts" from opposing points of view.' And I am inclined to go beyond actual case materials, as I will later show.

74  Ferguson, 'The Judicial Opinion,' 219.

75  I think the *Carnegie Report* is correct in positing (after Amsterdam and Bruner) 'that the narrative structure of legal reasoning provides a natural deep structure capable of uniting theory and practice.' Sullivan, *Educating Lawyers*, 42.

76  Neil MacCormick, 'Democratic Intellect and the Law,' *Legal Studies* 5 (1985): 172 at 177.

77  *Id.*, 180.

78  Llewellyn, *The Common Law Tradition*, 56–7.

79  Detmold, 'Law as Practical Reason,' 437.

80  *Id.*, 467–8.

81  See, for example, John Dewey, *Democracy and Education: An Introduction to the Philosophy of Education* (1916; New York: Free Press, 1997); Ronald Dworkin, *Is Democracy Possible Here? Principles for a New Political Debate* (Princeton: Princeton University Press, 2006).

82  *Id.*, 148–9.

83  Randy D. Gordon, 'How Lawyers (Come to) See the World: A Narrative Theory of Legal Pedagogy,' *Loyola Law Review* (forthcoming 2010).

84  Posner's most influential work in the law and economics vein began to appear in the early 1970s. See, for example, Richard A. Posner, 'Killing or Wounding to Protect a Property Interest,' *Journal of Law and Economics* 14 (1971): 201; 'The Economic Approach to Law,' *Texas Law Review* 53 (1975): 757. The seminal work in what we now think of as law-and-economics analysis traces to a decade earlier, especially with the work of (now Judge) Guido Calabresi and Ronald Coase. See Guido Calabresi, 'Some Thoughts on Risk Distribution and the Law of Torts,' *Yale Law Journal* 70 (1961): 499; Ronald Coase, 'The Problem of Social Cost,' *Journal of Law and Economics* 3 (1960): 1.

85  Posner, 'The Economic Approach,' 763–4.

86  Richard A. Posner, *Law, Pragmatism, and Democracy* (Cambridge, MA: Harvard University Press, 2003), 78.

87  See, for example, *Apani Southwest, Inc. v. Coca-Cola Enters.*, 300 F.3d 620, 628 (5th Cir. 2002) ('Where the plaintiff fails to define its proposed relevant market with reference to the rule of reasonable interchangeability and cross-elasticity of demand, or alleges a proposed relevant market that clearly does not encompass all interchangeable substitute products even when all factual inferences are granted in plaintiff's favor, the relevant market is legally insufficient, and a motion to dismiss may be granted').

88  Posner, 'The Economic Approach,' 764.

89  Ferguson, 'Untold Stories,' 84.

90  464 U.S. 238 (1984).

91  See Kelly Lynn Anders, 'Reviewing Silkwood at 25: The Reel Impact on Environmental Policy,' *South Texas Law Review* 49 (2007): 451.

92  *Silkwood v. Kerr-McGee Corporation*, 769 F.2d 1451, 1461 (10th Cir. 1985) (quoting *Smith v. Wade*, 461 U.S. 30, 52 [1983]) (emphasis added).

93  *Silkwood v. Kerr-McGee Corp.*, 464 U.S. 239, 241–2 (1984). I should note that I practised for a few years with the firm, Crowe & Dunlevy, that defended Kerr-McGee in *Silkwood*. The case had settled well before my arrival at the firm, so I had no involvement with any stage of the litigation. I do, of course, know and admire many of the lawyers involved, but I have based my discussion on the public record, not any particular insight I got from the firm.

94  The statement that Silkwood's death was 'unrelated' also appears in opinions of the Tenth Circuit, both before and after the Supreme Court opinion. *Silkwood v. Kerr-McGee Corp.*, 667 F.2d 908, 912 (10th Cir. 1981) and 769 F.2d 1451, 1453 (10th Cir. 1985).

95  In focusing on Karen Silkwood's personal story, I don't want to minimize the possibility that the jury was influenced generally by the growing public scepticism about nuclear energy or specifically by evidence allegedly suggesting that Kerr-McGee's plant was unsafely maintained and operated.

96  *Silkwood v. Kerr-McGee Corp.*, 485 F. Supp. 566, 590 (W.D. Okla. 1979).

97  667 F.2d 908, 915 (10th Cir. 1982).

98  Richard Rashke, *The Killing of Karen Silkwood*, 2d ed. (Ithaca: Cornell University Press, 2000).

99  485 F. Supp. at 492.

100  485 F. Supp. at 602.

101  Rashke, *The Killing of Karen Silkwood*, 344–6 (quoting testimony of union leader Steve Wodka and Silkwood's friend Wanda Jean Jung); see also 769 F.2d at 1464 (Doyle, J., dissenting).

102  Robin H. Conley and John M. Conley, 'Stories from the Jury Room: How

Jurors Use Narrative to Process Evidence,' *Studies in Law, Politics & Society* 49 (2009), http://ssrn.com/abstract=1510290, 25 at 37.

103  667 F.2d at 915.

104  See Alan M. Dershowitz, 'Life Is Not a Dramatic Narrative,' in Brooks, *Law's Stories*, 99.

105  Nora Ephron and Alice Arlen, *Silkwood Shooting Script*, (An ABC Motion Picture New York Office Production Office, 1982), 125–6, ¶¶ 203–4.

106  *Silkwood v. Kerr-McGee Corporation*, 769 F.2d 1451, 1470 (10th Cir. 1985) (Doyle, J., dissenting).

107  'Karen Silkwood,' like 'Three Mile Island' and 'Chernobyl,' has become a shorthand for all sorts of calamities in the nuclear industry. Her name is often invoked in regulatory contexts, especially those dealing with the handling and disposal of hazardous materials. See Anders, 'Reviewing Silkwood,' 454n.16.

108  Edward W. Said, *Humanism and Democratic Criticism* (New York: Columbia University Press, 2003), 71, 73.

## A Conclusion of Sorts

1  T.S. Eliot, 'Tradition and the Individual Talent,' reprinted in *The Norton Anthology of English Literature*, gen. ed. M.H. Abrams, vol. 2 (1919; New York: Norton, 1979), 2293. For an interesting take on law-as-tradition-as-narrative, see Dennis Patterson, 'Law's Pragmatism: Law as Practice and Narrative,' *Virginia Law Review* 76 (1990): 937 at 987–9.

2  *Id.* (italics added).

3  *Id.*

4  *Id.*, 2294.

5  *Id.* Alasdair MacIntyre states the deep issue here as one of 'an historically extended, socially embodied argument' that crosses generational lines. And narrative is crucial to this transgenerational argument: 'The history of a practice in our time is generally and characteristically embedded in and made intelligible in terms of the larger and longer history of the tradition through which the practice in its present form was conveyed to us; the history of each of our own lives is generally and characteristically embedded in and made intelligible in terms of the larger and longer histories of a number of traditions.' Alasdair MacIntyre, *After Virtue*, 3rd ed. (Notre Dame: University of Notre Dame Press, 2007), 222.

6  *Id.*, 2295.

7  Ronald Dworkin, *Law's Empire* (Cambridge, MA: Belknap, 1986), 227. Dworkin is not unaware of Eliot's essay, though he cites it only for a posi-

tion on authorial intention that he appears to eschew in favour of Gad-amer. *Id.*, 61n.11. See also Neil MacCormick, *Rhetoric and the Rule of Law: A Theory of Legal Reasoning* (Oxford: Oxford University Press, 2005), 233–6 (discussing possibility of normative coherence as narrative coherence).

8 *Id.*, 2294–5. Derrida makes a similar point when he asserts that 'to be just, the decision of a judge, for example, must not only follow a rule of law or a general law but also must assume it, approve it, confirm its value, by a reinstituting act of interpretation, as if ultimately nothing previously existed of the law, as if the judge himself invented the law in every case. No exercise of justice as law can be just unless there is a "fresh judgment" (I borrow this English expression from Stanley Fish ...). This "fresh judg-ment" can very well – must very well – conform to a preexisting law, but the reinstituting, reinventive and freely decisive interpretation, the respon-sible interpretation of the judge requires that his "justice" not just consist in conformity, in the conservative and reproductive activity of judgment.' Jacques Derrida, 'Force of Law: The "Mystical Foundation of Authority,"' *Cardozo Law Review* 11 (1989–90): 919 at 961.

9 I think this is also what Llewellyn is up to when he posits 'the law of Fit-ness and Flavor': 'The work of the job in hand, and even more the work of the job at large, must fit and fit into the body and the flavor of The Law.' Karl Llewellyn, *The Common Law Tradition: Deciding Appeals* (Boston: Little, Brown, 1960), 222.

10 Dworkin, *Law's Empire*, 238–9.

11 Eliot, 'Tradition and the Individual Talent,' 2295.

12 Patterson, 'Law's Pragmatism,' 988.

13 *Id.*

14 Eliot, 'Tradition and the Individual Talent,' 2295.

# Bibliography

**Works Cited**

*Books, Chapters, and Articles*

Abramson, Jeffrey. *We, the Jury: The Jury System and the Ideal of Democracy*. New York: Basic, 1994 and 2000.

Adler, Jonathan H. 'Fables of the Cuyahoga: Reconstructing a History of Environmental Protection.' *Fordham Environmental Law Journal* 14 (2002): 89.

– 'Smoking Out the Cuyahoga Fire Fable: Smoke and Mirrors Surrounding Cleveland.' *National Review Online*, 22 June 2004. http://www.nationalreview.com/adler/adler200406220845.asp.

Almog, Shulamit. 'As I Read, I Weep – In Praise of Judicial Narrative.' *Oklahoma City University Law Review* 26 (2001): 471.

Amsterdam, Anthony G., and Jerome Bruner. *Minding the Law*. Cambridge, MA: Harvard University Press, 2000.

Anders, Kelly Lynn. 'Reviewing Silkwood at 25: The Reel Impact on Environmental Policy.' *South Texas Law Review* 49 (2007): 451.

Andersen, William R., and C. Paul Rogers. *Antitrust Law: Policy and Practice*. 3rd ed. New York: Mathew Bender, 1999.

Angelo, Mary Jane. 'Embracing Uncertainty, Complexity, and Change: An Eco-pragmatic Reinvention of a First-Generation Environmental Law.' *Ecology Law Quarterly* 33 (2006): 105.

Areeda, Phillip, and Louis Kaplow. *Antitrust Analysis: Problems, Text, Cases*. 4th ed. Boston: Little, Brown, 1988.

Bailey, Thomas A. 'Congressional Opposition to Pure Food Legislation 1879–1906.' *American Journal of Sociology* 36 (1930): 52.

Baldas, Tresa. 'Movement Building to Abolish "Locality Rules" in Med-Mal

Litigation.' *National Law Journal,* 23 July 2007. http://www.law.com/jsp/article.jsp?id=1184956607754.

Balkin, J.M. 'Understanding Legal Understanding: The Legal Subject and the Problem of Legal Coherence.' *Yale Law Journal* 103 (1993): 105.

– 'Deconstructive Practice and Legal Theory.' *Yale Law Journal* 96 (1987): 743.

Bankowski, Zenon. 'How Does It Feel to Be on Your Own? The Person in the Sight of Autopoiesis.' *Ratio Juris* 7 (1994): 254.

– 'In the Judgment Space.' In *The Universal and the Particular in Legal Reasoning,* edited by Zenon Bankowski and James MacLean. Burlington: Ashgate, 2006.

– 'Legal Reasoning from the Inside Out.' In *Stressing Legal Decisions,* edited by Tadeusz Biernat et al. Krakow: Polonia, 2003.

– *Living Lawfully: Love in Law and Law in Love.* Boston: Kluwer, 2001.

– et al. 'Rationales for Precedent.' In *Interpreting Precedents,* edited by D. Neil MacCormick and Robert S. Summers. Aldershot: Ashgate/Dartmouth, 1997.

Barth, John, 'Frame-Tale.' In *Lost in the Funhouse.* Garden City: Doubleday, 1968.

Barthes, Roland. *Image Music Text.* 1977. Translated by Stephen Heath. New York: Noonday, 1988.

Baxter, Hugh. 'Autopoiesis and the "Relative Autonomy" of Law.' *Cardozo Law Review* 19 (1997–8): 1987.

Beyl, Caula A. 'Rachel Carson, *Silent Spring,* and the Environmental Movement.' *HortTechology* 2 (1992): 272.

Binder, Guyora, and Robert Weisberg. *Literary Criticisms of Law.* Princeton: Princeton University Press, 2000.

Bix, Brian H. 'Law as an Autonomous Discipline.' In *The Oxford Handbook of Legal Studies,* edited by Peter Cane and Mark Tushnet. New York: Oxford University Press, 2003. http://ssrn.com/abstract_id=315719.

Bolt, Robert. *A Man for All Seasons.* New York: Vintage, 1990.

Borowitz, Albert. '*The Ring and the Book* and the Murder.' *Legal Studies Forum* 29 (2005): 849.

Bosso, Christopher J. *Pesticides and Politics.* Pittsburgh: University of Pittsburgh Press, 1987.

Brooks, Paul. *The House of Life: Rachel Carson at Work.* Boston: Houghton Mifflin, 1972.

Brooks, Peter. 'Narrativity of the Law.' *Law and Literature* 14 (2002): 1.

Brooks, Peter, and Paul Gewirtz, eds. *Law's Stories: Narrative and Rhetoric in the Law.* New Haven: Yale University Press, 1996.

Brown, Darryl K. 'Plain Meaning, Practical Reason, and Culpability: Toward a Theory of Jury Interpretation of Criminal Statutes.' *Michigan Law Review* 96 (1998): 1199.

Browning, Robert. *The Ring and the Book*. 1868–9, edited by Richard D. Altick and Thomas J. Collins. Peterborough: Broadview, 2001.

Bryan, Patricia. 'Stories in Fiction and in Fact: Susan Glaspell's *A Jury of Her Peers* and the 1901 Murder Trial of Margaret Hossack.' *Stanford Law Review* 49 (1997): 1293.

Burns, Robert. *To A Mouse*. 1786.

Butler, Paul. 'Racially Based Jury Nullification: Black Power in the Criminal Justice System.' *Yale Law Journal* 105 (1995): 677.

Calabresi, Guido. 'Some Thoughts on Risk Distribution and the Law of Torts.' *Yale Law Journal* 70 (1961): 499.

Campbell, Tom. 'Legal Positivism and Deliberative Democracy.' In *Law and Democracy*, edited by Tom D. Campbell and Adrienne Stone. Burlington: Ashgate, 2003.

Camus, Albert. *The Stranger* [1942]. Translated by Matthew Ward. New York: Vintage, 1989.

Carson, Rachel. *Silent Spring*. 1962. Wilmington: Mariner, 2002.

Cho, Susie. 'Capital Confusion: The Effect of Jury Instructions on the Decision to Impose Death.' *Journal of Criminal Law and Criminology* 85 (1994): 532.

Clawson, Mark A. 'Telling Stories: Romance and Dissonance in Progressive Legal Narratives.' *Legal Studies Forum* 22 (1998): 353.

Coase, Ronald. 'The Problem of Social Cost.' *Journal of Law and Economics* 3 (1960): 1.

Conley, Robin H., and John M. Conley. 'Stories from the Jury Room: How Jurors Use Narrative to Process Evidence.' *Studies in Law, Politics, and Society* 49 (2009): 25. http://ssrn.com/abstract=1510290.

Cornell, Drucilla. 'The Violence of the Masquerade: Law Dressed Up as Justice.' *Cardozo Law Review* 11 (1990): 1047.

Cover, Robert M. 'Forward: *Nomos* and Narrative.' *Harvard Law Review* 97 (1983): 4.

Crane, Gregg D. 'The Path of Law and Literature.' *American Literary History* 9 (1997): 758.

Cremona, Marise. 'The European Neighborhood Policy: Legal and Institutional Issues.' CDDRL, Working Paper No. 25, 2004. http://cddrl.stanford.edu.

Crenshaw, Kimberle, and Gary Peller. 'Reel Time/Reel Justice.' In *Reading Rodney King*, edited by Robert Gooding-Williams. New York: Routledge, 1993.

Cunningham, Clark D., et al. 'Plain Meaning and Hard Cases.' *Yale Law Journal* 103 (1994): 1561.

Derrida, Jacques. *Acts of Literature*, edited by Derek Attridge. New York: Routledge, 1992.

– *Of Grammatology*. Translated by Gayatri Chakravorty Spivak. Baltimore: Johns Hopkins University Press, 1976.

– 'Force of Law: The "Mystical Foundation of Authority."' *Cardozo Law Review*
11 (1989–90): 961.

Dershowitz, Alan M. 'Life Is Not a Dramatic Narrative.' In *Law's Stories: Narrative and Rhetoric in the Law*, edited by Peter Brooks and Paul Gewirtz. New
Haven: Yale University Press, 1996.

DeStephano, John M. 'On Literature as Legal Authority.' *Arizona Law Review*
49 (2007): 522.

Detmold, M.J. 'Law as Practical Reason.' *Cambridge Law Journal* 48 (1989): 436.

Devitt, Amy. 'Integrating Rhetorical and Literary Theories of Genre.' *College
English* 62 (2000): 696.

– *Standardizing Written English: Diffusion in the Case of Scotland, 1520–1659.*
Cambridge: Cambridge University Press, 1989.

– *Writing Genres.* Carbondale: Southern Illinois University Press, 2004.

Devlin, Patrick. *Trial by Jury.* London: Stevens, 1966.

Dewey, John. *Democracy and Education: An Introduction to the Philosophy of Education* [1916]. New York: Free Press, 1997.

Dolin, Kieran. *A Critical Introduction to Law and Literature.* Cambridge: Cambridge University Press, 2007.

Dworkin, Ronald. *Is Democracy Possible Here? Principles for a New Political
Debate.* Princeton: Princeton University Press, 2006.

– 'Law as Interpretation.' *Critical Inquiry* 9 (1982): 179.

– *Law's Empire.* Cambridge, MA: Belknap, 1986.

– 'Moral Reading.' In *Law and Democracy*, edited by Tom Campbell and Adrienne Stone. Burlington: Ashgate, 2003.

– 'Objectivity and Truth: You'd Better Believe It.' *Philosophy and Public Affairs*
25 (1996): 87.

– 'Social Sciences and Constitutional Rights – The Consequences of Uncertainty.' *Journal of Law and Education* 6 (1977): 3.

Dyzenhaus, David. 'The Grudge Informer Case Revisited.' *New York University
Law Review* 83 (2008): 1000.

Eagleton, Terry. *Literary Theory: An Introduction.* Minneapolis: University of
Minnesota Press, 1983.

Eco, Umberto. *On Literature.* 2002. Translated by Martin McLaughlin. Orlando:
Harcourt, 2004.

Eliot, T.S., 'Tradition and the Individual Talent' [1919]. Reprinted in *The Norton
Anthology of English Literature.* 4th ed., vol. 2. New York: Norton, 1979.

Ephron, Nora, and Alice Arlen. *Silkwood Shooting Script.* An ABC Motion Picture. New York Office Production Office, 1982.

Ewick, Patricia, and Susan S. Silbey. 'Subversive Stories and Hegemonic Tales:
Towards a Sociology of Narrative.' *Law and Society Review* 29 (1995): 197.

Farber, Daniel A., and Suzanna Sherry. 'Telling Stories out of School: An Essay on Legal Narratives.' *Stanford Law Review* 45 (1993): 807.

Farmer, Lindsay. '"The Genius of our Law …": Criminal Law and the Scottish Legal Tradition.' *Modern Law Review* 55 (1992): 25.

Ferejohn, John, and Pasquale Pasquino. 'Rule of Democracy and Rule of Law.' In *Democracy and the Rule of Law*, edited by J.M. Maravall and A. Przeworski. New York: Cambridge University Press, 2003.

Ferguson, Robert A. 'The Judicial Opinion as Literary Genre.' *Yale Journal of Law and the Humanities* 2 (1990): 201.

– 'Untold Stories in the Law.' In *Law's Stories*, edited by Peter Brooks and Paul Gewirtz. New Haven: Yale University Press, 1996.

Fish, Stanley. 'Almost Pragmatism: Richard Posner's Jurisprudence.' *University of Chicago Law Review* 57 (1990): 1447.

– *Is There a Text in This Class?* Cambridge, MA: Harvard University Press, 1980.

– 'Working on the Chain Gang: Interpretation in the Law and in Literary Criticism.' *Critical Inquiry* 9 (1982): 201.

Fried, Charles. 'Jurisprudential Responses to Legal Realism.' *Cornell Law Review* 73 (1987–8): 331.

Frost, Robert. *Mending Wall* (1915).

Fry, Michael. 'The Whig Interpretation of Scottish History.' In *The Manufacture of Scottish History*, edited by Ian Donnachie and Christopher Whatley. Edinburgh: Polygon, 1992.

Fry, Paul H. *The Reach of Criticism: Method and Perception in Literary Theory*. New Haven: Yale University Press, 1983.

Fuller, Lon L. *The Morality of Law*. Rev. ed. New Haven: Yale University Press, 1969.

Fuller, Lon, and Melvin Eisenberg. *Basic Contract Law*. 3rd ed. St Paul: West, 1972.

Gallagher, Catherine, and Stephen Greenblatt. *Practicing New Historicism*. Chicago: University of Chicago Press, 2000.

Gibbs, Jewelle Taylor. *Race and Justice: Rodney King and O.J. Simpson in a House Divided*. San Francisco: Jossey-Bass, 1996.

Glaspell, Susan. 'Trifles.' In *Law and Literature: Text and Theory*, edited by Lenora Ledwon. New York: Garland, 1996.

Goetz, Charles J., and Fred S. McChesney. *Antitrust Law: Interpretation and Implementation*. 3rd ed. New York: Foundation, 2006.

Golan, Tal. *Laws of Men and Laws of Nature*. Cambridge, MA: Harvard University Press, 2004.

Gordon, Randy D. 'How Lawyers (Come to) See the World: A Narrative Theory of Legal Pedagogy.' *Loyola Law Review* (forthcoming 2010).

Graham, Michael H. *Evidence: Text, Rules, Illustrations, and Problems.* Rev. 2nd ed. Notre Dame: National Institute for Trial Advocacy, 1989.

Greenblatt, Stephen. *Renaissance Self-Fashioning: From More to Shakespeare.* Chicago: University of Chicago Press, 1980.

Habermas, Jürgen. *Between Facts and Norms* [1992]. Translated by William Rehg. Cambridge, MA: MIT, 1996.

Hamilton, Alexander. *The Federalist* No. 78.

Harwell, Patrick, with Robert Bentley. *Open to Language.* New York: Oxford University Press, 1982.

Hearn, Jonathan. 'Narrative, Agency, and Mood: On the Social Construction of National History in Scotland.' *Comparative Studies in Sociology and History* 44 (2002): 745.

Heinzerling, Lisa, and Mark V. Tushnet. *The Regulatory and Administrative State.* New York: Oxford University Press, 2006.

Hoeflich, M.H. 'On Reading Cases: The Law Student in Wonderland.' *Syracuse Law Review* 42 (1991): 1163.

Hogan, Patrick Colm. *Cognitive Science, Literature, and the Arts: A Guide for Humanists.* New York: Routledge, 2003.

Holmes, Oliver Wendell, Jr. *The Common Law.* Boston: Little, Brown, 1881. Excerpted in Stephen B. Presser and Jamil S. Zainaldin. *Law and Jurisprudence in American History.* 2nd ed. St Paul: West, 1989.

– 'The Path of the Law.' *Harvard Law Review* 10 (1897): 457.

Howarth, David. 'Is Law a Humanity (or Is It More Like Engineering)?' *Arts and Humanities in Higher Education* 3 (2004): 9.

Hughes, Langston. *Harlem* (1951).

Hume, Baron. 1 *Commentaries on the Law of Scotland Respecting Crimes*, edited by B. Bell. 4th ed. Edinburgh: Bell and Bradfute, 1844.

Jackson, Bernard S. *Law, Fact, and Narrative Coherence.* Roby: Deborah Charles, 1988.

Johnson, Barbara. 'The Execution of Billy Budd.' In *The Critical Difference.* Baltimore: Johns Hopkins University Press, 1980.

Jones, Daryl. *The Dime Novel Western.* Bowling Green: Popular Press of Bowling Green University, 1978.

Jones, Harry. 'The Plain Meaning Rule and Extrinsic Aids in Interpretation of Federal Statutes.' *Washington Law Quarterly* 25 (1939): 2. Reprinted in Norman Singer. *Sutherland Statutes and Statutory Construction* 2A. 6th ed. (2002): 785.

Jonson, Ben. 'Discoveries.' In *The Works of Ben Johnson*, edited by Francis Cunningham. Vol. 3. London: Chatto and Windus, 1903.

Kafka, Franz. 'Before the Law.' In *The Penal Colony: Stories and Short Pieces* [1919]. Translated by Willa and Edwin Muir. New York: Schocken, 1961.

Kehoe, Terence, and Charles Jacobson. 'Environmental Decisionmaking and DDT Production at Montrose Chemical Corporation of California.' *Enterprise and Society* 4 (2003): 640.

Kissam, Philip C. *The Discipline of Law Schools: The Making of Modern Lawyers*. Durham: Carolina Academic Press, 2003.

– 'Lurching Towards the Millennium: The Law School, the Research University, and the Professional Reforms of Legal Education.' *Ohio State Law Journal* 60 (1999): 1965.

Langbaum, Robert. '*The Ring and the Book:* A Relativist Poem.' *PMLA* 71 (1956): 131.

Lear, Linda J. *Rachel Carson: Witness for Nature*. New York: Holt, 1997.

Leiter, Brian. Introduction to *Objectivity in Law and Morals*, edited by Brian Leiter. New York: Cambridge University Press, 2001.

Lerner, Renée Lettow. 'The Intersection of Two Systems: An American on Trial for an American Murder in the French *Cour D'Assises*.' *University of Illinois Law Review* (2001): 791.

Levinson, Sanford. 'The Rhetoric of the Judicial Opinion.' In *Law's Stories: Narrative and Rhetoric in the Law*, edited by Peter Brooks and Paul Gewirtz. New Haven: Yale University Press, 1996.

Libecap, Gary D., and Mark T. Law. 'Corruption and Reform? The Emergence of the 1906 Food and Drug Act and the 1906 Meat Inspection Act.' International Center for Economic Research, Working Paper No. 20, 2003. http://www.icer.it/docs/wp2003/Libecap20-03.pdf.

Linquist, Stefanie A., and Frank B. Cross. 'Empirically Testing Dworkin's Chain Novel Theory: Studying the Path of Precedent.' *New York University Law Review* 80 (2005): 1156.

Llewellyn, Karl N. *The Common Law Tradition: Deciding Appeals*. Boston: Little, Brown, 1960.

– 'Some Realism about Realism – Responding to Dean Pound.' *Harvard Law Review* 44 (1931): 1222.

Luhmann, Niklas. *Social Systems*. Translated by John Bednarz, Jr, and Dirk Baecker. Stanford: Stanford University Press, 1995.

MacCormick, Neil. 'Democratic Intellect and the Law.' *Legal Studies* 5 (1985): 172.

– *Institutions of Law: An Essay in Legal Theory*. Oxford University Press, 2007.

– 'Jurisprudence, Democracy, and the Death of the Weimar Republic.' *Texas Law Review* 77 (1999): 1095.

– *Legal Reasoning and Legal Theory*. 2nd ed. Oxford: Clarendon, 1994.

– 'Notes on Narrativity and the Normative Syllogism.' *International Journal for the Semiotics of Law* 4 (1991): 163.

– *Practical Reason in Law and Morality*. Oxford: Oxford University Press, 2009.
– *Rhetoric and the Rule of Law: A Theory of Legal Reasoning*. Oxford: Oxford University Press, 2005.
MacIntyre, Alasdair. *After Virtue*. 3rd ed. Notre Dame: University of Notre Dame Press, 2007.
Maravall, Jose Maria. 'The Rule of Law as a Political Weapon.' In *Democracy and the Rule of Law*, edited by Jose Maria Maravall and Adam Przeworski. New York: Cambridge University Press, 2003: 261.
McCracken-Flesher, Caroline. 'Thinking Nationally/Writing Colonially? Scott, Stevenson, and England.' *Novel* 24 (1991): 296.
Melville, Herman. *Billy Budd and Other Stories* [1924]. New York: Penguin, 1986.
Montrose, Louis Adrian. 'The Purpose of Playing: Reflections on a Shakespearean Anthropology.' *Helios* 32 (1980): 28.
Morgan, Thomas D. *Cases and Materials on Modern Antitrust Law and Its Origins*. 3rd ed. St Paul: West, 2005.
Murfin, Ross, and Supryia M. Ray. *The Bedford Glossary of Critical and Literary Terms*. 2nd ed. Boston: Bedford/St Martin's, 2003.
Murphy, Colleen. 'Lon Fuller and the Moral Value of the Rule of Law.' *Law and Philosophy* 24 (2005): 239.
Newman, Randy. 'Burn On.' On *Sail Away*. Warner Bros. Records, 1972.
Nin, Anais. *Seduction of the Minotaur*. Denver: Swallow, 1961.
Note. 'Second Circuit Holds that Juror's Intent to Nullify Is Just Cause for Dismissal.' *Harvard Law Review* 111 (1998): 1347.
Nozick, Robert. *Anarchy, State, and Utopia*. New York: Basic, 1974.
– *Invariances: The Structure of the Objective World*. Cambridge, MA: Belknap, 2001.
Nussbaum, Martha. 'Equity and Mercy.' In *Sex and Social Justice*. New York: Oxford University Press, 1999.
– *The Fragility of Goodness: Luck and Ethics in Greek Tragedy and Philosophy*. New York: Cambridge University Press, 1986.
O'Donnell, Guillermo. 'The Quality of Democracy: Why the Rule of Law Matters.' *Journal of Democracy* 15 (2004): 32.
Orgel, Stephen. 'The Role of King.' In *The New Historicism Reader*. Edited by H. Aram Veeser. New York: Routledge, 1994.
Papke, David Ray, and Kathleen H. McManus. 'Narrative and the Appellate Opinion.' *Legal Studies Forum* 23 (1999): 449.
Parenti, Michael. *Democracy for the Few*. New York: St Martin's, 1974.
Patterson, Dennis. 'Law's Pragmatism: Law as Practice and Narrative.' *Virginia Law Review* 76 (1990): 937.

Posner, Richard A. *Cardozo: A Study in Reputation*. Chicago: University of Chicago Press, 1990.

– 'Conventionalism: The Key to Law as an Autonomous Discipline?' *Toronto Law Journal* 38 (1988): 333.

– 'The Decline of Law and an Autonomous Discipline: 1962–1987.' *Harvard Law Review* 100 (1987): 761.

– 'The Economic Approach to Law.' *Texas Law Review* 53 (1975): 757.

– 'Jurisprudential Responses to Legal Realism.' *Cornell Law Review* 73 (1987–88): 326.

– 'Killing or Wounding to Protect a Property Interest.' *Journal of Law and Economics* 14 (1971): 201.

– *Law and Literature*. Rev. ed. Cambridge, MA: Harvard University Press, 1998.

– 'Law and Literature: A Relation Reargued.' *Virginia Law Review* 72 (1986): 1351.

– *Law, Pragmatism, and Democracy*. 2003. Cambridge, MA: Harvard University Press, 2004.

Postema, Gerald. 'Objectivity Fit for Law.' In *Objectivity in Law and Morals*, edited by Brian Leiter. New York: Cambridge University Press, 2001.

Potter, Rachel. 'Waiting at the Entrance to the Law: Modernism, Gender, and Democracy.' *Textual Practice* 14 (2000): 253.

Powell, H. Jefferson. 'The Original Understanding of Original Intent.' *Harvard Law Review* 98 (1985): 885.

Presser, Stephen B. 'Some Realism about Orphism or The Critical Legal Studies Movement and The New Great Chain of Being.' *Northwestern Law Review* 79 (1984–5): 869.

Railton, Peter. 'Marx and the Objectivity of Science.' In *The Philosophy of Science*, edited by Richard Boyd et al. Cambridge, MA: MIT, 1991.

Rashke, Richard. *The Killing of Karen Silkwood*. 2nd ed. Ithaca: Cornell University Press, 2000.

Raz, Joseph. 'The Rule of Law and Its Virtue.' *Law Quarterly Review* 93 (1977): 195. Reprinted in *The Authority of Law*. New York: Oxford University Press, 1979.

Regier, C.C. 'The Struggle for Federal Food and Drugs Legislation.' *Law and Contemporary Problems* 1, no. 1 (1933–4): 3.

Rehg, William. 'Habermas' Discourse Theory of Law and Democracy: An Overview of the Argument.' In *The Handbook of Critical Theory*, edited by David M. Rasmussen. Malden: Blackwell, 1996.

Reid, John Phillip. *Law for the Elephant: Property and Social Behavior on the Overland Trail*. San Marino: Huntington Library Press, 1996.

Renoe, Curtis E. 'Seeing Is Believing? Expert Testimony and the Construction of Interpretive Authority in an American Trial.' *International Journal of Semiotics* 9 (1996): 115.

Resnik, Judith. 'Singular and Aggregate Voices: Audiences and Authority in Law and Literature and in Law and Feminism.' In *Law and Literature*, edited by Michael Freeman and Andrew D.E. Lewis. Oxford: Oxford University Press, 1999.

Roosevelt, Theodore. *Theodore Roosevelt: An Autobiography*. New York: Scribner's, 1920.

Rorty, Richard. 'Solidarity or Objectivity?' In *From Modernism to Postmodernism*, edited by Lawrence Cahoone. Malden: Blackwell, 1996.

Rosenfeld, Michael. Review: 'Law as Discourse: Bridging the Gap between Democracy and Rights.' *Harvard Law Review* 108 (1995): 1163.

Said, Edward W. *Humanism and Democratic Criticism*. New York: Columbia University Press, 2003.

Sandburg, Carl. *Always the Young Strangers*. New York: Harcourt, 1952.

Scalia, Antonin. 'The Rule of Law as a Law of Rules.' *University of Chicago Law Review* 56 (1989): 1175.

Selden, Raman. *A Reader's Guide to Contemporary Literary Theory*. Lexington: University Press of Kentucky, 1985.

Severance, Lawrence J., et al. 'Toward Criminal Jury Instructions That Jurors Can Understand.' *Journal of Criminal Law and Criminology* 75 (1984): 198.

Shakespeare, William. *The Complete Works of Shakespeare*. 3rd ed., edited by David Bevington. Dallas: Scott, 1980.

Shelley, Percy. *A Declaration of Rights* [1812]. http://terpconnect.umd .edu/~djb/shelley/declaration1880.html.

Shepard, Sam. *True West*. New York: Samuel French, 1981.

Sinclair, Upton. *The Jungle* [1906]. New York: Penguin, 1985.

Smith, Marie Hockenhull. 'The Lawyer, the Novelist, and the Discourse of Authority.' In *Law and Literature*, edited by Michael Freeman and Andrew Lewis. Oxford: Oxford University Press, 1999.

Somers, Margaret R. 'The Narrative Constitution of Identity: A Relational and Network Approach.' *Theory and Society* 23 (1994): 605.

Sophocles. *Antigone*. In *The Three Theban Plays*. Translated by Robert Fagles. New York: Penguin, 1984.

Stern, Simon. 'Literary Evidence and Legal Aesthetics.' Forthcoming in *Teaching Literature and Law*, edited by Austin Sarat, Matthew Anderson, and Catherine Frank. New York: MLA, 2010. http://ssrn.com/abstract=1378337.

Stone, Geoffrey R., et al. *Constitutional Law*. Boston: Little, Brown, 1986.

Stone, Lawrence. 'The Revival of Narrative: Reflections on a New Old History.' *Past and Present* 85 (1979): 3.

Sullivan, Lawrence A., and Warren S. Grimes. The Law of Antitrust: An Integrated Handbook. 2nd ed. St. Paul: Thomson/West, 2006.

Sullivan, William, et al. Educating Lawyers: Preparation for the Profession of Law. San Francisco: Jossey-Bass, 2007.

Taine, Hippolyte. History of English Literature [1864]. Translated by Henry von Laun. Rev. ed. New York: Colonial, 1900. Excerpted in The Modern Tradition, edited by Richard Ellman and Charles Feidelson, Jr. New York: Oxford University Press, 1965.

Teubner, Gunther. 'How the Law Thinks: Toward a Constructivist Epistemology of Law.' Law and Society Review 23 (1989): 727.

– 'Introduction to Autopoietic Law.' In Autopoietic Law: A New Approach to Law and Society, edited by Gunther Teubner. New York: de Gruyter, 1988.

Thomas, Brook. The New Historicism and Other Old-Fashioned Topics. Princeton: Princeton University Press, 1991.

– 'Reflections on the Law and Literature Revival.' Critical Inquiry 17 (1991): 510.

Tocqueville, Alexis de. Democracy in America [1835 and 1840]. Edited by J.P. Mayer, translated by George Lawrence. New York: Harper, 1988.

Tolstoy, Leo. War and Peace [1865–9]. Translated by Aylmer Maude. vol. 2. New York: Oxford University Press, 1933. Excerpted in The Modern Tradition, edited by Richard Ellman and Charles Feidelson, Jr. New York: Oxford University Press, 1965.

Turner, Frederick Jackson. The Frontier in American History [1893]. New York: Holt, 1920.

Tushnet, Mark. 'Constitutional Interpretation and Judicial Selection: A View from The Federalist Papers.' Southern California Law Review 61 (1988): 1669.

Twain, Mark. Roughing It. Hartford: American, 1873. http://www.mtwain.com/Roughing_It/49.html

Van Dunne, Jan M. 'Narrative Coherence and Its Function in Judicial Decision Making and Legislation.' American Journal of Comparative Law 44 (1996): 463.

Veeser, H. Aram. 'The New Historicism.' In The New Historicism Reader, edited by H. Aram Veeser. New York: Routledge, 1994.

Veyne, Paul. Writing History. Translated by Mina Moore-Rinvolucri. Middletown: Wesleyan University Press, 1984.

Waldron, Jeremy. 'The Concept and the Rule of Law.' New York University Law School Colloquium in Legal, Political, and Social Philosophy, Paper No. 2, 2006, 12–13. http://papers.ssrn.com/sol3/papers.cfm?abstract_id=1273005.

Ward, Ian. Law and Literature: Possibilities and Perspectives. Cambridge: Cambridge University Press, 1995.

Wargo, John. Our Children's Toxic Legacy: How Science and Law Fail to Protect Us from Pesticides. 2nd ed. New Haven: Yale University Press, 1998.

Warren, Robert Penn. *All the King's Men* [1946]. New York: Bantam, 1971.

Watson, Alan. 'Legal Education Reform: Modest Suggestions.' *Journal of Legal Education* 51 (2001): 91.

Watt, Ian. 'Realism and the Novel Form.' Excerpted in *Law and Literature*, edited by Lenora Ledwon. New York: Garland, 1996.

– *The Rise of the Novel: Studies in Defoe, Richardson, and Fielding*. Berkeley: University of California Press, 1957.

Weisberg, Richard H. 'Literature's Twenty-Year Crossing into the Domain of Law: Continuing Trespass or Right by Adverse Possession?' In *Law and Literature*, edited by Michael Freeman and Andrew D. E. Lewis. Oxford: Oxford University Press, 1999.

– *Poethics and Other Strategies of Law and Literature*. New York: Columbia University Press, 1992.

Wesson, Marianne. 'Particular Intentions: The Hillmon Case and the Supreme Court.' *Law and Literature* 18 (2006): 343.

– '"Remarkable Stratagems and Conspiracies": How Unscrupulous Lawyers and Credulous Judges Created an Exception to the Hearsay Rule.' *Fordham Law Review* 76 (2007): 1675.

West, Robin. 'Constitutional Fictions and Meritocratic Success Stories.' *Washington and Lee Law Review* 53 (1996): 995.

– *Narrative, Authority, and Law*. Ann Arbor: University of Michigan Press, 1993.

White, Hayden. 'The Value of Narrativity in the Representation of Reality.' *Critical Inquiry* 7 (1980): 5.

White, James Boyd. 'The Judicial Opinion and the Poem.' Reprinted in *Law and Literature*, edited by Lenora Ledwon. New York: Garland, 1996.

Wigmore, John Henry. *Evidence in Trials at Common Law* 1. 3rd ed. Boston: Little, Brown, 1940.

Wiley, Harvey W. *The History of a Crime against the Food Law*. Washington: Wiley, 1929. http://www.soilandhealth.org/03sov/0303critic/030305wylie/030305toc.html.

Williams, Melanie. '*Tess of the D'Urbervilles* and the Law of Provocation.' In *Law and Literature*, edited by Michael Freeman and Andrew D.E. Lewis. Oxford: Oxford University Press, 1999.

Wimsatt, W.K., and Monroe C. Beardsley. 'The Intentional Fallacy.' In *The Verbal Icon: Studies in the Meaning of Poetry*. Lexington: University Press of Kentucky, 1954.

Witteveen, William. 'The Hidden Truth of Autopoiesis.' In *Law and Literature*, edited by Michael Freeman and Andrew D.E. Lewis. Oxford: Oxford University Press, 1999.

Wittgenstein, Ludwig. *Philosophical Investigations* [1953]. 3rd ed. Translated by
    G.E.M. Anscombe. Malden: Blackwell, 2001.
Yeats, William Butler. *Easter 1916* [1920].
Young, James Harvey. 'The Long Struggle for the 1906 Law.' *FDA Consumer* 1,
    June 1981. http://www.fda.gov/AboutFDA/WhatWeDo/History/Centen-
    nialofFDA/TheLongStrugglefortheLaw/default.htm.
– *Pure Food*. Princeton: Princeton University Press, 1989.

## Cases

*Ake v. Oklahoma*, 470 U.S. 68 (1985).
*Alexander v. Russo*, 571 P.2d 350 (Kan. App. 1977).
*Allen v. Greyhound Lines, Inc.*, 656 F.2d 418 (9th Cir. 1981).
*Apani Southwest, Inc. v. Coca-Cola Enters.*, 300 F.3d 620 (5th Cir. 2002).
*Atkins v. Virginia*, 536 U.S. 304 (2002).
*Ball v. U.S.*, 163 U.S. 662 (1896).
*Batson v. Kentucky*, 476 U.S. 79 (1986).
*Baur v. Veneman*, 352 F.3d 625 (2d Cir. 2003).
*Berry v. Chaplin*, 169 P.2d 442 (Cal. App. 1946).
*Bockweg v. Anderson*, 402 S.E.2d 627 (1991).
*Bowers v. Hardwick*, 478 U.S. 186 (1986).
*Brown v. Board of Education of Topeka*, 347 U.S. 483 (1954).
*Brown v. Simpson*, Case No. SC036876 (LA Sup. Ct.).
*Brunswick Corp. v. Pueblo Bowl-O-Mat, Inc.*, 429 U.S. 477 (1977).
*Bushell's Case*, 124 Eng. Rep. 1006 (C.P. 1670).
*Caminetti v. United States*, 242 U.S. 470 (1917).
*Dodd v. Henkel*, 84 Cal. App.3d 604 (Cal. App. 1978).
*Dred Scott v. Sanford*, 60 U.S. (19 How.) 393 (1857).
*Dr. Miles Medical Co. v. John D. Park & Sons*, 220 U.S. 373 (1911).
*Environmental Defense Fund v. Environmental Protection Agency*, 598 F.2d 62
    (D.C. Cir. 1978).
*Goings v. United States*, 377 F.2d 753 (8th Cir. 1967).
*Goldman v. Simpson*, Case No. SC036340 (LA Sup. Ct.).
*Goldsmith v. Learjet, Inc.*, 917 P.2d 810 (Kan. 1996).
*Gonzales v. Carhart*, 127 S. Ct. 1610 (2007).
*Grider v. USX Corp.*, 847 P.2d 779 (Okla. 1993).
*Grutter v. Bollinger*, 539 U.S. 306 (2003).
*Harnett v. Parris*, 925 F. Supp. 1496 (D. Kan. 1996).
*Harnett v. Parris*, 1995 WL 55036 (D. Kan).
*Herron v. Miller*, 220 P. 59 (Okla. 1923).

*Hynes v. New York Cent. R. Co.*, 176 N.Y.S. 795 (N.Y. App. Div. 1919).

*Hynes v. New York Cent. R. Co.*, 231 N.Y. 229 (N.Y. 1921).

*IBP, Inc. v. Alvarez*, 339 F.3d 894 (9th Cir. 2003).

*Jackson v. Prairie Oil & Gas*, 222 P. 1114 (Kan. 1924).

*Lawrence v. Texas*, 539 U.S. 558 (2003).

*Leegin Creative Leather Products v. PSKS Inc.*, 127 S. Ct. 2705 (2007).

*Lepak v. McClain*, 844 P.2d 852 (Okla. 1992).

*Lochner v. New York*, 25 S. Ct. 539 (1905).

*Miller v. California*, 413 U.S. 15 (1973).

*Morris v. Wise*, 293 P.2d 547 (Okla. 1955).

*Muller v. Oregon*, 208 U.S. 412 (1908).

*Mutual Life Ins. Co. of New York v. Hillmon*, 145 U.S. 909 (1892).

*Old Chief v. United States*, 519 U.S. 172 (1997).

*Planned Parenthood of Southeastern Pa. v. Casey*, 505 U.S. 833 (1992).

*Plaut v. Spendthrift Farm, Inc.*, 514 U.S. 211 (1995).

*Plessy v. Ferguson*, 163 U.S. 537 (1896).

*Prince v. Leesona Corp., Inc.*, 720 F.2d 1166 (10th Cir. 1983).

*Roe v. Wade*, 410 U.S. 113 (1973).

*Roper v. Simmons*, 125 S. Ct. 1183 (2005).

*Scott v. Harris*, 127 S. Ct. 1769 (2007).

*Silkwood v. Kerr-McGee*, 464 U.S. 238 (1984).

*Silkwood v. Kerr-McGee*, 759 F.2d 1451 (10th Cir. 1983).

*Silkwood v. Kerr-McGee*, 667 F.2d 908 (10th Cir. 1981).

*Silkwood v. Kerr-McGee*, 485 F. Supp. 566 (W.D. Okla. 1979).

*Solid Waste Agency of Northern Cook County v. U.S. Army Corps of Engineers*, 351 U.S. 159 (2001).

*Stanford v. Kentucky*, 492 U.S. 361 (1989).

*State v. Hodges*, 716 P.2d 563 (Kan. 1986).

*State v. Hundley*, 693 P.2d 475 (Kan. 1985).

*State v. Lawrence*, 135 P.3d 1211 (Kan. 2006).

*State v. Martin*, 658 P.2d 1024 (Kan. 1983).

*State v. Scott*, 21 P.3d 516 (Kan. 2001).

*State v. Smith*, 174 P. 551 (Kan. 1918).

*State v. Stewart*, 763 P.2d 572 (Kan. 1988).

*Taft v. Hyatt*, 180 P. 213 (Kan. 1919).

*Taylor v. Louisiana*, 419 U.S. 522 (1975).

*U.S. v. Barry*, No. 90-0068, 1990 WL 174907 (D. D.C.).

*U.S. v. City of Chicago*, 870 F.2d 1256 (7th Cir. 1989)

*U.S. v Espy*, 145 F.3d 1369 (D.C. Cir. 1998).

*U.S. v. Microsoft*, 253 F.3d 34 (D.C. Cir. 2001).

**Miscellaneous**

President's Science Advisory Committee. *Use of Pesticides.* 1963.

*Hearings on S. 1250 and S. 1251 Before the S. Comm. on Commerce*, 88th Congress 1 sess. (1963) (Statement of Rachel Carson).

*Interagency Coordination in Environmental Hazards (Pesticides): Hearings Before the U.S. Senate Subcommittee on Reorganization and International Organizations of the Committee on Government Operations*, 4 June 1963, 88th Congress 1 sess. (1963) (testimony of Rachel Carson).

Ohio Historical Society. 'Cuyahoga River Fire.' *Ohio History Central: An Online Encyclopedia of Ohio History.* http://www.ohiohistorycentral.org

http://www.cnn.com/NATURE/9906/22/saving.cuyahoga

Richard J. '"Diamond Dick" Tanner Dime Novels.' Nebraska State Historical Society. http://www.nebraskahistory.org/lib-arch/research/treasures/diamond_dick_tanner.htm.

**Works Consulted**

Baghramian, Maria. *Modern Philosophy of Language.* Washington: Counterpoint, 1999.

Barthes, Roland. *The Rustle of Language.* Berkeley: University of California Press, 1989.

Brest, Paul. 'Indeterminacy and Interest.' *Stanford Law Review* 34 (1982): 765.

Brink, David. 'Legal Theory, Legal Interpretation, and Judicial Review.' *Philosophy and Public Affairs* 105 (1988): 17.

Davidson, Donald. *Inquiries into Truth and Interpretation.* Oxford: Oxford University Press, 1984.

Derrida, Jacques. *Negotiations.* Stanford: Stanford University Press, 2002.

– *Without Alibi.* Stanford: Stanford University Press, 2002.

– *Writing and Difference.* Chicago: University of Chicago Press, 1978.

Dummett, Michael. *Frege: Philosophy of Language.* 2nd ed. Cambridge, MA: Harvard University Press, 1981.

Eskridge, William. 'The New Textualism.' *UCLA Law Review* 37 (1989): 621.

Fiss, Owen. 'Objectivity and Interpretation.' *Stanford Law Review* 34 (1982): 739.

Floyd, Juliet, and Sanford Shieh, eds. *Future Pasts: The Analytical Tradition in Twentieth-Century Philosophy.* Oxford: Oxford University Press, 2001.

Gadamer, H.G. *Truth and Method.* 2nd rev. ed. New York: Continuum, 1990.

Gay, Peter. *The Enlightenment: An Interpretation.* New York: Knopf, 1966.

Gell-Mann, Murray. *The Quark and the Jaguar.* New York: Freeman, 1994.

Greenawalt, Kent. 'Interpretation and Judgment.' *Yale Journal of Law and Humanities* 9 (1997): 415.

Hartman, Geoffrey. *Saving the Text: Literature/Derrida/Philosophy*. Baltimore: Johns Hopkins University Press, 1981.

Haskell, Thomas. *Objectivity Is Not Neutrality*. Baltimore: Johns Hopkins University Press, 1998.

Leiter, Brian, ed. *The Future for Philosophy*. Oxford: Oxford University Press, 2004.

– 'Objectivity and the Problems of Jurisprudence.' *Texas Law Review* 72 (1993): 187.

Levinson, Sanford. 'Law as Literature.' *Texas Law Review* 60 (1982): 373.

Marshall, Donald. 'The Inflation of Theory.' *Partisan Review* 48, no. 2 (1981): 294.

Omnés, Roland. *Quantum Philosophy*. Princeton: Princeton University Press, 1999.

Phelps, Teresa, et al. 'Questioning the Text: The Significance of Phenomenological Hermeneutics for Legal Interpretation.' *St. Louis University Law Journal* 29 (1985): 353.

Price, Huw. *Time's Arrow and Archimedes' Point*. Oxford: Oxford University Press, 1996.

Rorty, Richard. *Objectivity, Relativism, and Truth*. Cambridge: Cambridge University Press, 1991.

Tushnet, Mark V. 'Defending the Indeterminacy Thesis.' In *Analyzing Law: New Essays in Legal Theory*, edited by Brian Bix. Oxford: Clarendon, 1998.

Wittgenstein, Ludwig. *Philosophical Grammar*. Berkeley: University of California Press, 1974.

Wright, Crispin. *Truth and Objectivity*. Cambridge, MA: Harvard University Press, 1992.

# Index